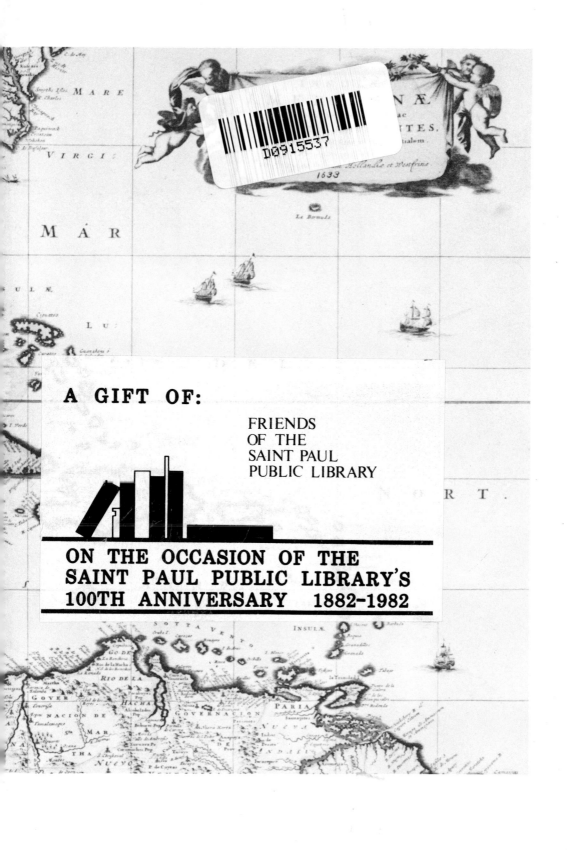

Alabama and the Borderlands

Alabama

Edited by

R. REID BADGER *and* LAWRENCE A. CLAYTON

A Dan Josselyn Memorial Publication

and the Borderlands

From Prehistory to Statehood

THE UNIVERSITY OF ALABAMA PRESS

Library of Congress Cataloging in Publication Data

Main entry under title:

Alabama and the borderlands.

   Essays evolved from a symposium held at the University of
Alabama, Sept. 1981, sponsored by the College of Arts and Sciences.
   Bibliography: p.
   Includes index.
   1. Alabama—History—To 1819—Congresses. 2. Indians of North
America—Alabama—History—Congresses.
I. Badger, R. Reid.   II. Clayton, Lawrence A.
III. University of Alabama. College of Arts and Sciences.
F326.5.A39 1985   976.1   83-17957
ISBN 0-8173-0208-5

Contents

Illustrations

ILLUSTRATIONS

Preface

This book was born of a concern with Alabama's past and the need to explore and explain that legacy, so often hidden by the veils of time, ignorance, or misunderstanding. In 1981 The University of Alabama celebrated its 150th anniversary, and each College contributed to the celebration by sponsoring a special symposium. The College of Arts and Sciences decided to bring together the nation's leading scholars on the prehistory and early history of Alabama and the Southeastern United States, and for two memorable days in September 1981 several hundred interested listeners heard those scholars present their interpretations of Alabama's remarkable past.

The organizers of the symposium deliberately chose to focus on Alabama's history before statehood. Alabama as a constituent state of the Old South is well known. Alabama as a home of Indian cultures and civilizations of a high order, as an object of desire, exploration, and conquest in the sixteenth century, and as a borderland disputed by rival European nationalities for almost 300 years is less well known. We trust the following essays prove as interesting, enlightening, and provocative to the casual reader as to the professional scholar, for we intended to reach for Everyman's attention in exploring among the artifacts and documents that reveal the realities and romance of that older Alabama.

The College of Arts and Sciences symposium, "Alabama and the

Borderlands," found its genesis in three principal areas: the administration of the College, the Department of History, and among the anthropologists on campus. In the Dean's Office, Douglas E. Jones and Reid Badger, Dean and Assistant Dean respectively, initiated the project and supplied the momentum from the beginning. From anthropology, Richard A. Krause and Joseph O. Vogel provided the principal ideas and suggestions for the first and second sections, and Lawrence A. Clayton, in history, suggested most of the participants for the third section. Krause subsequently contributed the introductory essay to the first section and Badger and Clayton edited the volume for publication.

Many individuals and organizations beyond the immediate University community contributed time or money (or both) as the project evolved from idea to symposium to book, and we gratefully acknowledge the assistance of the following gracious people and kind organizations: the Alabama Alumni Association, the Alabama Archaeological Society, the Committee for the Humanities in Alabama, Mr. Jack Warner of Gulf States Paper Corporation, Sr. D. Roberto Bermudez of the Ministry of Cultural Affairs of the Embassy of Spain, and Mr. Wilton Dillon of the Smithsonian Institution. Donna Peters, of the Alabama Museum of Natural History; Joan Mitchell, of the College of Arts and Sciences; and Margaret Searcy, of the Anthropology Department, contributed their unique talents. Emily Ellis and Frances Caroline Webber deserve special thanks for their enthusiasm and many long hours devoted to the project.

We dedicate this book to the memory of all those people who gave Alabama its legacy and, more specifically, to the memory of John H. Parry, formerly Gardiner Professor of Oceanic History at Harvard. John Parry gave one of the most delightful and insightful presentations in that September seminar of 1981. It is included in this volume, and may be the last major work that Professor Parry prepared. He died in late August 1982, but we trust that this work will be as fresh and invigorating as his memory is to those who knew him.

Alabama and the Borderlands

Introduction

Alabama and the Borderlands: From Prehistory to Statehood appears, at first glance, a curious title for a volume of scholarly essays. The central focus is Alabama, which was recognized officially as a territory of the United States of America only in 1817 and which gained admission to the Union as a state two years later. Until just prior to statehood, then, Alabama did not exist as a distinct political, cultural, or even geographic entity. This volume, in addressing the complex and sweeping period of Alabama history prior to statehood, is concerned with a time when Alabama was *not* Alabama but was included within and divided among a number of broader patterns of cultural and historical experience. Because the period is transitional, bridging prehistory and modern recorded history, such general patterns as have emerged are due largely to the concerted efforts of scores of individuals interested not only in the history of the region but, necessarily, in archaeology and anthropology as well.

As an introduction to the Alabama region's early history, the present collection of essays is arranged in three, roughly chronological parts: "The Prehistoric Background," "The Age of Exploration," and "Colonization and Conflict." Each of these parts includes a summary of current knowledge about the era and analysis of a particular event, issue, or theme within each era that is of special significance in the history of the region now known as Alabama.

Part I, "The Prehistoric Background," presents the earliest chapter in the story of human culture in the region and encompasses, by far, the broadest expanse of time. It is also the most inaccessible historical period. The major patterns which can be confidently drawn, therefore, are for the most part very general.

Beginning around 10,000 B.C., when the glaciers of the last Ice Age (the Wisconsin) began to recede, the earliest Alabamians moved into the southern regions of North America, following the herds of prehistoric game upon which their nomadic subsistence culture depended. As the large animals became scarce, partly as a result of the efficiency and skill of the hunters, and as the population increased, hunting began to give way to a mixed hunting and harvesting economy, which in turn led to agriculture and a more settled mode of social organization. These changes took place over thousands of years and culminated in what has come to be known as the "temple mound" or Mississippian period of Native American (Amerindian) history. Extending roughly from A.D. 850 until just prior to the first European contact with the New World, the Mississippian period and culture are the focus of part I.

While much remains to be fully documented, archaeologists and anthropologists agree that characteristic Mississippian societies first appeared in the Central Mississippi Valley (which contains the largest known Mississippian site at Cahokia, Illinois), then spread into an area encompassed by eastern Oklahoma, Texas, and Louisiana (with their major center at Spiro, Oklahoma), and the Tennessee-Cumberland drainage (with large centers at Etowah, in Georgia, and Moundville in western Alabama). Having developed an economy based upon the cultivation of maize, beans, and squash on stretches of self-fertilizing alluvial soil, the Mississippians achieved dense populations that harnessed impressive amounts of energy. Powerful chiefs commanded the loyalty and labor of widely scattered farming communities, directed the construction of monumental public works, conducted long-distance trade, and sustained (by their authority) the elaborate ceremonialism which both supported and reflected the most complex social order developed by Native Americans in Eastern North America.

While archaeologists and anthropologists generally agree upon the largest patterns, or stages, of cultural change in the prehistoric period, the material evidence which explains the localized trends in particular cultural patterns, such as the Mississippian, is yet to be discovered. In the opening essay of "The Prehistoric Background,"

Professor Richard A. Krause argues that although we must await the accumulation of new facts, it is equally important that we continue to take the questions raised by present theoretical assumptions seriously, together with their logical implications.

Archaeologists operate much like other scientists, in that their work involves not only the familiar gathering and sifting of material evidence uncovered in the field or the laboratory, but also continuous formulation and reformulation of the theoretical structure which both accounts for the empirical facts and gives them meaning and directs the design of future programs of research. One of the major assumptions which has guided archaeologists, and to which Dr. Krause calls attention, is the belief that state and empire formulation is a natural, universal tendency in human culture and that therefore, given time and the absence of external interference, all human societies inevitably progress toward states and empires. When Europeans first encountered the native cultures of the Western Hemisphere, they found impressive evidence, in Mexico and South America, to sustain this progressive theory of civilization. In North America, however, similar examples of state and empire formulation were absent, save for the remnants of what is now called Mississippian. Did these societies prefigure the emergence of states in North America, and if so, why did they not continue to develop? Or, on the other hand, do the Mississippians offer evidence which cannot be accommodated to the theory of the inevitable "march toward civilization," and is the theory, therefore, in need of serious modification? In Dr. Krause's review of the evidence and his analysis of the paths which research must take to answer these questions, it is made abundantly clear that the importance of our knowledge of Mississippian culture extends beyond mere curiosity with this fascinating chapter of Southeastern history, and has far-ranging implications for our most basic assumptions about the nature of human culture.

In the second essay of part I, Professor James B. Griffin provides a detailed survey of the evolution of knowledge about these ancient people, beginning with early nineteenth-century reports of literate and curious nonprofessional observers who puzzled over the remains of the great mound cities. Dr. Griffin traces the efforts of early professional archaeologists to organize and systematize the academic field of Eastern North American prehistory through development of such sophisticated methods as the carbon 14 test, which allowed greater accuracy in dating artifactual evidence and in identification and classification. One result of this process is that ceramics—once thought to be the most important key to identification and classification of the prehistoric Indian peoples—has given ground to a broader cultural definition that emphasizes general environmental adaptation and organization, as well as technological or stylistic attributes.

Not surprisingly, while much has been learned through the efforts of early students, and a substantial body of more or less scientific literature has emerged, lively debate continues as to the nature of Mississippian culture, including questions about its origin, growth, and development, the meaning and function of its religious and ceremonial activities, the character of its social and political order, and the reasons for its passing. In his conclusion, Professor Griffin joins the debate by questioning the validity of "Mississippian" as indicating a single cultural tradition. In his view, the term is properly used only in the broadest sense of reflecting "the continuing areal interaction of ideas and practices over the broad Eastern wooded area which during a 1,000-year period reached levels of development not attained earlier."

In the final contribution to the section, Dr. Bruce D. Smith challenges this broad definition of Mississippian by calling attention to the underlying environmental patterns that are beginning to emerge from recent archaeological research. The true Mississippians, he argues, are those groups which developed roughly similar subsistence strategies, utilizing six primary food-resource groups. These societies developed only in certain river-valley floodplains of Eastern North America because it was here that easily worked, self-renewing soils and seasonally abundant plant and animal life were available to support such complex energy-consuming societies. While regional differences exist—and Dr. Smith does not underestimate the difficulties in uncovering hard evidence of the importance of various plant and animal resources—recognition of a general Mississippian pattern of subsistence provides a more accurate definition of these people and points to a potentially more fruitful direction for investigation.

Within the state of Alabama, of course, the major Mississippian site is in Hale County at Moundville, in the west-central part of the state. Since a large portion of the bottomland of the Black Warrior Valley is annually renewed by spring flooding, the location fits the general requirements of "Mississippian" suggested by Smith. The Moundville site is especially important because few of the other

4

large centers have been as fortunate in escaping the ravages of modern urban American life. At the time of this writing, excavation of the fortifications which once surrounded the 300-acre complex— the first systematically conducted at a Mississippian site—is proceeding slowly but surely. When completed, it should be possible to gain not only a more complete understanding of Mississippian engineering techniques, but also a fuller grasp of the social and political organization that produced and maintained such extensive defensive works. This painstaking research may also assist in explaining why, sometime before 1540, the major regional centers of Mississippian life, such as Moundville, began to decline in importance and why, therefore, when the first Spanish explorers entered the Black Warrior Valley, no great chief from Moundville was borne out from the city on a litter to meet them.

Although the prehistoric backgrounds of Alabama and Southeastern North America remain the primary province of the archaeologist and the anthropologist, Alabama's early history, beginning with the great voyages of Columbus at the end of the fifteenth century, entered upon a new chapter, one that enlists the skills and perspectives of the historian as well. As the promise of potential and real American riches spread through the ports and palaces of Europe in the early sixteenth century—especially those of Spain, Portugal, France, and England—adventurers of high and low birth alike searched with increasing frequency for fortune and fame in the New World. The conquest of native American peoples began in the Caribbean in the last decade of the fifteenth century and extended north, south, and west toward the continents and Central America. Española, Puerto Rico, and Cuba were all subdued by 1513 when a group of Spaniards, led by a well-born soldier-adventurer with the odd surname of Ponce de León (Paunch of the Lion), sailed north in search of the legendary island of Bimini and chanced instead upon the Florida peninsula. Juan Ponce de León's discovery of La Florida—so named in honor of the *Pasqua de Flores*, or Easter Sunday— and his encounter with North American Indians presaged a long period of European exploration, discovery, conquest, and settlement of lands that today constitute the American Southeast. For the next 300 years, this territory was an arena for European rivalry and for proselytizing the faith.

Ponce de León represented Spain and her very real domination of American affairs in the first half of the sixteenth century. Fired by religious zealotry from their recent completion of the reconquest of Spain from the Moors and by fervor from their conquests of Mexico and Peru, Spaniards (after Ponce de León) turned northward from the Caribbean and Mexico in search of new empires to conquer and Christianize. Although challenged by France and England in the latter half of the century, early European expansion into this border-lands area is the story of Spanish enterprise, and the subject of part II of this volume.

Spanish interest in North America developed slowly, as Professor John H. Parry explains in his essay "Early European Penetration of Eastern North America," which provides the introduction to part II. Old myths and long-standing preconceptions had directed the early explorers south from the Caribbean in their quest for gold and their dream of finding an easy passage to the rich markets of Asia. In 1539, after the discovery and subjugation of the great Amerindian civilizations of Central America, a well-equipped expedition, led by the brash Hernando de Soto, landed in Florida, expecting to find fabulous plunder in the interior of the northern continent. "Soto," writes Dr. Parry, "had amassed a fortune in Peru by extorting treasure from living Indians and by robbing the tombs of dead ones, and he proposed to do the same in North America." For the next three years, Soto and his men wandered through territories which now comprise the states of Florida, Georgia, North Carolina, Alabama, Tennessee, Arkansas, Mississippi, and Louisiana.

The importance of the Soto *entrada*, which receives special attention in the three essays which follow Parry's introduction, lies not in its success; it was a failure by almost any contemporary or current measure. Spanish hegemony in the New World was not increased appreciably as a result, nor were settlements or positive relationships with the Indians (which might have proved of value to Spain) effected. The Conquistador did not find the great treasure he passionately sought; rather, he perished beside the Mississippi River in 1542. Even as explorers, Soto and his men accomplished little, adding only minor strokes to Europe's picture of the interior of the North American continent.

The expedition was important, nevertheless, because Soto and his men were the first Europeans to travel extensively through the Southeast and the first to leave written records (however vague) of the landscape they traversed and the peoples they encountered. Many years would pass before more personal observations would be added to the historical record, and by then the native population of the region had undergone substantial change. The chronicles left by survivors of the Soto expedition, therefore, provide the best firsthand account of the Mississippian (or early post-Mississippian) period of Southeastern prehistory and may, perhaps, be a key to understanding the decline of that tradition.

A second important reason for the continuing interest in Soto is a strong suspicion that such unexpected and dramatic contact between Europeans and Native Americans, despite its brevity, may have had significant contemporary (as well as subsequent) impact upon the Indian culture.

To pursue these questions further, it is necessary to trace with much greater accuracy than has been possible in the past the route of Soto's army and to establish the points of contact between Soto and the native population. "In other words," as Dr. Jeffrey P. Brain points out, "we have to reconstruct the route of Soto." Fortunately, in 1939 the United States De Soto Commission, under the direction of John R. Swanton, arrived, after careful study, at what was believed to be the most likely route of the expedition. The Swanton Report provides the starting point from which all subsequent Soto studies have begun, but it is no longer thought to provide the definitive account, for two major reasons: the commission gave too much weight to the vague and undependable accounts and descriptions of the expedition, and it did not have the benefit of archaeological evidence which has been uncovered in recent years.

Dr. Brain, in "The Archaeology of the Hernando de Soto Expedition," describes the kinds of archaeological data required to prove the passage of the army through a particular locale, and he examines the "Swanton route" in detail. He concludes: Although we "cannot trace the route of Soto with precision," we have a "much better idea of what to look for archaeologically, and the archaeological picture itself is slowly coming into focus." That the picture is beginning to clear is due largely to the efforts of such scholars as Professor Charles M. Hudson and his students, who are willing and able to combine detailed, comparative analysis of the historical and archaeological evidence with imaginative, empirical research.

DePratter, Hudson, and Smith's essay, "The Hernando de Soto Expedition: From Chiaha to Mabila," which is the third contribution to part II, presents compelling new evidence of the army's movements from May of 1540 to October of the same year, when Soto and his men fought the forces of Chief Tascaluza in what is believed to be the most massive battle of its kind in the history of

7

the region. The team is convinced that it has precisely located the Indian town of Chiaha, which Soto visited in June of 1540 (which now is submerged under Douglas Lake). From this "fix," DePratter, Hudson, and Smith plot day by day (much like navigators) the subsequent movement of the army. In the process, they find support for their reconstruction of the route (which takes Soto farther north than anyone had previously thought) from archaeological evidence, the historical record, and the coincidence of similar place names. The significance of this fascinating and detailed work is that it not only permits greater precision in the historical particulars of the Soto expedition, but allows us "to link together sixteenth-century Southeastern history and archaeology in a way that has not been achieved before."

In the final essay of part II, Dr. Charles H. Fairbanks begins his "From Exploration to Settlement: Spanish Strategies for Colonization" in a manner similar to his predecessors. He starts with the Swanton Report of the Soto *entrada*. After analyzing the evidence of the early Spanish presence in Florida, he shifts his focus (and time frame) to later Spanish explorations and to the major reorganization of Indian culture which followed the Soto expedition. Whatever the effect of the *entrada* upon the native culture, Fairbanks is concerned also about the effect that Spanish recognition of Indian depopulation and deculturization had upon Spain's settlement policy. By the time of Pedro Menéndez de Avilés and the founding of St. Augustine in 1565, the Spaniards appear to have become convinced that "direct exploitation of the Indians to provide food and export materials was a losing gambit." Another strategy was required, and, if it also proved unsuccessful, it was not for "lack of planning." It was because the "Spaniards failed to understand how much damage had been done to Southeastern Indian populations by the excesses of the Soto expedition."

The four papers which comprise the final section of the volume represent the various interests that have focused on Alabama and the Borderlands in the post-Soto period. Professors Wilcomb Washburn and Michael Scardaville express concern over the great gaps in Borderlands scholarship, while Professor Eugene Lyon and William and Hazel Coker try to fill some of those gaps. Washburn views the Southeast from the point of view of a New England scholar, while Scardaville looks north from Mexico with his expertise as a Latin-Americanist. Each has approached the Borderlands in his scholarly endeavors, and each calls for clearer recognition of the vital role that Alabama and the Borderlands have played in the histories of England, Spain, and France, and of course the United States. (The sources that Washburn and Scardaville draw upon and weave into their essays are a wide and valuable survey of the literature of the region and offer a number of important insights and suggestions that challenge basic assumptions about this critical but poorly understood aspect of our country's history.)

Lyon's "Continuity in the Age of Conquest: The Establishment of Spanish Sovereignty in the Sixteenth Century" relates Spanish efforts to dominate North America as an extension of Spain's earlier conquests in the Caribbean and Mexico. To the Spaniard of the sixteenth century, the Southeast presented a challenge of major proportions, and Dr. Lyon focuses upon Pedro Menéndez de Avilés, one of Spain's greatest admirals and strategists of the time, and the individual most responsible for permanently establishing the Spanish in the Southeast.

William and Hazel Coker's "The Siege of Mobile, 1780" details one of the most successful military campaigns waged by Spanish forces during the American Revolution. Led by Bernardo de Gálvez, the governor of Louisiana, the Spanish ousted the British—not only from their stronghold at Mobile but from their fortifications along the Lower Mississippi and from Pensacola as well. These defeats, combined with their disaster at Yorktown in the fall of 1781, helped convince the British of the futility of crushing the American Revolution.

The historical issues addressed by Lyon and the Cokers roughly bracket the chronological limits of Alabama and the Southeast as a borderland or "debatable land" (as the great historian Herbert E. Bolton described this region during the age of "Conflict and Revolution").

Although the Spanish explored Alabama and the Southeast first, their European rivals, especially France, lagged only briefly behind. By 1562 a group of French Huguenots, led by Jean Ribaut, had landed on the coast of South Carolina, intending to establish a French colony. The presence of these French Protestants not only insulted a deeply pious and Catholic Spain but also, as a threat to Spanish shipping, represented a direct challenge to Spain's claims in the area. A fleet, under the command of Pedro Menéndez de Avilés, was dispatched by Philip II in 1565 to establish a permanent Spanish settlement on the coast and to evict the French intruders. After a bitter and bloody campaign, the French were destroyed and Spain's predominance was reasserted, not to be challenged again until, 100 years later, Spain's *mare nostrum* (the Caribbean) began to slip from Spanish control.

When Spain's European rivals approached Alabama and the Borderlands in the latter third of the seventeenth century, they did not come as they had in the sixteenth century; this time they were the vanguards of expanding colonial empires whose power had grown as Spain's had declined. In 1670 Spain was forced by the Treaty of Madrid (also called the American Treaty) to recognize English sovereignty over those New World areas that England then possessed. "Effective occupation" became the criterion for territorial claims in the Borderlands, superseding claims by right of discovery and token occupation, which had underpinned the Spanish position. This victory for England encouraged her adventurous people to make even bolder incursions to the south and west over the next several decades, which culminated in the War of the Spanish Succession (or Queen Anne's War) in the early eighteenth century. English traders, settlers, and expansion-minded leaders, such as Governor James Moore of South Carolina, assaulted the small Spanish garrisons that dotted the Georgia coast and the interior of Florida, Georgia, and Alabama. The Peace of Utrecht, signed in 1713, formally brought the war to an end. Nonetheless, hostilities continued in the Borderlands, on the principle that New World rivalries were not necessarily governed by Old World diplomacy.

Complicating the struggle between England and Spain was the entry, once again, of France. In 1682, Sieur de La Salle had discovered that the Mississippi emptied into the Gulf of Mexico. This prompted the French to attempt a settlement at its mouth, hoping thereby to secure control of the river and lay claim to the vast valley—the heartland of America—which it drained. This effort, also led by La Salle, though ultimately unsuccessful, alarmed the Spanish. Nightmares about French pirates, privateers, and adventurers in the service of Louis XIV, descending upon the silver mines of Mexico, provoked the arthritic and embattled Spanish empire to action.

Between 1689 and 1699, several Spanish expeditions, by land and by sea, reconnoitered the Gulf Coast while handfuls of missionaries and soldiers established outposts in East Texas. Despite several setbacks, the Spanish settlement of Texas was accomplished by

1716. To the east along the Gulf, the Spanish debated an appropriate response to the French, and chose finally to establish a defensive position at Pensacola Bay. French ambitions, at the same time, remained very much alive. Excited by the promise of a lucrative fur trade with the Southern Indians, Pierre le Moyne led the effort to found Mobile in 1702, and was followed by Jean Baptiste le Moyne, who realized La Salle's dream of anchoring the French empire in America on the Lower Mississippi by founding New Orleans in 1718.

In 1732 General James Oglethorpe, philanthropist and imperialist, established the city of Savannah in Georgia and by this act widened English claims farther south and west. During the War of Jenkins' Ear (1739–1744), a conflict born of trade rivalries in the Caribbean between the English and Spanish, Oglethorpe pushed the Spaniards hard on the southern frontier. He attacked and laid siege to St. Augustine in 1740, and although that redoubtable fortress held, the Spanish were forced to concede further recession of their borders.

By midcentury, the center of European competition on the North American continent had shifted north, from Florida and Louisiana to the Ohio Valley, where clashes between French and English frontiersmen and regular soldiers precipitated the Seven Years' War (1756–1763). In the end, the war went badly for the French and their Spanish allies: English fleets captured Spanish Manila and Havana, and British armies destroyed French power along the St. Lawrence, in the heart of the French empire in North America. By the terms of the Peace of Paris of 1763, France was eliminated as a colonial power in North America. England expanded her western frontier to the Mississippi River and acquired Florida from Spain, which in turn acquired Louisiana from France as compensation for joining France in the losing cause. With the exception of New Orleans, all Spanish territories were now west of the Mississippi. Although England discouraged her American colonists from leaving the Atlantic Coast, American farmers and frontiersmen continued to move in ever increasing numbers into the southern and western regions in search of land and trade, and the American Revolution hastened this trend.

Although Florida was reacquired by the Spanish, according to provisions of the Peace of Paris of 1783, which brought the Revolution to a close, the American penetration—economic, cultural, and military—of the entire region continued. The informal alliance between Spain and the inchoate United States during the Revolution (which led to the capture of Mobile, for example) rapidly disintegrated once the common enemy, England, had been vanquished. Competition revived between Spain and England's successors, the Americans, and in this new contest the Spanish attempted several strategies. One of these was to strangle United States expansion by closing the port of New Orleans to American traffic; another was to attempt to convert Americans into loyal Spanish citizens; a third was to incite the Indians against the Americans. In the end, all these strategies failed, and the Spanish court concluded a treaty in 1795 (San Lorenzo or Pinckney's, depending on one's point of view) which recognized American rights to navigate the Mississippi and to use New Orleans for transshipment of American goods, and yielded to the United States' interpretation of a boundary dispute over Florida.

By 1800 Spain had become tied to the fortunes of France, then ascending to new imperial heights under Napoleon Bonaparte. European intrigues proved more enticing to the Spanish court than protecting the wilderness of Louisiana, and that province was secretly retroceded to France. From Louisiana, Napoleon hoped to reestablish France's American empire. Again, however, Europe took priority, and in Napoleon's grand strategy Louisiana became expendable. He sold it to the United States in 1803, leaving Spanish Florida even more isolated by the expanding American nation.

The acquisition of Florida by the United States became a mere matter of time, complicated by the War of 1812 but hastened by the dissolution of Spain's Latin America empire. The Adams-Onís Treaty of 1819 (ratified in 1821) yielded Florida to the Americans and fixed the Spanish–Texas/American–Louisiana border. By this time, Spain had precious little to negotiate, for Mexico was entering the last stage of her independence movement and would inherit all Spanish possessions in North America.

With the acquisition of Florida, the entire Southeastern United States—again, as in the sixteenth century, under Spain—fell under the sovereignty of one nation. The American settlers, however, were different from the Spanish conquistadors and missionaries. The latter were outriders of a mighty empire which rarely viewed this portion of the world as more than a borderland, to be fortified but sacrificed (if need be) for greater, and richer, colonies elsewhere. The Americans came to settle, and they remained.

Thus the struggle for the Southeast among Europeans, their

descendants, and their American allies and adversaries fashioned attitudes and policies that bear heavily on our understanding of the history of the region and the combatants who vied for the treasure, glory, promise, and patrimony that Alabama and the Borderlands represented.

R.R.B.
L.A.C.

I

This painting by John Douglass provides an accurate reconstruction of life at the Gypsy Joint site, a thirteenth-century Mississippian farmstead excavated by Smith in 1978 in southeast Missouri. A nearby ceremonial mound is visible in the background. (Courtesy of Smithsonian Exposition Books)

The Prehistoric Background

1

Trends and Trajectories in American Archaeology: Some Questions about the Mississippian Period in Southeastern Prehistory

Richard A. Krause

From the nonperishable debris of extinct societies, archaeologists have created a picture of pervasive change in the details of material culture.[1] Viewed in hemisphere-wide perspective and through broad spans of time, the record of change in the New World seems reasonably regular. Big-game hunters and the lifestyle this mode of subsistence engendered preceded a lifestyle that depended on smaller, more scattered game. Increases in the efficiency of hunting and collecting preceded a settled lifestyle and prepared the way for agricultural modes of production. Agriculture, in turn, set the stage for material productions of greater sophistication and complexity and for such social enterprises as state and empire building.[2] Yet detailed comparisons of artifact inventories, burial practices, domestic and public architecture, and subsistence and settlement patterns reveal localized trends and trajectories of restricted duration. Here, there may be stability in artifact style; there, remarkable variability. Here, there may be stability in burial practices; there, rapid alterations. A shift from "surrounds" to ambushes may characterize the hunting practices in one region; "drives" may be the dominant and persistent pattern in a nearby region. It is precisely these short-term trends and trajectories, and the contrasts in lifestyle they reveal, that most severely challenge the archaeologist's imagination.[3]

It is commonly assumed, for instance, that trends were created by events and trajectories were maintained by processes.[4] Hence from trends and trajectories purposely looked for and compared with others, of like or different kind, archaeologists may infer the events which created them and the processes which maintained them. Making the inference is, of course, operational. And it is true that the adequacy of inferences must ultimately be judged by confrontation with a suitable program of archaeological tests, which is truly exciting work. Unfortunately, this ultimate aim—that is, design of a testing program for previously inferred events and processes—must (for now) lie beyond the scope of our inquiry. Our immediate interest must perforce be with the trends and trajectories themselves and their portent for issues of broader scope. The former, the trends and trajectories we perceive and the inferences they elicit are detailed in the essays by Griffin and Smith. The latter, the portent of trajectories and trends we perceive, will be the primary concern of this essay. I will join the issue of portent by (1) examining the implications of a contemporary scheme of cultural historical classification and (2) explicating some assumptions in archaeological reasoning. First, the implications of cultural historical classification.

The most popular scheme of cultural historical classification organizes the prehistory of the Western Hemisphere into a succession of configurational stages: Lithic, Archaic, Formative, Classic, and Post Classic.[5] The Mississippian manifestation represents the zenith of the Formative stage.[6] It is preceded by the less populous and less complex formulation, traditionally called Woodland, and is followed by the less populous, less complex formulation termed Protohistoric. More to the point, however, is that while remains attributed to the Lithic, Archaic, and Formative stages have been found in North America, representatives of the Classic and Post-Classic stages are absent north of the Rio Grande.[7] Put more simply, colonial Euroamericans encountered Amerindian confederacies and small-scale chiefdoms (social forms representative of the Formative stage) during their westward expansion. They did not find the states and empires (social forms representative of Classic and Post-Classic stages) that confronted the Spanish in Mexico and western South America.

Why states and empires flourished in Latin America but not in North America is an intriguing and vexing question. That a satisfactory answer requires reference to the advent of agriculture, technology, and population growth cannot be doubted.[8] Several papers which follow touch upon this issue; but can the brief experience as cultivators account for the absence of Native American states and empires in North America? To restate the issue: Given sufficient time, would North American Indians have become state and empire builders? An affirmative answer requires belief in an orderly march toward civilization and implies that all Amerindian societies responded to the beat of the same drummer, some more slowly than others. A negative answer calls into question the end toward which all Amerindian societies were moving and implies, as Caldwell put it, that "civilization might indeed be something rather special, possibly an abnormal, as it certainly can be an uncomfortable, condition of cultural development."[9]

To sharpen our focus a bit, let us ask: Do the Mississippian manifestations in Alabama, and by extension those of the Mississippi River drainage as a whole, prefigure the emergence of states and empires? If so, then the protohistoric organizational simplification and population decline were but an interlude, a brief hiatus, in the gathering of momentum. States and empires would have been inevitable if Euroamerican conquest had not intervened. If not, then the Mississippian manifestations discussed herein represent a culture climax, a pinnacle of momentum, an example of the ultimate in the potential of a social, economic, and political structuring which could, in and of itself, have gone no further. From the latter perspective, the protohistoric simplification of social, political, and economic life was more than an interrupted interlude. It was, instead, a waning of momentum, a dissipation of organizational force which, in the absence of additional—and most probably external—pressures, could not have been reformulated to the end of state and empire building.

I have alluded to a conflict in perspective which, as yet, is unresolved and will be for some time to come. Nevertheless, it affects what archaeologists see in their research and how they describe the archaeological evidence at hand. There are those so firmly committed to the inevitability of state and empire formation that they describe at least *some* Mississippian manifestations as states, although the evidence is unconvincing.[10] Others, no less sanguine in their view, argue that Native American achievements, the Mississippian enterprise among them, exemplify a pattern of development which, in and of itself, would never have led to statehood.[11] They interpret the evidence as demonstrating a pattern of development which is "non-nuclear," that is, a set of social, political, and economic adjustments which, once established, impeded—rather than promoted—the spread of state- and empirehood. Since the adherents of both views base their conclusions on the patterning presumed to inhere in the archaeological record, it might be well to examine that record before we continue.

Few would doubt that all Native American groups can ultimately, and by various routes, be traced to an Asian heartland.[12] Controversy, however, swirls about the details of when and how the Western Hemisphere was peopled.[13] Nevertheless, if three components of the general question of how the peopling occurred are considered, a reasonable model of that process can be developed. The three components are (1) glacial dynamics, (2) population dynamics, and (3) environmental/cultural interaction; and the role of each component may be briefly stated as follows. Glacial dynamics provided, ever so slowly, the available space for the process of New World settlement. Population dynamics provided the motive or propelling force. Culture and environment provided the facilitating mechanisms through which the effects of both motive force and available space were realized.

More specifically, there seems to have been a dynamic balance between sea level and glacier size during past episodes of glacial advance and retreat. During periods of glacial advance, the sea level was lowered; during glacial retreat, it was elevated. Thus, at the maximum extent of the Wisconsin glacier growth, a vast territory, an eastward extension of the Siberian Plain called Beringia, joined the Eurasian land mass to what is today Alaska. We may presume that Beringia was created very slowly and was likewise slowly populated with animals, plants, and human beings. We may also suppose that the motive force for the spread of animals, plants, and human beings to the newly emergent portions was population pressure on available resources.

The human population was almost certainly composed of arctic-adapted hunting and gathering groups that used highly portable tools, implements, shelters, and containers. We may assume a division of labor by age and sex, and decision making by consensus, with the role of leader falling to the male most capable of shaping and expressing that consensus. A balanced reciprocity was probably the dominant form of economic integration. Religious beliefs and practices were presumably centered on attempts to ensure, through ritual and magic, the well-being and availability of those game animals and collectable plants needed for group survival. Most importantly, however, it was a lifestyle in which people moved to food, rather than vice versa. Hence human behavior was organized to fit a daily and annual round of economic practices which, in turn, depended upon the availability of wild plants and the behavior of animals.

Like most hunting and gathering folk, the earliest inhabitants of Beringia must have existed in dynamic balance with their food supply. In other words, when food supply grew, the human population, after a modest lag, also grew; when food supply declined, population, after a lag, also declined. Put another way, the human population did not—at least for long—exceed the available food. But with a growth in food supply, we may predict a growth in the number of humans, and their expansion in both numbers and area occupied, until a new balance was struck. When such a balance was struck in Beringia and the glacial ice (which had, in a manner of speaking, created the new landscape) began to wane, new pressures must have slowly but steadily forced people and animals to seek new solutions to old problems. The sea level was rising to cover formerly dry lands; an ice-free corridor, axial to the Mackenzie drainage, was opening to the south; and hunting/collecting peoples spread southward toward unknown and uninhabited but richly stocked lands. The vast stretches of virgin territory seem to have witnessed an explosive population increase and an equally impressive rate of population spread.[14]

The speculative events I have recounted occurred sometime between 30,000 and 20,000 years ago.[15] We know that 15,000 years ago hunting and gathering peoples had spread throughout western North America and Mexico, and perhaps beyond.[16] Their southward spread reached Tierra del Fuego at the southern tip of South America by 10,000 years ago.[17] Their spread eastward to the Atlantic seaboard seems to have been equally rapid.[18] Hence by 8,000 B.C., or perhaps a bit earlier, the Western Hemisphere was settled by hunting and harvesting peoples whose lifestyles seem remarkably homogeneous.[19] This homogeneity—which may be more apparent than real—nonetheless allows us to use the Great Plains of North America as a kind of test area for anticipating the patterning of social development expected of early hunting groups farther south and east.

In the Great Plains of North America, two distinct forms of fluted projectile points—one found exclusively with the mammoth and the other with extinct bison, and the stratigraphic superposition of the two—established a sequence of early mammoth hunters and later bison hunters.[20] The food requirement of mammoths presumably exceeded the potential of the short steppe grasses that now dominate the region; hence a more luxuriant plant cover must be posited.[21] The general picture that has emerged from research on this element of an early human ecology is of a cooler, moister climate which supported a lush prairie grassland. Many of the mammoth kills in this region were found, in fact, in or near ancient ponds, streams, or river channels. Further, a significant proportion of the beasts slaughtered at these locales was female, young, or immature. This evidence led some to infer selectivity on the part of the hunters and to suggest a pattern of single elephant kills at favored hunting stations.[22] With the disappearance of the elephant (for reasons not yet satisfactorily explained), hunting/gathering peoples turned to smaller but more abundant grazing animals, and chief among them was a bison of larger than modern size.[23] Mass kills resembling drives, or "pounds," and opportunistic surrounds or ambushes at waterholes or in breaks along watercourses or drainage ways replaced the earlier pattern of repetitious single-animal kills.[24] This shift from single, large-animal kills to the mass slaughter of smaller animals may have been far more important than we assume. It could, for instance, have forced the emergence of those basic principles of personnel management and conflict resolution upon which larger and more stable population aggregates were ultimately built. At any rate, it was from the protean base provided by early hunters and harvesters, whether in Mexico, the Great Plains, or elsewhere, that the events of succeeding millennia shaped a rich diversity of lifestyles.

For the next 6,000 years the multiplex web of human, animal, and plant relationships expanded and intensified as the economies of hunting and gathering groups responded to the food potentials of different regions. The early post-Pleistocene food potentials of Mexico, the Southwestern United States, the Great Plains of North America, and perhaps parts of the Southeast were set, in part, by the altithermal, a period characterized by higher temperatures and lower rainfall than is typical today.[25] In Mexico and the American Southwest, lush, well-watered plains were slowly replaced by arid lands with a xyrophilic plant cover.[26] To the north in the Great Plains, short-grass communities expanded into areas of tall grasses; parts of the modern short-grass plains (e.g., the Bighorn and Wyoming basins) possessed a Great Basin type of ecology; and stands of oak-hickory forest along upland tributaries were reduced or eliminated.[27] There is intriguing evidence for episodic shifts from forest-edge to prairie biotypes in the Ozarks.[28] The effects of the altithermal (if any) have yet to be adequately measured farther east, but there may have been an eastward spread of grasslands to portions of the Southeastern United States.[29]

The effects of the altithermal were felt in Mexico as early as 7,000 B.C., and the course of subsequent events there is exemplified by the pattern of development in the Tehuacan Valley, south of Mexico City. Here, dessication led to a gradual redistribution of plants and animals which ultimately concentrated them about water sources. The human inhabitants responded by adjusting their hunting tools and techniques, extending and intensifying their collecting practices, and equipping themselves with more efficient tools and implements for the preparation of plant foods. The better-watered regions now served as focal areas, pockets of periodic but intense man/plant interaction.

People still subsisted as hunters and harvesters, but as millennium followed millennium the focalization of humans and plants led first to plant tending, then to full-scale cultivation. Full-scale cultivation, and perhaps some of the forms of plant tending which preceded it, forced incremental increases in residential stability, such that by 3,000 B.C. clusters of timber, grass, and dirt—covered pit houses were built near better-watered strips of tillable land.[30] These earth-lodge clusters are good presumptive evidence for the emergence of a mixed hunting, collecting, and farming economy, adjusted to a seasonal cycle that featured periods of village life interspersed with periods of hunting and gathering. The first, faltering steps toward full-scale farming and year-round village life had been taken. In Mexico, once this threshold had been passed, there was no turning back; the economic import of farming continued to grow at the expense of hunting and gathering.

By 1,000 B.C., Mexico was occupied by village-dwelling farming folk.[31] The prevailing pattern of settlement was small, autonomous farming communities, each dependent upon locally available resources. The inhabitants of such communities presumably had equal access to the means of production, and the exploitative tasks performed in one community were similar in type and scheduling to the tasks performed in every other. At any rate, the tools and strategies for procuring and processing locally available raw materi-

23

als seem to have been similar for most groups. Under such conditions, seasonal differences in intergroup surpluses must have been minimal; trade in foodstuffs, raw materials, or indigenous manufactured goods must have been restricted; and the economic incentives for supracommunity management of social and natural resources must have been limited. Yet the foundations of a kinship-based, internally ranked authority structure must have been laid in these early communities. The earliest suprahousehold forms of authority were probably a response to the need for conflict resolution and the need to organize and schedule community labor. Whatever the case, early authority structures seem to have been weakly developed and purely local. The overall picture is one of a sparse populace, gathered together in small communities, and each independent of the comings and goings of others: each, in effect, a nation unto itself.[32] However, an important transition had been fully realized. Food was now moved to and among people. Upon this foundation a new and stratified—as opposed to ranked—social order was raised.

Mexico's regionally distinct village farming traditions formed the weft threads in the emergent tapestry of state and empire. The warps were provided by commerce and conquest. Both were driven, in slightly different ways, by the shuttle of population growth. In more prosaic terms, we may see two pathways, or routes, to state- and empirehood: one through conquest, which emerged in environmentally circumscribed areas; the other through the pull of market centers in areas with uneven distribution of important natural resources.

State formation through conquest requires an initial phase in which population growth produces demographic stress, which may be temporarily relieved by the reorganization of labor and technology to the end of irrigation, terracing, or reclamation of swamps and other marginal lands. If, however, population continues to grow, with no relief by emigration, demographic stress will again assert its influence, promoting competition for available resources and inciting conquest warfare. Conquest warfare, with its incorporation of vanquished by victor, will lead, we presume, to multicommunity forms of economic integration and will produce the administrative apparatus that is needed to direct and control newly acquired human and natural resources.[33]

For state formation by means of the market, we must assume that a multicommunity exchange network, in an area characterized by an uneven distribution of resources, became focused upon a

24

strategically located settlement and converted it to a trade center. Further, we must assume that this trade center attracted and at least partially supported religious functionaries, artisans, craftsmen, merchants, and other specialists or quasi specialists who augmented the local population and added to the natural growth rate of the community. We must also contend that during this process some of the community's specialists or quasi specialists (most probably those with combined civil and religious responsibility) acquired power and prestige by virtue of liens against the goods and services channeled through the market, such that they formed the administrative nucleus needed to organize and direct conquest warfare, if that became necessary. Thus when the local populace swelled to the demographic stress point and the demands for an inflow of goods exceeded the available supply, the center had both the organizational structure and the manpower to extend its demands upon the productive power of the hinterland, either by (1) economic threat and intimidation or (2) military venture. Population densities in the hinterland may have remained low and a pattern of fight and flight may have still obtained there, unless or until formerly autonomous communities were incorporated into the network of control cast by the market center.[34]

In Mexico these two patterns of growth were not mutually exclusive. Singularly or jointly, by 800 B.C. they stimulated the formation of states, and the Olmec civilization of Vera Cruz and Tabasco is a good example.[35] The Monte Alban formulation in Oaxaca is another. The Valley of Mexico spawned the equally early market center of Tlatilco, and by the first century A.D. had become the home of the greatest of all precolumbian Mexican commercial centers, Teotihuacan.[36] Teotihuacan was a true city, an unequivocal example of urbanism, which at its height contained 20 square kilometers of temples, plazas, workshops, palaces, apartments, slums, drainage systems, waterways, and reservoirs organized about a grid system of avenues and streets.[37] Teotihuacan was also the center of a vast commercial empire that serviced populations in Vera Cruz, Tabasco, Oaxaca, and the Mayan regions of Mexico and Guatemala.[38]

North of Mexico and west of the Mississippi River, the postaltithermal rhythmic process was different. Along the Pacific Coast, the abundant plant and animal life permitted a remarkable fine-tuning of postaltithermal hunting and harvesting economies. Once a workable balance had been achieved here, it proved extremely durable. There were, to be sure, periodic economic adjustments as a consequence of human initiative or variations in the behavior of plants and animals, but they never exceeded the limits of a dynamic equilibrium as realized within the confines of a hunting and harvesting lifestyle.[39] Across the coastal mountains in the arid and semi-arid basins and plateaus to the east, a desert culture, reminiscent of the earliest postaltithermal adjustments in Mexico, led to sparse and mobile populations which, once integrated with a scarce resource base, proved equally resistant to change. The desert culture that was achieved in this region persisted virtually unaltered into historic times.[40]

In the American Southwest, particularly in regions suitable for dry farming and small-scale-irrigation agriculture, a desert-culture lifestyle gave way to a mixed farming and hunting economy. Here and there, clusters of timber, grass, and dirt-covered pit houses (some lined with stone slabs) were built near the better-watered stretches of tillable land. Like their counterparts in the Tehuacan Valley, these earth-lodge settlements indicate a seasonal cycle of village life interspersed with hunting and gathering. In subsequent millennia, semisedentary village life lapsed into either (1) full-scale village farming, centered upon blocks of adjacent masonry rooms, or (2) large-scale-irrigation agriculture which supported sizable villages of aboveground timber, grass, and earth-covered houses. Isolated masonry room blocks gave way to the multistoried, multiroom pueblo towns of the fourteenth, fifteenth, and sixteenth centuries. Similar towns and their lifestyle persisted into historic times. Large-scale-irrigation agriculture and the sizable earth-lodge villages it supported collapsed by the fifteenth century A.D.[41]

A seriously reduced carrying capacity during the altithermal seems to have forced the inhabitants of the Great Plains into oasis areas or peripheral regions where they developed a diversified lifestyle.[42] It was from this diversified lifestyle that postaltithermal differences in fauna and flora shaped a mosaic of adjustments. Among the elements of this mosaic were (1) a highly mobile herd-animal hunting and high-plains foraging pattern in the Western short-grass plains, (2) a less mobile, mixed woodland–tall-grass-plains form of hunting or harvesting the creeks and river courses in the central plains, and (3) a yet more sedentary woodland-adapted pattern of hunting and gathering, focused upon the broad, forested bottomlands of the major river valleys and feeder streams which edged the plains on the east.[43]

A mixed hunting and farming lifestyle, characterized by hamlets and homesteads composed of square earth lodges; by the cultivation of maize, beans, squash, sunflowers, and tobacco; and by the hunting of buffalo, deer, antelope, and smaller, more solitary game animals, appeared in the central and eastern portions of the plains by A.D. 800. Larger farming villages of long rectangular earth-covered houses, surrounded by dry moats and palisades, appeared about the same time, but were confined to the trough of the Missouri River and its immediate environs in northern Iowa and southern South Dakota.[44]

The next millennium was marked by shifts in population density and distribution. There were, for example, (1) abandonment of the western reaches of settlement, (2) intensification of population scattering farther to the east, (3) the emergence of large farming villages, composed of circular earth lodges along the northern and eastern margins of the plains, and (4) the extension of maize agriculture and village farming to its northern limit in northern North Dakota. Nevertheless, the village level of sociocultural integration was never superseded. Nor were multicommunity aggregates of any size or permanence formed.[45]

A still different developmental patterning may be discerned east of the Mississippi River, in that vast region classified as the Eastern Woodlands. Since the southern portion of the region is of greatest interest to us here, we shall focus upon it and treat its trends and trajectories in greater detail than if an equally balanced account of the whole region were our aim. If Quimby is right, some of the earliest inhabitants of the Eastern Woodlands followed a pancontinental coniferous zone into the Northeastern forests and worked their way southward.[46] Quimby's forest-adapted immigrants may well have settled the Northeast, but it seems equally reasonable to suppose that lands to the south may have been settled from the plains. T. M. N. Lewis, for example, noted a correlation between fluted-point occurrences in the Southeast and the distribution of relic prairies.[47] He inferred an eastward spread of grasslands during the altithermal, as well as an eastward spread of big-game hunters.

Some of those who first came to the Southeast may, indeed, have brought with them a hunting and harvesting tradition that was shaped by prior experience with a plains or prairie environment. Hence we may expect an initial pattern of single elephant kills at favored hunting stations in relic prairielands. Nevertheless, with the disappearance of the elephant in the East we should not expect a shift to the plains-grassland pattern of herd-animal hunting (i.e., mass kills resembling drives or pounds) and opportunistic surrounds in the breaks along watercourses or drainage ways. We may expect, instead, a fine-tuning of the hunting and harvesting economy, adjusted to increasing efficiency in using the forest. This fine-tuning should be manifested in the emergence of (1) a forest analogue to grassland forms of ambush hunting, (2) seasonal cycles of movement and resource use, expressing a forest rhythm, and (3) the discovery and use of forest-based sources of natural plant and animal foods. This, in fact, seems to be the pattern discernible in the eastern Archaic. It is also a pattern which, though in place by the second millennium B.C., culminated later in the intimate integration of human behavior with natural resources that Caldwell described as "primary forest efficiency."[48]

As "primary forest efficiency" was achieved, sometime between 2000 B.C. and A.D. 700, groups that lived in areas with abundant natural foods (fish, forest products, and shellfish) experienced a level of residential stability which promoted the full potential of a hunting/harvesting lifestyle. Our picture of this Woodland period in the Southeast is one of peoples who were still hunters and harvesters—among whom plant cultivation, if known, made slow headway. Use of the bow and arrow, improved hunting techniques, new methods of harvesting and using forest products, and improved fishing techniques seem to have hindered the growth of emphasis upon food production. Nevertheless, those Southeasterners who were more settled than their predecessors seem also to have been wealthier. Timber, brush, and bark-covered houses of various sizes and shapes, exquisite ornaments, well-developed traditions of potting and weaving, and elaborate burial ceremonialism (frequently interpreted as signaling differences in rank) are found among them.[49] This expressed potential was, we suspect, of primary import in providing a foundation for later developments. Once in place, it fostered an institutional structure and plan of organization from which many later peoples departed reluctantly, or not at all.

The advent of intensive forms of food production in the Southeastern United States is a matter of great interest and some debate. The debate centers less upon *when* than upon *how* crop growing reached the region. There are three contrasting views: (1) about A.D. 1000, immigrant Mississippian farming populations displaced resident Woodland groups; (2) from A.D. 700 to 900, resident Woodland

28

hunting and gathering groups were transformed (i.e., "Mississip-pianized") through the diffusion of ideas and practices typical of crop-growing peoples in other regions, and (3) from A.D. 800 to 900, a limited influx of cultivators introduced ideas and practices which transformed resident hunters and harvesters and stimulated a fusion of resident with immigrant to produce local versions of a Mississip-pian lifestyle.[50]

Arguing the immigration view requires (1) identifying a parent population from which most, if not all, immigrant groups were derived, (2) adducing reasons for reasonably large-scale migrations, (3) demonstrating that most, if not all, Southeastern Mississippian communities were what Rouse called "site unit intrusions," and (4) showing that resident Woodland populations were expelled.[51] Advancing the second position (that the Mississippian lifestyle consti-tuted a diffusion-induced transformation) requires (1) identifying compatible Woodland predecessors, (2) demonstrating trajectories in Woodland manufacturing and economic practices which, under suitable conditions, could produce elements of succeeding life-styles, and (3) isolating what Rouse called "trait unit intrusions," which could stimulate "Mississippianization."[52] Defending the third position (limited immigration and immigrant-resident fusion) requires demonstrating that (1) suitable newcomers were in some portions of the Southeast and that (2) a fusion of Woodland resident with Mississippian migrant could explain those transformations in subsistence, settlement, and manufacturing practices which oc-curred throughout the Southeast. These issues are joined, with varying success and from subtly different perspectives, in the essays by Griffin and Smith (which follow).

Precise knowledge of how crop growing achieved its economic status in the Southeast is also of import to the question posed earlier: Were Mississippian peoples on the road to statehood? If, for example, food-production techniques were brought to the Southeast via large-scale immigration, we might suggest that population pressure elsewhere was the motive force, that is, farmable lands to the north and west were exhausted or in short supply. Thus if immigrant populations were large, they were, in effect, colonists, fleeing the effects of population pressure in their homelands and ultimately subject to reincorporation by the parent population, if and when this became feasible. (It never did.) Further, if these putative colonial populations grew at a typical rate, and if Smith's assertion that Mississippian peoples confined themselves to "linear, environmentally circumscribed flood plain habitats" is also correct, they should have filled the space available to them quite rapidly.[53] Once the available space was filled, we might expect either programs of land improvement, like those in Mexico or the Southwestern United States, or competition for unimproved lands and unmanaged natural resources. We have little, if any, evidence for programs of land improvement or intensive natural resource management.[54]

There were, however, elaborate fortifications around the large Mississippian towns.[55] Most archaeologists identify them as a response to competition over unimproved lands and unmanaged resources. That such competition led to a raiding and feuding pattern of warfare seems a reasonable inference. But some see the bastioned, fortification walls, guarded gateways, and dry moats of the Southeast as evidence for the emergence of conquest warfare.[56] If these scholars are right, then Mississippian peoples may have been taking the first steps toward building conquest states. Reference to the developmental patterning discernible in other regions of North America does not, however, support this view. Fortifications of similar plan and construction appear in the northern plains at about the same time, but few Plains specialists consider them evidence for wars of conquest.[57] Drastic defensive measures were also taken by the prehistoric residents of the American Southwest, and again, few would consider them evidence for attempts at conquest.[58]

In sum, large-scale incorporation of vanquished by victor, which presumably played a role in Mexican state building, seems alien to the pattern of development north of the Rio Grande. Nevertheless, if the Southeast *was* settled by large-scale immigration, it could be an exception.

In this volume, Griffin discusses the migration hypothesis, but clearly prefers the view that resident hunting and gathering groups were "Mississippianized" by the introduction of maize and the consequences of maize farming:

While maize, probably coming in from the Southwest, is securely known in the East by about A.D. I, it is not a significant part of the food supply until in the A.D. 700 to 900 period, when it appeared in quantities over a wide area. Apparently it took over a half-millennium to acquire adequate cultivation, seed-selection, food-preparation, and storage techniques to transform this seed crop into the valuable food supply it became in most prehistoric Eastern societies after A.D. 900. The view adopted here is that this major addition to their already sophisticated hunting and gathering skills permitted population growth that resulted in a need for mechanisms of societal control and hastened the changes in societal structure.[59]

The major questions raised by Griffin's interpretation are: Why was the potential of full-scale maize cultivation unrealized for 500 years? and Why was there a rapid growth in maize cultivation from A.D. 700 to 900? Definite answers elude us, but—as usual in such cases—potentially fruitful speculations may be advanced.

Most Southeastern prehistorians have noted the abundance of the Eastern forests and the progressively intense integration of natural plant and animal foods into the region's Archaic and Woodland economies.[60] For millennia, the Southeast seems to have been like the Pacific Coast. Its human population was in dynamic equilibrium with its food supply. To be sure, technological innovations may, from time to time, have increased the natural foods available, and human populations, as a consequence, may have grown until a new balance was struck. Nevertheless, people still moved to food, with the rhythm and range of such movement determined, in large part, by their knowledge of the distribution and behavior of plants and animals. Under such circumstances, the introduction of maize via trade or diffusion would render that food an oddity.

That maize could be grown or tended may have been realized from the outset, but full-scale cultivation would have hindered the efficiency of established and successful subsistence practices. Maize, in limited quantities, may have been tangentially incorporated into Woodland economies, perhaps as an item of religious attention or as a delicacy, in regions where the abundance and geographical juxtaposition of natural foods stimulated the greatest residential stability. Full-scale cultivation, however, would require narrowing the range of intense natural resource use and greater residential stability than most groups had achieved prior to about A.D. 700 or 800. Hence future archaeological inquiry might be directed toward those forces which could have promoted a narrower range of intensive natural food use, as well as evidence for full-scale cultivation. It is from this perspective that the third option for the introduction of cultivation to the Southeast merits closer attention.

If it can be demonstrated that a limited influx of cultivators introduced ideas and practices which stimulated a fusion of resident with immigrant, then a plausible account could be created of how a narrower range of intensive resource use was achieved. Let us suppose, for the moment, that from A.D. 700 to 900 those regions with abundant natural foods were sustaining peak hunting and harvesting populations. Let us further suppose that periodically used but economically important portions of one region were successfully claimed by immigrant cultivators. A part of the region would thus be removed from the reach of resident hunters and harvesters, creating an intense, if local, disruption of the natural resource/population balance. Hunting and gathering groups could temporarily redress the problem by extending their range. Nevertheless, in the long run this solution would merely disrupt the balance between population and natural resources in a broader area, putting pressure on neighboring groups either to extend their territory or to narrow their range of intense natural resource use. Such pressure should encourage intergroup competition and conflict. If some of the most populous and settled groups responded by intensifying the harvesting portion of their subsistence to retain the advantage of massed manpower, then crop growing might provide them a minimally disruptive alternative to intense, if periodic, overuse of harvestable wild foods. An increased commitment to crop growing could then provide the impetus for partial "Mississippianization," which might prepare the way for full-scale incorporation into a Mississippian lifestyle via continued population growth and additional resource-range narrowing.

In short, competition, conflict, and a preadaptive response wave may have preceded the advent of cultivators in a given region, easing their acquisition of new lands and adding substantially to their natural rate of population increase. Further, if the newly expanded cultivating populace continued to grow and spread, the process would feed upon itself, gaining momentum as it occurred in one region after another, until the "linear environmentally circumscribed flood plain habitats" of the Southeast were filled. There would still be territories beyond the effective reach of cultivators that might have remained hunter and harvester strongholds. Indeed, the continued presence of a potentially hostile hunting and harvesting folk may in part (at least) have been responsible for the construction of Mississippian fortifications.

Both the emergence of food production, through the diffusion hypothesis, and limited immigration, with the fusion-of-immigrant-and-resident hypothesis, require events and processes which fit the developmental patterning seen elsewhere in Native North America. Either could have produced a settled lifestyle. Thus if either hypothesis can be considered compatible with a move toward statehood, we must show that the subsequent patterning was significantly different in the Southeast from elsewhere. For such evidence, we must, however, turn to what we know—or at least think we know—about sociopolitical events that shaped the conduct of life in ancient Mississippian communities. Settled populations, tied to a narrow range of intensively used resources, pose managerial problems. Chief among them are the need to adjudicate disputes, allocate land, organize and direct labor, and regulate the flow of food and other commodities. Mississippian mound building and burial ritual can be seen as organized and, presumably, managed investments of community resources which emphasized the legitimacy and promoted the durability of traditional patterns of authority.[61] The precise role such traditional authority played and the structure of past forms of managerial effort are, of course, exciting points to consider.

There can be little doubt that the social core of ancient Mississippian communities was an aggregate of consanguineous kinsmen.[62] That is, each community contained a network of interlocking parent–child and sibling ties that served as the social charter for distributing rights and duties, privileges, and obligations. Of the two kinds of social bonds, parent–child links must be considered primary and sibling links secondary. This is because siblings are offspring with at least one parent in common. Thus recognition of a sibling tie requires the prior existence of a parent–offspring link. In any case, the existence of a parent–child or sibling tie implies an *assumed* biological relationship, or bond of descent, between persons. The assumed relationship may be traced through a single parent (patrilateral if male, matrilateral if female) or through both parents (bilaterally). Since most Southeastern Amerindian societies have been characterized as unilateral (usually matrilateral), it has been assumed that a unilateral principle of descent was typical of ancient Mississippian societies (whether patrilateral or matrilateral is, for the moment, unimportant).[63] It should be noted, however, that a complementary social bond between offspring and nondescent-related parent may have been important in special circumstances.

The archaeological evidence seems to indicate that not all parent–child and sibling bonds were of equal value. After death, some Mississippians were interred in temple mounds, or other special places, with sumptuous grave goods. Others were buried beneath their houses, or in cemeteries, with a much more modest supply of grave goods—or no grave goods at all.[64] The differential

treatment accorded the dead may be interpreted as indicating in-
equalities of rank within the society at large or as signaling the rank
of the deceased. The first interpretation merely states that some
members of a Mississippian community were set apart from others
by virtue of their birth and/or personal accomplishments and may
have constituted an indigenous, if nascent, aristocracy. The second
holds that the indicated rank was that of the deceased. Thus if lavish
burial treatment was given an infant, we may infer ascribed status.
From this second perspective, children of high-status persons were
expected, by virtue of birth alone, to assume positions of power and
prestige, with little (if any) need to validate themselves by personal
effort or initiative.

The first interpretation is the more cautious and fits the pattern
of Native American status striving somewhat better than the second. Throughout much of Native North America status was
achieved, or enhanced, by the distribution or destruction of wealth,
rather than by its accumulation. This distribution or destruction
often took place at group ceremonials, such as burials. The wealth
that was interred with an infant at burial, therefore, might mark the
status-striving efforts of a living relative, rather than the rank of the
deceased. I am not arguing that this was invariably the case, only
that it could have been, and this must be carefully considered if
more elaborate interpretive edifices are to be built on the analysis of
burial practices. At any rate, the basis for inequality of rank in
Mississippian societies needs further attention.

Let us take the more cautious view and assume that rank was a
product of genealogical position that required validation through
personal accomplishment. In other words, let us assume that the
number of parent–offspring and sibling links to a high-ranking
ancestor could be used to claim a particular rank if and when it
seemed warranted by personal achievements. In such a system, the
fewer the links to a ranking ancestor, the higher the rank that could
be claimed. Lineal links, however, should be distinguished from
collateral links. The former are to be construed as any concatena-
tion of parent–child ties; the latter are sibling ties in any biological
generation other than one's own. Thus two lineal links connect any
individual to his father's father. One lineal and one collateral link
connect any person to his father's brother. Now if we can assume
primogeniture in calculating the genealogical links from an individual to an ancestor, chains of kin ties that include a collateral link
will be longer than those that include only lineal links.

34

In kin groups of the kind considered here, there will always be many fewer lineals than collaterals. As a population grows, the number of people who must count a collateral link to claim descent from a common ancestor will increase much faster than the number who are able to trace the relationship through lineal links alone. For example, let us assume an ancestor who produces two offspring, each of whom produces two offspring, and so on. After four generations, four descendants will be able to claim lineal links, twelve must include collateral ties. After eight generations, still only four descendants will be able to claim lineal links alone, whereas 252 must include collateral ties. If access to status and prestige were to be justified by such a genealogical network, and in the manner described, then the potential for seeking community rewards might be characterized as flowing downward from ancestor to descendants and outward from higher-ranking lineal to lower-ranking collateral kinsmen. In sum, we suspect that a few members of any descent group had, by reason of their accomplishments and genealogical position, the right to decide what goals were desirable and to direct the attention and labor of other descent-group members toward attaining them. One of these goals, we think, was temple mound building.

Temple mounds apparently played a dual social role. On one hand, Mississippian mounds were tangible representations of the right to legitimate exercise of power and authority by a select few. On the other, they represented the community's wealth, glory, and capability. Hence Mississippian mounds may be interpreted as both public and private monuments, as community shrines (perhaps dedicated to gods), and as markers of a cardinal social principle (symbols of ranking).[65] Then too, Mississippian mounds required massed manpower to construct—manpower thus committed to the authority the mounds represented. At the same time, working toward a common goal promoted worker solidarity, if suitable rewards were forthcoming. In the case at hand, rewards would have taken the tangible form of a monument, and the intangible form of civic pride and a community fund of prestige in which all might have shared, albeit differentially.

There were, however, limits to the rewards that could be adequately distributed and the authority that could be maintained through mound building. It has been noted that lineals could claim the greatest share of a monument's prestige yield, near-collaterals could claim less, and distant collaterals still less. Yet even the most distant collaterals must have provided construction labor. The disparity between labor owed and rewards received would have grown as group size increased and the kinship and social gulf between lineals and collaterals widened. Thus there would come a time in the group's growth when the vast majority of members were related only distantly to the leaders; therefore, they could claim little of the glory and power these authorities represented. When this happened, resentments could have resulted, and dissatisfied portions of the population might have begun to question traditionally held assumptions about the legitimate transfer and use of power. These dissidents would have formed a potential body of followers, should disputes over succession to status or title have emerged among competing descent-group members who claimed higher rank.

Ethnographic evidence indicates that in unilateral descent groups disputes over succession to status or title occur most frequently among half-brothers, that is, a high-ranking man's descendants by several wives.[66] Each descendant has a claim (although some claims may be stronger than others) and each may call upon his nondescent-related kinsmen for support—that is, make use of the complementary bond noted earlier. As the struggle over leadership unfolds, the number and disposition of each competitor's relatives may play an important role. Nevertheless, only one competitor can win. Each loser, however, has identified himself as a potential leader and a potential threat to the established order. Such a man may become the focal point for other dissidents, who see in him a means for advancing their cause. Thus a claimant to title and high status, though unsuccessful, may attract a sufficient number of determined followers among his kinsmen and dissatisfied segments of the population to set himself up as an authority, should he so choose.

After identifying a willing body of relatives and other supporters, a potential authority figure may consider several moves. If his challenge has created bitterness and suspicion, he may choose to found an independent settlement. However, conditions for such a move must be favorable. Suitable land must be available beyond the parent community's reach. Moreover, founding a totally independent settlement requires a following of sufficient size and vigor to provide for the common defense and economic security. If conditions for founding an independent community are *not* favorable but suitable space is available in the parent community's hinterland, the dissident authority may found a colony that retains social, ceremonial, and economic ties to its parent while establishing an independent or pseudo-independent local-authority structure. Finally, if suitable hinterland space is not available or the military and/or economic risks of removal are prohibitive, the potential leader may choose to remain within the parent community and seek other means to promote recognition of his claims. By manipulating affinitive alliances and kin ties, through success in war, trade, and various economic enterprises, a shrewd potential leader might marshal the wealth and support necessary to further his ambitions. If these ethnographic considerations can be applied to the political process in Mississippian communities, they might shed new light on mound-building practices. For example, an emergent Mississippian leader, whether resident, colonist, or independent migrant, might have advanced his cause and consolidated his position by building a mound for his ancestors, his followers, and his descendants, but especially for himself.

This admittedly speculative model of the Mississippian political process may account for two infrequently discussed aspects of mound building. The first of these is the large number of multimound settlements. If mound building had the social significance and solidarity-promoting effects envisioned, multiple contemporary mounds are the predictable consequence of population growth and competition for status and prestige in favorably located and politically mature settlements. Moreover, the propensity to rebuild, refurbish, and enlarge existing mounds—behavior often relegated to religious fervor alone—assumes new meaning. Major rebuilding and enlargement, in this model, reflect succession to leadership. In other words, changes of leadership that accompany the death or removal of an authority are marked by the beginning of a major new construction episode. From this point of view, Mississippian mound building chronicles succession to office and title, as well as ritual purification. The model also contains developmental implications that bear upon our original question.

By A.D. 900, population growth and resource range narrowing had led to the creation of farming communities whose authority and prestige-distribution practices centered on the construction and maintenance of earthen temple-tombs. Between A.D. 900 and 1400, the authority and prestige-distribution limits inherent in mound building and other public works programs combined with continued population growth to produce a dispersed pattern of populous cen-

37

ters, satellite communities, hamlets, and homesteads.[67] Internal ranking both created these developments and accompanied them as opposition between original settlers and newcomers, senior and junior descent lines, those rising to prominence, and those in decline hardened into a locally and regionally stratified social order. Once maturity was achieved, modifications of the social order could be attained through demographic growth or decline, successful or unsuccessful management of resources, people, or alliances, and victory or defeat in war.

Successful competitors might, for instance, translate otherwise temporary social gains into genealogical claims, but there was a limit to the growth that could be thus sustained. As a chief or other leader drew a greater following through judicious management, he reached a point at which his radius of action was checked by his kinsmen and their allies protecting their own interests. By virtue of a competitor's growth, an ambitious yet less powerful authority could, for a while at least, offer greater immediate returns. Thus, centers of power and prestige as they grew larger spawned their own competitors and by virtue of their growth yielded the advantage to them. To supersede the limitations of a monument-based prestige yield system and the kin order which it exemplified, an authority had to gain independent access to reliable and renewable resources of his own. One means to this end was control of commerce, and some of the populous late Mississippian communities participated in a moderate commerce, which may have promoted a craft specialization and other forms of entrepreneurship.

Greater commercial prosperity might have ultimately broadened the base provided by traditional forms of prestige distribution, and temporarily at least, allowed entrenched authorities to control a larger following. Indeed, if commerce had expanded farther, Mississippian communities might have moved toward those forms of sociocultural integration that promote the formation of states; but without external forms of wealth in sufficient volume, there were limits to the population that could be controlled by traditional means. Lacking a substantial and renewable external form of wealth, Mississippian societies were forced to depend upon the management of locally available resources, which would have limited the economic growth their technology could sustain. Ultimately, continued population growth would combine with limited economic potential, intensified intra- and intergroup competition, and ecological mismanagement (or stress) to produce severe strains in the fabric of Mississippian society.

In the fifteenth century—here faster, there more slowly—elaborate expressions of mound building and other public works were discontinued.[68] We may presume that the organizing social and political force behind them had, in part at least, collapsed.[69] In sum, Mississippian sociopolitical organization contained the seeds of its own destruction, namely, the prestige-distribution limits inherent in monument building for expressing and maintaining authority.

This model of the Mississippian political process, should it prove tenable, would be consonant with the view that the protohistoric simplification of social, political, and economic life represented a waning of momentum, a dissipation of organizational force, which—without the intercession of additional and probably external pressures—could not have been reformulated to the end of state and empire building. Nevertheless, as the essays in this volume show, these matters are far from resolved.

2 Changing Concepts of the Prehistoric Mississippian Cultures of the Eastern United States

James B. Griffin

It is appropriate that The University of Alabama Sesquicentennial include a symposium on the last major phase of prehistoric Indian development in the Eastern United States. The name of the state and the names of many of its rivers, counties, cities, and towns are derived from Indian languages. Within the borders of the state, thousands of locations were occupied by Indian societies for about 12,000 years. Hundreds of sites represent the prehistoric populations of the Mississippian period from about A.D. 900 to 1700, including the major Moundville site and supporting satellites, a primary focus of this session.

The earliest field work recorded at Moundville was by Thomas Maxwell in 1840, and he subsequently noted and described materials and data on activities at the site by nature and by man.[1] Nathaniel T. Lupton, a president of the University of Alabama from 1871 to 1875, excavated at Moundville in 1869, at the request of the secretary of the Smithsonian Institution. Lupton shared his interest in archaeology with Eugene A. Smith, state geologist, professor of geology, and founder-director of the Alabama Museum of Natural History. One of Smith's students was Walter B. Jones, who played a major role in the development of archaeology in the state and in the acquisition of Moundville as state property. The first and largest part of the monument was purchased from the Griffin estate in 1929 with funds raised by public subscription.

40

About this same time, Jones must have met Carl E. Guthe, director of the Museum of Anthropology at the University of Michigan and chairman of the Committee on State Archaeological Surveys of the National Research Council. In an effort to allow prominent anthropologists of that period to view the recently acquired site of Moundville, a Conference on Southern Pre-History was organized by Guthe, met in Birmingham in mid-December 1932, and a "Not for Publication" document of the meeting was issued. Its unnamed compiler and editor was Guthe,[2] and it has since been reissued and dedicated to Dr. Walter B. Jones and David L. DeJarnette, a student and protégé of Jones who was to become, from the 1930s to 1970s, the premier Alabama archaeologist and curator of Mound State Monument (for twenty-five years). DeJarnette received archaeological training at the University of Chicago Field School in Fulton County, Illinois, in 1932; was in charge of the Relief Labor programs in the 1930s in Alabama; and was associated with Guthe in excavations at the Bessemer site for Birmingham-Southern College in 1934–35.[3] Later, he was responsible for training most of the best Alabama students in archaeology. My association with Jones, and particularly with DeJarnette, began in the mid-1930s and has continued (with David) to the present.

Many other interrelations of that small portion of American society that is actively interested in archaeology cannot be given here, and may never be recorded, but they provide continuity and they enrich the pursuit of an adequate, though always incomplete and fragmentary, reconstruction of prehistoric life in Alabama and the Eastern United States. My presence at this symposium reflects a Tuscaloosa–Ann Arbor connection which has flourished, and faltered, for over fifty years.

From the time of the discovery (or rediscovery) of the Western World by Columbus there have been many attempts, fabulous and fatuous, to connect its inhabitants to known historical peoples and cultures of Eurasia and Africa. Until reasonably accurate assessments of the age of human beings on earth, and of the age of the world and the universe, were made, interpretations of the derivation of Indian populations and their length of stay in the New World were handicapped. A full review of these ideas would produce a very large volume; but an engaging and delightful summary was prepared by Robert Wauchope in which he provides a list of erroneous ideas: that the Indians "were once Tyrian Phoenicians, Assyrians, Ancient

Egyptians, Canaanites, Israelites, Trojans, Romans, Etruscans, Greeks, Scythians, Tartars, Chinese Buddhists, Hindus, Mandingoes or other Africans, Madagascans, the early Irish, Welsh, Norsemen, Basques, Portuguese, French, Spaniards, Huns, or survivors of the Lost Continents of Mu or Atlantis."[4] Publishers have always been ready to sponsor any fantasy, if it is readable and they can make money on it.

The only acceptable proposal for the presence of prehistoric people in the New World is that they crossed the Bering land bridge, connecting Siberia and Alaska, between 15,000 and 30,000 years ago, gradually occupying the Americas and slowly developing, over thousands of years, the great variety of cultural patterns that were observed by Europeans.[5] Very few people, however, have been privileged to see a major Mississippi site before it was ravaged by various forms of alteration, and to record their observations with accuracy and sobriety. One such was Henry M. Brackenridge, whose 1811 observations are described in a chapter called "Antiquities in the Valley of the Mississippi."[6] There is a sketch of the major platform mounds on the west side of the river in the St. Louis area, but his views of the evidence of occupation on the east side are even more valuable. He viewed with awe and admiration what is now called Monks Mound, and the time and labor it took to construct it. The American Bottom, from the mouth of the Kaskaskia to that of the Cahokia River, was rich in natural foods and its nutrient soils were suitable for cultivation. Among the several mound groups, which he believed to number some 150 mounds, were many small rises which seemed to reflect order in their placement. Near them were fragments of pottery and pieces of flint. His estimate of the population of the American Bottom was that it was equivalent to Philadelphia's and its vicinity. (In the 1810 United States census, Philadelphia was credited with 53,722 persons.) His concluding observation, made without the benefit of having studied anthropology, is also of interest:

Amongst a numerous population, the power of the chief must necessarily be more absolute, and where there are no laws, degenerates into despotism. This was the case in Mexico, and in the nations of South America; a great number of individuals were at the disposal of the chief, who treated them little better than slaves. The smaller the society, the greater consequence of each individual. Hence, there would not be wanting a sufficient number of hands to erect mounds or pyramids.[7]

The population estimate of Philadelphia in 1810 was based on an organized head count within a time frame of no more than one year. However, the evidence of prehistoric occupation of the American Bottom is the accumulation of 500 to 700 years. Nor has the temporal factor that made Brackenridge's population estimate inaccurate been eliminated in recent estimates by archaeologists. The importance of the floodplain environment and agriculture for population growth, and the implication that the large population and numerous platform mounds denote an advanced social organization, are shared by observers to the present day. Brackenridge also observed that evidences of prehistoric occupation "invariably occupy the most eligible situations for towns or settlements. . . . I have heard a surveyor of the public lands observe, that wherever any of these remains were met with, he was sure to find an extensive body of fertile land."[8] This agrees with contemporary assessments that most Mississippian sites are on or near the most fertile and easily worked soils.

One of the earliest sound attempts to characterize a prehistoric unit that included many remains now considered Middle Mississippi was that of Frederick Ward Putnam, curator and director of the Peabody Museum of American Archaeology and Ethnology of Harvard University. He was involved with excavations and collections from the central United States, and made extensive explorations in central Tennessee. Before the Bureau of American Ethnology was founded, he summarized what was known of the stone-grave populations of the Nashville area and stated that many of its archaeological features were also found in southern Illinois and Missouri.[9] This indicated to Putnam that one great nation or people, with many subdivisions of tribes and villages, formerly covered the heartland of what is now called the Middle Mississippi complex. Putnam was one of the first to recognize the temporal priority of what is now called Early and Middle Woodland over Mississippian.

In the 1880s the mound survey of the Eastern United States by the Bureau of American Ethnology, Smithsonian Institution, was directed by Cyrus Thomas and supervised by J. W. Powell. In many ways, this was the "New Archaeology" of the latter part of the nineteenth century, and Thomas used that phrase to describe it.[10] The survey was designed to be, essentially, a sampling procedure for recognizing similarities and differences of earthwork construction over the entire area of mound distribution. Thomas's instructions to his field men were to obtain information in the most scientific way and to provide data on archaeological problems as they were conceived. The analysis concentrated on the formal features of sites, but included functions where they were recognizable.

For Thomas, Powell, and other commentators, "the first and chief question to be considered may be stated briefly as follows: were all the mounds and other ancient works of the mound area as above defined, constructed by the Indians, in the restricted sense above mentioned, or are they wholly, or in part, to be attributed to other and more highly cultured races, as the Nahuatl tribes, the Mayas, the Pueblo tribes, or some lost race of which there is no historical mention?"[11] Thomas concluded that only the ancestors of the Indians and the early historic Indian tribes were responsible for the mounds and other remains.

One of his primary archaeologic units was the "mound-builders" section, and within it were a number of units, such as the Illinois, Ohio, Tennessee, Arkansas, and Gulf districts. Platform, pyramidal, and domiciliary mounds and their associated features were identified in these districts and connections were indicated between them. Thomas also included their earthworks and artifacts, with little or no attempt to define or distinguish what could now be called Mississippian Culture features from other remains in these districts. He felt that platform mounds were the substructures for council houses, residences of chiefs, and possibly of temples. He did not make the mistake of implying, by the term he called them, that they were all "Temple Mounds."

Thomas's study was not the first to equate the mounds and other ancient remains with the ancestors of the Indians, but it separated serious and professional students from those who thrived on myth, mystery, and misinformation. It made all earlier attempts to attribute prehistoric remains or developments in the United States to European, Mediterranean, African, and central or southern Asian peoples so much wasted effort. The same can be said of subsequent (and contemporary) proposals to recognize Libyans, Phoenicians, Norse, Germanics, and Hebrews (or individuals from outer space) as founding fathers for prehistoric cultures and populations.

During the late 1870s and the 1880s, W. H. Holmes worked on a description and classification of Eastern United States prehistoric pottery, designed to be a comprehensive statement on ceramics. It was prepared as a grouping of ceramics and not prehistoric societies.

His first major paper was on the Mississippi Valley collections, which he subdivided into three major provinces: Upper, Middleland, and Lower.[12] "Middle Mississippi province" was a geographic term, while "family" and "ware" referred to related forms and constructional features of the pottery. He recognized that the paste was tempered with pulverized shell or powdered potsherds. In quality, he equated the shapes of these vessels to those of the Southwest, adding that they were superior to Central and Northern Europe, but were not as fine as those of Middle America, Peru, and the Mediterranean.

The Middle Mississippi province was "the greater part of the States of Missouri, Arkansas, and Tennessee, covers large portions of Mississippi, Kentucky, and Illinois, and reaches somewhat into Iowa, Indiana, Alabama, and Louisiana and Texas."[13] In terms of quantity and quality of pottery, the Central area of the Mississippi Valley, which is the contiguous parts of Missouri, Arkansas, and Tennessee (with Pecan Point, Arkansas, as the center), was identified as preeminent. He recognized that the major rivers were responsible for the spread and location of the Middle Mississippi pottery family. He believed the "family" had been in existence many centuries before Soto (in the sixteenth century) and a number of European writers (in the early eighteenth century) noted it, and that the producers of the pottery were builders of earthen mounds. He recognized that this pottery complex continued into the historic period.

Holmes's major monograph had a map with colored dots, with the Middle Mississippi family identified with red dots (the distribution is given in figure 2-1).[14] Typical specimens were found in the Chicago area, near Pittsburgh, Augusta, along the Gulf Coast, and even into eastern Oklahoma. To Holmes, this broad distribution implied that Algonquin, Siouan, Muskogean, Natchez, and Caddoan tribes were involved in the production of this complex. It was primarily an indigenous development, although some exotic features were suggestive of influences from Mexico. From the locations of the red dots, I infer that Fort Ancient products in the Ohio Valley, Oneota and Fisher in northern Indiana and Illinois, Illinois Valley 1, Larson phase, and Nebraska pottery in western Missouri and eastern Kansas were all included, as well as Caddoan pottery in the contiguous parts of Oklahoma, Arkansas, Louisiana, and Texas. Central Alabama, with its large funerary jars, was regarded as part of the

45

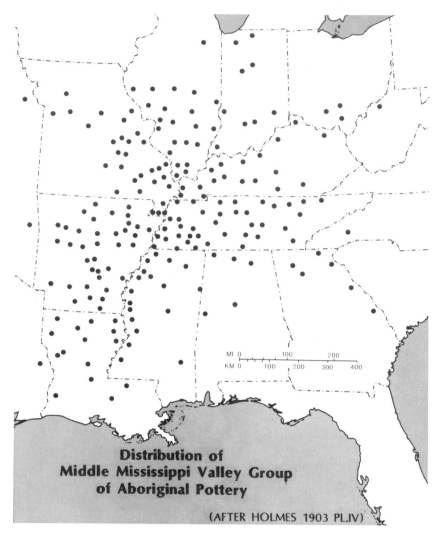

FIGURE 2-1. *Distribution of Middle Mississippi Valley Group of Aboriginal Pottery (After plate IV in "Aboriginal Pottery of the Eastern United States," by William H. Holmes)*

Lower Mississippi group, which was very similar to the Middle Mississippi family. His Gulf group was confined to Weeden Island wares and their descendants.

In discussions of Eastern United States pottery, Holmes emphasized familial relations of the ceramics and identified their major locations as "provinces." In his paper on prehistoric culture areas, his Middle and Lower Mississippi Valley was his Area III.[15] His presentation included some of the distinctive features of various periods and cultures, and did not emphasize or elaborate on his Middle Mississippi province or family.

Up to the 1930s, probably the best characterization of Middle Mississippi societies was by G. P. Thruston, who had extensively explored the late-prehistoric sites in the Nashville area.[16] He recognized that the fortified towns and other settlements he investigated had been occupied by agricultural societies that were more advanced than the Indian tribes of the eighteenth and nineteenth centuries but had not reached the level of the ancient civilizations or even semicivilizations. The Nashville Basin people were in the same class as the village Indians of the Southwest and of Mexican village Indians. They were similar in culture to contemporary populations in southeast Missouri, Arkansas, southern Illinois, and southwestern Indiana, and there is evidence of tribal and trade relationships among them. The remains of their art and industries, which he described and illustrated, indicate they were as highly developed as any society in United States territory. He believed that their culture was "the original, independent product . . . of the Stone Grave race, the mound builders of Tennessee. The traces here and there of Mexican, southern, or Pueblo culture save in occasional instances were probably but the outgrowths of customs and tendencies derived from a common ancestry. The mound building tribes doubtless lived during many generations, upon various planes of development, in the fertile and widely extended territory in which their monuments are discovered."[17] This statement, if transposed into modern terminology, is close to some modern opinions.

The major survey and excavation work of Clarence B. Moore, along Southeastern rivers and coasts from the late 1880s through the first two decades of the 1900s, did not make many references to Holmes's ceramic groups until, in publication of the volume on the Ouachita River, Holmes provided a brief characterization of the pottery. "It embraces features of form and embellishment indicating close alliance with the wares of the middle Mississippi province and of the Gulf Coast as far east as Florida."[18] The next year, discussing the vessels excavated in northeastern Arkansas, Moore wrote that "the St. Francis valley forms part of the Middle Mississippi region which region was defined by Holmes."[19] One of Moore's concerns was to recognize Holmes's different areas, and he concluded that the Arkansas River is a convenient dividing line between the Middle and the Lower Mississippi regions.[20] In the volumes in which he presented the results of his efforts to archaeologists, no significant effort was made to identify and define cultural complexes; instead, he commented on his findings in terms of regions. This was, I think, because of the emphasis at the time on the definition of cultural areas in both ethnological and archaeological circles. Moore did not regard himself as a "professional archaeologist" and, I believe, was hesitant to try to do more than report the results of his surveys.

One of the curious facets of archaeological writing after Holmes's two papers is that his terminology was not often used by archaeologists during the fairly long span between 1900 to 1930, and to some degree until the 1940s. Even when citations were made to Holmes's publications, they referred to vessel shapes or functions and were more interested in comparing and identifying recently excavated material to more localized cultural units. Even when examples of Middle Mississippi vessels were reproduced by She-trone, Holmes's term for their "family" was not used, and everything known—from St. Louis south to the Gulf, Caddoan material to the west, and to Moundville on the east—was placed in "the Lower Mississippi Area."[21] In the papers of the Conference on Southern Pre-History, very few references were made.[22] "Holmes and Moore make this river (Arkansas) the dividing line between the Middle and Lower Mississippi cultures. The pottery of the Middle Mississippi is markedly inferior to that of the Lower Mississippi."[23] The emphasis in the archaeological papers was on areal grouping or localized cultures. A rather small "Effigy Ware and Moundville Culture" was identified on the archaeological culture map.[24]

Even as late as his "Analysis of Indian Village Site Collections from Louisiana and Mississippi," J. A. Ford identified his problems as obtaining a time scale and recognizing "the insidious phenomenon of cultural change."[25] He rejected the Midwest taxonomic classification of McKern and others as inapplicable and not appropriate to his aims.

I do not remember when I first became aware of the concepts "Middle Mississippi" and "Upper Mississippi," but I believe it was during the summer field-work program of the University of Chicago in Fulton County, Illinois, in 1930. Certainly, during the school year 1931-32 the use of such terms was common, and they were definitely employed in the "Illinois Pre-History" papers at the anthropology meetings of the Illinois Academy of Science in the spring of 1932. The papers of McKern, Snodgrasse, Gilbert, Eggan, and Deuel all make reference to one or the other of those cultural units. Identification of Middle Mississippi was based primarily on earlier investigations of the Dickson mound, with the University of Chicago's excavations of the Fulton County mounds and village sites providing additional data to round out a cultural complex. At the 27th Annual Meeting of the Illinois Academy of Science (in 1934), Thorne Deuel presented a paper, "Basic Cultures of the Mississippi Valley and Their Illinois Representatives," which was later published in *American Anthropologist,* and Anson Simpson portrayed the "Kingston (Illinois) Focus of the Mississippi Culture."[26]

These early papers reflected the ideas that developed into the "Midwestern taxonomic method," as McKern later called it, but it was known to all of its practitioners and devotees as the McKern Classification.[27] It was the "New Archaeology" of the 1930s in the Midwest and the method was designed to bring order out of the chaos of archaeological units of varying size and complexity, for many of which the term "culture" was used. As accurately as possible, "trait lists" defined remains from what was judged to be a cultural unit of either a single site, which was a "component," or of a group of closely related sites, called a "focus." A series of foci might be regarded as closely related and form a "unit," such as the Fort Ancient Aspect. A number of "aspects" could be grouped into a "phase," such as the Middle Mississippi or Upper Mississippi phases, and both of these into the Mississippi "pattern." Some archaeologists preferred to define patterns and phases, and others began with components and foci. In any event, the schema attempted to provide a full and precise characterization of archaeological culture and give some idea of size and complexity. (It is curious that the much maligned McKern Classification provided the stimulus for the first "cultural" definition of the several Mississippi phases, which were regarded as part of a Mississippi pattern.)

From the formal proposal in May 1932, classification terminology was discussed by correspondence and in consultation at meetings until December 1935, when a group of archaeologists was invited by Carl Guthe to the Indianapolis Archaeological Conference, which included a May 1934 discussion of culture-classification problems in Middle Western archaeology by McKern.[28] Under a Middle Mississippi phase, the conference classified the Monks

Mound aspect, consisting of a Rock River focus, with the Aztalan site in Wisconsin as the sole component, and the Spoon River and Kingston foci in the Illinois Valley. It did not define or describe the Middle Mississippi phase, but used the term "pattern" to include the Upper and Middle phases. In his paper and in the discussions, Deuel placed the Kincaid, Tolu, and Wickliffe sites of the Lower Ohio Valley, the Gordon-Fewkes sites in the Nashville Basin, Etowah, the Spoon River sites, and Cahokia in Middle Mississippi. Deuel's paper, "Basic Cultures of the Mississippi Valley," had already appeared, in which he placed the sites south of Cahokia in a Lower Mississippi phase. In a paper published in 1937, Deuel presented his revised statement and listed fifteen "determinants" for the Mississippi pattern, an additional eleven determinants of Middle Mississippi, and five not-generally-reported determinants which also served to identify Middle Mississippi.[29] The eleven Middle Mississippi determinants were as follows, and each was given a weighting of 1.

Truncated pyramidal mounds, often in groups, employed primarily as substructures.

Houses with rectangular floor outlines.

Wattle-and-daub house walls, as indicated by lumps of dried clay exhibiting cane or grass impressions.

Equal armed pipe in varieties other than the projecting stemmed.

The employment of marine shells, cut marine shells, and pearls for personal adornment.

Pottery: effigy, beaker, plate, and other specialized forms of common occurrence.

Pottery: two or more wares present.

Pottery: narrow-trailing, incising (while clay is plastic), scratching, etching, etc. (after drying or firing), are the chief techniques of decoration.

Pottery: designs commonly include bands or chains of hatchured triangles, arches, scrolls, and spirals.

Pottery trowels.

"Awl-sharpeners."

This approach defined Middle Mississippi with five pottery features, three constructional features, a pipe shape, marine shell and pearls, and "awl-sharpeners" as determinants, with the last weighted equally with house form, use of platform mounds, and variety of vessel forms. Aztalan, Etowah, Moundville, Gordon, and two Spoon River sites in the Illinois Valley were the Middle Mississippi sites identified. The Middle Mississippi traits, not generally listed, were:

1. Copper-covered wooden earspools and other objects similarly treated.
2. Engraved gorgets of shell and *repousse* copper plaques depicting human, animal and bird forms.
3. Elaborate ornaments or insignia in copper, stone, and other materials and/or shown on engraved shell gorgets and plaques of *repousse* copper.
4. Textile-impressed pottery.
5. Ceremonial swords of skillfully chipped flint 12–30 inches in length.

Agriculture was not mentioned in the pattern or phase determinants because it was regarded as part of the identification of the "Basic Culture," which included both the Woodland and Mississippi patterns. "Basic Culture" was identified by the primary adaptation of the culture to its environment.

When the Relief Labor Program of the Depression years got under way in the Southeast in 1933 and 1934 (to continue about seven years), many participants had been indoctrinated in the Midwest taxonomic system. They included the chief archaeologist in the TVA program, W. S. Webb, in northern Alabama and Kentucky; T. M. N. Lewis in Tennessee; A. R. Kelly in Georgia; the field director in northern Alabama, David L. DeJarnette; the archaeological laboratory director in Knoxville, Madeline Kneberg; and the primary archaeologist in North Carolina, Joffre Coe. Most of the archaeologists in field excavations were University of Chicago graduate students or they had participated in the summer-school field program.[30] (Those who had been trained at other institutions were quickly "infected.") Many Mississippi sites were excavated, described, and identified as units of various kinds within the Mississippi pattern.

The impact of this classification device during the 1930s and 1940s on the thinking of many archaeologists is reflected in most of the essays in *Archeology of the Eastern United States*.[31] However, the decline of emphasis on classification in a taxonomic scheme began with the sequential frameworks developed in Illinois, from 1926 to 1939; in Louisiana, from the late 1920s to 1940; and with the Relief Labor Program in many areas of the Southeast. These demonstrated that Mississippi cultures were uniformly late in the sequence and that earlier and later Mississippi units could be recognized. Most of the authors who wrote on the Southeast spoke of Spiro on the west (to Savannah II) and Etowah on the east as Middle

51

Mississippi. Some of them transposed Coles Creek from the Temple Mound I classification of Ford and Willey into Middle Mississippi.[32] Almost all commentators of the time felt that Middle Mississippi had received a strong infusion of new practices and beliefs from Middle America.

One of the major difficulties with the interpretive structure of Eastern archaeology between World Wars I and II was the conviction that most of the cultural developments represented by Woodland and Mississippi were quite late and, particularly, that the Mississippi complexes were in existence from about A.D. 1400 to 1700. While there was recognition of cultural elements that indicated local development from Late Woodland to Mississippi, these elements were scattered occurrences. Furthermore, many archaeologists expected to find in the central Mississippi area an early "parent" Middle Mississippi assemblage which then radiated outward to central Georgia, eastern Tennessee, western Illinois, and west toward the Southern Great Plains. In effect, it was a continuation of the culture-area and culture-center concepts which were so strong in American anthropology around the turn of the century. The definitions of Middle Mississippi were based on the developed practices of the societies at their peak, and it was impossible to find such cultural units in Early or Proto-Mississippi levels.

In a paper written largely in the late 1930s, the view was expressed that

a single center of origin of the Mississippi "Pattern" is not recognized here. Instead, a gradual growth throughout the valley is postulated. In other words, various ideas and complexes developed in several centers, the whole to be welded into classic Middle Mississippi. Finally, in late proto-historic or perhaps even historic times, the culture expanded to cover a wide area in central North America. This expansion was accompanied by the rapid spread of the cultural art styles identified in archaeological circles as the "Buzzard Cult." Because of this, Middle Mississippi is now found from points near the Georgia coast, west to Spiro, in Oklahoma, and from central Illinois south to Selzertown.[33]

I suggested that a socioeconomic base had developed on which Mississippi culture was later grafted, that a transition from Woodland to Mississippi culture led into the Small Log Town House sites of northeast Tennessee, that in the Cahokia area there was a gradual shift from Woodland to Mississippi, and that research should be devoted to recognition and definition of specific cultural units, and a chronological arrangement of them, in the Cumberland area, in northern and central Alabama, in northern Mississippi and western Tennessee, in the lower Arkansas, in the St. Francis Valley, along the Mississippi in the Pecan Point and New Madrid area, in southwestern Illinois, and in western Kentucky.[34]

To many, the studies which produced assessments of Middle Mississippi by archaeologists who applied the methodology of the Midwest taxonomic system were unsatisfactory, and even distasteful. In the mid-1930s, however, they helped motivate Philip Phillips to write an "Introduction to the Archaeology of the Mississippi Valley," his Ph.D. thesis at Harvard.[35] The Peabody Museum had extensive collections, largely gathered when Putnam was the director, from the Nashville Basin, southeast Missouri, and northeast Arkansas. Phillips' effort provided fuller consideration of the societies that could be included within Middle Mississippi, for (as indicated above) the Indianapolis conference had identified only a Monks Mound aspect. Phillips' analysis resulted in identification of the Cumberland, Cairo Lowland, and Eastern Arkansas "aspects," but no attempt was made to define a Middle Mississippi "phase." Quotation marks were employed for the classificatory terms to indicate tongue-in-cheek acceptance of their meaning and of the Midwest taxonomic system in general. Although the thesis was not published, it was a major reference work and the initial stimulant for some forty-five years of Peabody Museum concentration on the prehistory of the physiographic Lower Mississippi Valley.

The extensive survey of the Middle Mississippi collection at the Peabody and other museums enabled Phillips to prepare, then publish, his "Middle American Influences on the Archaeology of the Southwestern United States" in the volume in honor of Alfred M. Tozzer.[36] In this, Phillips avoided taxonomic terms and wrote about Middle Mississippi culture without attempting a short definition, providing instead a short description of some of its salient features. He referred to regional variations within his acceptable concept of Middle Mississippi and said that "many of our supposed Middle American features far outrun the more fundamental aspects of Middle Mississippi culture."[37] The examples he cited of this outrunning were the Etowah and Spiro complexes. Comparing Southeastern late-prehistoric complexes and Middle America, he indicated various potential Mexican sources, over a wide area, in various cultures and periods.

In their paper in the fall of 1940, while students at Columbia University, James A. Ford and Gordon R. Willey used what they called "chronological profiles" or "transects" along the Mississippi, Ohio, Missouri, Red, and Tennessee river valleys, and a sequence of "stages" called "Archaic," "Burial Mound I," "Burial Mound II," "Temple Mound I," and "Temple Mound II."[38] The transects or profiles were composed to show that, after the Archaic, the succeeding major cultural developments had their origins in the Louisiana-Mississippi portions of the Lower Mississippi River Valley and gradually spread north, east, and west. This was based on the idea (not clearly expressed) that pottery, agriculture, and many elements of the ceramic groups in the Eastern United States had come from Mexico. Some of these changes were brought by an infiltration of populations; but the profiles were so obviously slanted, and the assignment of local units so carelessly done, that acceptance of the presentation was jeopardized. Furthermore, "stage" was not defined, and their four ceramic "stages" bore a close resemblance to more commonly used concepts of Early and Middle Woodland and Early and Late Mississippi. They began the Temple I stage with a series of traits, such as platform mounds around a plaza, clay elbow pipes, small and very thin projectile points, pottery trowels, small solid-clay figurines, rectangular houses, and other features which were said to be characteristic of the Lower Mississippi Valley Troyville culture. This was not the case, and was a poor prophecy for the future. They *did* use the terms "early" and "late Middle Mississippi" within the Temple Mound I and II stages. No concise definition of Middle Mississippi was attempted, and their scenario followed many well-known interpretations of the times. While it may be called a historical developmental framework, the "history" was strongly biased and the developments were based primarily on ceramic changes through time, as interpreted by Ford.

The research problem of "Archaeological Survey in the Lower Mississippi Alluvial Valley, 1940–1947" (by Philip Phillips, James A. Ford, and James B. Griffin) was to determine what ceramic complexes preceded Middle Mississippi and to obtain information on the latter's origin and development, including areal and temporal divisions.[39] Although our attempt to recognize and describe the origin of Middle Mississippi was unsuccessful, we identified early ceramic materials, particularly in the lower levels of Rose Mound in Cross County, Arkansas. Also, a number of different settlement patterns were identified and described, and their areal patterning was mapped for the Pre-Mississippi temporal and cultural units and for those within the Mississippi period. It was also stated that these patterns were associated with distinctive cultural assemblages. This was a model for later studies in other areas, such as Peru. A two-climax model of Eastern prehistory was proposed; the first was associated and interrelated with the Hopewell culture of Ohio and the second with the Mississippi climax, which had a period of growth and then declined. One of the surprising results of the field work (to this participant) was the large number of sites identified; unfortunately, however, we did not appreciate the significance of the few non-mound sites we found or that there were many more locations that represented special activity areas and were an integral part of Mississippi settlement systems.

In the late 1940s, comparative studies of eastern Texas, the central Mississippi Valley, and the Southwest suggested that the Eastern United States chronological framework was much too late and that the complex agricultural societies in the Southwest and Eastern United States had developed at approximately the same time.[40] A short time later, radiocarbon dating made its appearance and forced the gradual recognition that elements of Mississippi culture could be found that dated to A.D. 700 and Early Mississippi culture to A.D. 900.

A major handicap in interpreting Mississippi culture units was that no site had been completely excavated before the late 1960s or the 1970s, and the small farmsteads and other economic support locations were not recognized as part of an organized societal system for the maintenance of the major center. Excavations were primarily of major population centers, platform mounds, and a few houses in major centers or villages, as well as test pits to acquire cultural sequence. The main modifications of the 1950s and 1960s in interpreting Mississippi cultures included (1) greater ability to identify changes in material culture during the A.D. 500–900 period that were gradually incorporated into regional Mississippi societies, (2) stronger emphasis on hypotheses about social, political, and religious changes, and (3) new interest in studies of the several settlement patterns and the interaction of the societies with their environment. There were brave attempts to interpret the origins and spread of Mississippi cultures, emphasizing facets thought to be important by the various authors.[41] The term "Tradition" (with a

55

capital T) became common, and "Mississippian" was used to indicate cultural complexes that were *not* Middle Mississippi but had many similarities to that long-recognized concept.

An influential monograph of the 1950s, *Method and Theory in American Archaeology* by Willey and Phillips, refers to a Mississippi period of the New World Formative stage. The latter was primarily defined as resulting from "the diffusion, or diffusions of native American agriculture,"[42] and the authors provided a brief characterization:

The features of this period (Mississippi) that seem reliably reflective of an intensive agricultural village life, i.e., a full-blown Formative Stage, are the rectangular "temple" or "town-house" mounds, the arrangement of these mounds around a central plaza, compact villages of substantial pole-and-thatch or wattle-and-daub houses with deep and extensive refuse (other than shell middens), and the frequent and abundant finds of maize itself. Such features, along with certain characteristic pottery styles and artifact types, are known to be associated with, though not confined to, the Mississippi ("or Middle Mississippi") culture. Many of these elements appear to have derived from Middle American sources. They are clearly post-Hopewellian arrivals in the eastern United States. The mechanisms and routes of their presumed diffusion from Middle America are still completely unknown, although there has been no lack of speculation on the subject.[43]

Willey and Phillips regarded the nuclear area of Mississippi culture as the *Central* Mississippi Valley, from St. Louis to Cairo, and the adjoining Lower Ohio Valley–Tennessee–Cumberland regions. They excluded southeast Missouri and northeast Arkansas. Their identification of important Mississippi centers, however, extended to eastern Tennessee, central Georgia, and Moundville. They regarded the iconography of the "Southern Cult" and associated materials as a horizon style of the late pre-contact Mississippi traditions within, and extending far beyond, the periphery of an expanded nuclear area.

At about the same time, with no collusion, Willey and Griffin produced similar expansions of the term "Mississippian." Within the Mississippian Tradition, Willey included Coles Creek and Plaquemine in the Lower Mississippi Valley, Caddoan complexes on the west, those in the east as far as the Georgia coast in post–A.D. 1000 times, and Fort Ancient and Oneota in the Ohio and Upper Mississippi valleys.[44] Griffin placed the major sites of Middle Mississippi, South Appalachian Mississippian, and Caddoan Mississippian on a map. Fort Ancient and Oneota were not identified as Mississippian, nor was Coles Creek. (My use in that paper of the term "Mississippian" referred "to the wide variety of adaptation made by societies which developed a dependence on agriculture for their basic, storable food supply.")[45] The discussions of both authors further elaborated the developments within the Mississippian period and looked to Mexico for stimuli for some of the changes that were important in the restructuring of Southeastern economics and society. Looking to the glamorous civilizations of Mesoamerica for the injection of people, concept, and behavior was an established practice in interpreting Eastern United States archaeology for about 200 years.

In the 1960s and 1970s, one of the changes in understanding prehistoric social and political structure was more detailed analysis of burial patterns, particularly at three major Mississippian sites. These patterns have been shown to have had important differences, but in general they reveal the structured rank societies which were reported in the sixteenth and seventeenth centuries by early European exploiters.[46] None of the studies, however, presented the variety of status positions recorded for the seventeenth-and eighteenth-century Hasinai, a Caddoan confederacy in northeast Texas. The historical data for the Hasinai, after careful scrutiny by Don G. Wycoff and Timothy G. Baugh, disclosed that there were seven important status positions, and yet that three individuals were able to make decisions for all members of the confederacy. Two of the positions were hereditary, and one was an elected status. They also presented a summary of the archaeological evidence that might be expected from sites occupied by Hasinai in late prehistoric times.[47] It is a reasonable supposition that the large Mississippian societies of A.D. 1100–1500 would have had more official positions and status holders than the Hasinai.

Adequate funding for intensive surveys and excavation resulted in recognition of the complexity of Mississippian functioning societies. Instead of viewing them from the information obtained from the larger towns and villages, it now can be seen that large centers were integrated with small villages, farmsteads, or hamlets; hunting or fishing stations; lithic procurement quarries; and other special-activity areas. Improved recovery techniques have produced a wider variety of plant remains which furnished foods and medicines, but these still do not approach the quantity or variety known from historical documentation. Refined studies of animal remains have

57

indicated seasonality of procurement and hunting strategies, and
have provided, with the floral evidence, a better understanding of
the prehistoric environment. Trace-element analyses have contributed more accurate assessment of the source of raw materials and
their widespread distribution by trade and exchange. Differences
between the trade patterns of status symbols and items of more
mundane use emphasize that there was not a single system of
exchange within and between areas.

Recent writings about Middle Mississippi and Mississippian in
Mississippian Settlement Patterns[48] reflect the growing sophistication of archaeologists in understanding the variety of adaptations by
local societies to their environments within the Mississippian period, together with a number of common strategies which identify
similar organizational principles. On the western border of the
Eastern Woodlands, for example,

The Arkansas Valley Caddoan represents the westernmost population of
advanced Mississippian cultural systems. Even though the drainage patterns favor cultural interaction to the east and west, the Arkansas Valley
tradition aligns with Caddoan systems to the south to form a cultural zone
west of the Mississippi lowlands.[49]

While there has been, and continues to be, disagreement as to
whether the Caddoan archaeological complexes should be included
as a western expression of Mississippian, Brown and his associates,
whose knowledge of those complexes is outstanding, believe that, in
spite of local Caddoan differences, "the similar organization of
communities around civic-ceremonial centers with platform
mounds, combined with a basic agricultural technology based on
hoe cultivation of maize, attests to the fundamental unity of the
two areas [Middle Mississippi and Caddoan]. Their essential continuity can be traced to a common economic base on the one hand
and to the dominating influence of Mississippi ideology on the
forms of Caddoan social integration on the other."[50]

In the same volume, we find that Roy Dickens, dealing with the
late prehistoric period in the Appalachian Summit area, identifies
two sequential complexes as Mississippian phases but finds they
had a somewhat "lower" level of social complexity than other south
Appalachian societies, such as those at Etowah.[51] For occupations in
the state of Mississippi in, or along, the "Delta" or floodplain, Brain
does not include the Coles Creek societies from about A.D. 700 to
1100 within Mississippian, but accepts the interpretation that the

Plaquemine societies of A.D. 1100–1700, developing from Coles Creek, became increasingly "Mississippianized."[52]

The editor, in the concluding chapter of the settlement-pattern volume, proposed boundary conditions "to define Mississippian as a cultural adaptation to a specific habitat situation and as a particular level of sociocultural integration."[53] This was a result of the dissatisfaction of some archaeologists with older views which had emphasized ceramic characteristics, such as shell-tempered pottery or variety of vessel forms, platform mounds, or the Southern iconography, in their definitions. In *his* definition, the environment is recognized as important in providing the necessary energy to support increasingly larger and more complex societies.

I would like to propose that the term "Mississippian" be used to refer to those prehistoric human populations existing in the eastern deciduous woodlands during the time period A.D. 800–1500 that had a ranked form of social organization, and had developed a specific complex adaptation to linear, environmentally circumscribed flood plain habitat zones. This adaptation involved maize horticulture and selective utilization of a limited number of species groups of wild plants and animals that represented dependable, seasonally abundant energy sources that could be exploited at a relatively low level of energy expenditure. In addition, these populations depended significantly upon an even more limited number of externally powered energy sources. Defining "Mississippian" in part, in terms of an adaptive niche is useful, I think, for a number of reasons.[54]

This definition was preferred at the time because it allowed variations of social and ideological subsistence and settlement pattern subsystems. Also, it was not rigid, but allowed investigation of temporal and regional variables and their interdigitation into contemporary functioning societies. Smith's chapter in this volume also provides an analytical framework for identifying development of an effective maize economy until its gradual disintegration under the impact of European empire building. While this definition is too restrictive in its environmental requirements, it is an improvement on those that preceded it and is, of course, subject to change.

The discussion of the Mississippian Tradition by Charles Hudson does not provide a concise definition but offers a brief description of the many characteristics and the development and location of Mississippian societies. His volume, *The Southeastern Indians*, concentrates primarily on historical accounts of their lifeways,[55] and several chapters—"Social Organization," "The Belief System," "Subsistence," "Ceremony," "Art, Music and Recreation"—discuss the topics' importance in understanding data from prehistoric Mississippian sites. Such contributions by ethnohistorians and ethnologists have been of value to prehistorians for many years, and notable among them are the publications of John R. Swanton, who devoted many years to compiling data on the Indians of the Southeast. Goldstein's is a contemporary and generally admirable identification of "Mississippian":

In sum, the Mississippian cultural system, when compared to that of the preceding Late Woodland period, represents a vastly increased level of complexity in the technological, social and organizational realms. Mississippian had agriculture and specialization of labor trade and social ranking—theirs was a cultural system which required a diversity of material forms and social positions.[56]

Such condensations, while having some validity, are more or less forced to ignore germinal developments throughout the large Eastern area, changing at different rates in different societies, as some were widely and others were only locally adopted. As populations increased because of the productivity of agriculture (with its obvious dependence on weather), shifts in the social structure were necessary, and changing religious practices transformed their world view as the more tangible material culture produced different forms. It may be doubted that there was a single Mississippian system in the Early, Middle, or Late Mississippian. Instead, an increasing cultural florescence in all phases of life, with societies in strategical locations becoming dominant through force of numbers and improved political strategies, is probable. Others, in less favorable locations, lagged in development and did not fully participate in the climactic Mississippian period. While there may be enough "regularities" to allow the concept of Mississippian some acceptance, the many deviations in every societal area, in historical heritage, and in participation in common themes make the concept of a single "system" in the Southeast unwise.

For years, many archaeologists have felt that an original "tradition," founding the Mississippi culture, appeared almost full blown along the Central Mississippi Valley and radiated outward, primarily by population movement. However, there were some who recognized the probability of gradual change (in some features of local societies) into an Early Mississippi complex. These ideas were not presented in a widely acceptable manner. So little work had been done on sites of the Late Woodland societies that gradual changes in material culture and settlement were not recognized. Many features that were thought to be associated only with Mississippi societies are now known to have occurred in earlier periods, or to have been foreshadowed in Late Woodland. One of these is a shift in house form from circular (or oval) to square and rectangular, with the houses built around a central courtyard. Stockaded villages, in western Pennsylvania and Ontario, are another example of Late Woodland societies in the period A.D. 800–900.

Additionally, small low-platform mounds were used to support charnel houses and for burial preparation in the Lower Mississippi Valley about A.D. 100, and may be the prototype for the low-platform mounds of the early to middle Coles Creek, of about A.D. 700–850. As community size increased, the mounds became larger and they were placed around a central plaza, where communal activities took place. Gradual changes in ceramic shapes and methods of manufacture and greater variety of forms are known from Alabama, Tennessee, Arkansas, Missouri, southwestern Indiana, and Illinois. The bow and arrow became a common addition to hunting and raiding by at least A.D. 700, and seems to have been introduced from the Plains into the Mississippi Valley. Prototypes of artifact forms, often thought to be typical of the Mississippi period, are now recognized in Late Woodland. These include the spud, discoidals, elbow pipe, and engraved shell gorgets.

While maize, which probably came from the Southwest, was known in the East by about A.D. 1, it was not a significant part of the food supply until the period A.D. 700–900, when it appeared in quantity over a wide area. Apparently it took more than a half-millennium to acquire adequate cultivation, seed-selection, food-preparation, and storage techniques to transform this crop into the valuable food supply it became in most of the prehistoric Eastern societies after A.D. 900. By the early historic period, the Natchez are said to have had 42 maize dishes. Our view is that this major addition to their already sophisticated hunting and gathering skills permitted population growth, resulting in a need for mechanisms of societal control and thereby hastening changes in societal structure. Villages became large and the populations more sedentary as the planters protected their maize fields and their stored yields from birds, animals, and neighboring societies. The beneficial—or disastrous—effect of weather patterns emphasized the importance of placating the pervasive supernatural forces that governed nature. Long-established interaction patterns between societies disseminated new cultural developments throughout much of the area, so that it is extremely difficult, even with radiocarbon dating, to determine where many of these changes first took place. We are aware of the growth of regional societies with distinctive character- istics, in particularly favorable locations for maize agriculture and a diverse subsistence base, and in strategic situations along trade and exchange routes, either by water or by trails.

By A.D. 1000–1200, these pan-Southeastern changes allow iden- tification of many communities with similar (but rarely identical) patterns, artifact forms, economic bases, and social structures as Mississippian. Craft specialization is implied by the wide dissemi- nation of distinctive and well-made ceramic forms, hoes of south- western Illinois flint, engraved marine-shell gorgets and containers of distinctive styles, copper effigies (such as the "long-nosed god" masks), large effigy pipes, and status symbols of quarried flint. The apogee of Mississippian development in most areas was A.D. 1200 to 1450, with the trade and exchange of ceremonial and status items, the largest populations, and mound and fortification constructions. The sixteenth and seventeenth centuries saw population move- ment, abandonment of areas formerly occupied, and a decline in the number of indicators of interareal exchange. At least part of these changes may be attributed to European colonization, exploration, missions, and shifts of trading patterns which undermined the native economy, as well as its social and political structure, and introduced European diseases which swept through the Southland in epidemics.

Intentionally or inadvertently, many archaeologists have neg- lected to specify their conception of "Mississippian," and some have even questioned the suitability of the term.[57] Muller has suggested that it might be advisable to return to Holmes's ceramic construct for Mississippian, although Holmes does not use that term.[58] There- fore, I will try again to adduce a reasonable construct for "Mississip- pian." It should *not* include specific artifact forms which have areal and temporal limitations. It should *not* be restricted to specific constructional features, such as platform mounds, palisaded towns, or rectangular house forms. It should *not* be limited to a few arbitrary categories of cultural evolution. It should *not* be confined to narrowly defined habitat zones or to the geographic Southeast. Instead, "Mississippian" should reflect the continuing areal inter- action of ideas and practices over the broad Eastern wooded area which, during a 1,000-year period, reached levels of development not attained earlier.

The Mississippian societies of the Eastern United States may be identified as those which:

Developed many cultural innovations over much of the culturally defined Southeast between A.D. 700 and 900.

Added these disparate innovations to local cultural inventories by contact between neighboring and distant groups.

Increased in population, resulting from an augmented energy input from a more effective agronomy.

Constructed planned permanent towns and ceremonial centers, villages and subsidiary support hamlets, farmsteads, and other extractive camps.

Had regional and temporal variations of a hierarchical social, political, and religious structure.

Participated in an area-wide belief system that integrated and emphasized the complex interaction of the spirit world and man, and ritualized these concepts in an elaborate symbolic iconography on marine shells, copper, ceramics, and stone.

Had an extensive trade network, of rivers and trails, over which manufactured symbolic and mundane items and raw materials were moved either to neighboring or distant societies.

Reached an area-wide cultural crest between A.D. 1200 and 1500, and slowly receded to less formally organized and controlled groups of the post–A.D. 1700 colonial period.

3   Mississippian Patterns of Subsistence and Settlement

Bruce D. Smith

Extending from around A.D. 850 until the Soto *entrada* of 1539–43, the Mississippian or "temple mound" period spans the final seven centuries of prehistory in the Eastern Woodlands. During this 700-year span the major river valleys of the East, from Illinois to north Florida and from North Carolina to Oklahoma, were occupied by Indian groups who shared a number of similarities in material culture, as well as the common practice of building earthen mounds to support public buildings and the houses of their leaders. Because of similarities in their tools of bone and stone, in their pottery vessels and houses, and in their villages and "temple mounds," these prehistoric groups have been lumped together under the general label "Mississippian."

These Mississippian groups were similar in another, very fundamental way: they all lived in essentially the same environmental setting or habitat—river-valley floodplains. This river-valley floodplain habitat was much the same throughout the wide geographical range of these Mississippian groups. Although no two river valleys (or even different segments of the same valley) were exactly comparable, all contained the same general landscape of opportunities, obstacles, and challenges. And it was, of course, the muddy waters of the rivers that shaped floodplain landscapes into a characteristic, if ever changing, pattern.

Most major rivers of the East are *aggrading* streams, whose

64

floodplain slopes down and away from the river toward the valley edge, rather than toward the river. This seeming impossibility—that a river can be higher than much of the valley through which it flows—is due to the differential deposition of soil during floodstage. The velocity of rushing floodwaters suddenly drops as the waters rise and overflow the river bed, and large amounts of suspended silt, sand, and nutrients are deposited. The lighter sediments, such as clay, are carried greater distances away from the river, toward the valley edge, before they settle to the bottom. This deposition of large amounts of soil along the edges of the river bed forms *natural levees*—low ridges that parallel the river and confine it during the long seasonal intervals between floods. Periodically, rivers break through these naturally formed low levees of sand and silt at various points along their courses, abandoning some channel segments as they cut new ones. Over time, as a result of this continual meandering process of channel formation, a river becomes flanked by a wide zone or belt of superimposed and coalesced abandoned channel segments and their associated natural levees. This *meander belt*, with its undulating hill-and-swale topography of oxbow lakes, canebrakes, and low sand ridges, is in turn bordered on either side by lower-elevation *back swamps*. In these areas the floodwaters of spring become the shallow, stagnant, and slowly shrinking back-swamp ponds of summer and early fall, forming a seasonal barrier of sorts between the meander belt and the uplands.

This, then, is the natural setting, the environmental backdrop, that Mississippian groups shared. Even though they were distributed over a wide geographical area, the settlements and way of life of these temple mound builders were narrowly restricted to the sinuous meander belts of major rivers (figure 3-1). What attractions did these riverine landscapes hold for Mississippian groups? Why did they seek out and settle in these meander belts, rather than in the vast, intervening expanses of upland forest?

One of the most important attributes of these floodplain meander belts was their levee soils. Sandy, well drained, and easy to work, these soils were ideal for growing the corn, beans, squash, and other cultigens of these Mississippian groups. Annually, in addition, these soils received "natural fertilization" in the form of new soil and nutrients deposited by floodwaters.

The floods of spring also carried nutrients of another sort, so that catfish, bullheads, and suckers moved out of the main channels to feed and spawn in the shallow oxbow lakes and back swamps.

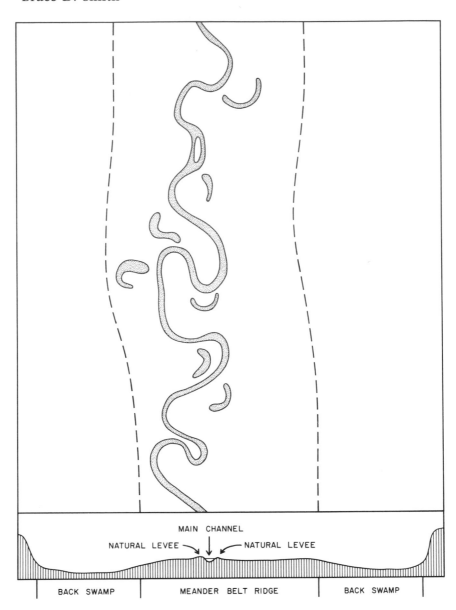

FIGURE 3-1. *The Main Features of a River-Valley Floodplain (Illustration by G. Robert Lewis)*

Because the receding floodwaters of late spring trapped these fish in the ever smaller and shallower pools of summer and fall, prehistoric temple mound builders had easy access to an almost unlimited supply of fish protein. The millions of waterfowl that passed through the Mississippi and Atlantic flyways in their spring and fall migrations were another important seasonal item in the menu of Mississippian groups. Matching the abundance and easy accessibility of these aquatic resources was a variety of floodplain forest plants and animals. Explaining why Mississippian populations settled almost exclusively in the river-valley floodplains of the Eastern Woodlands is thus not very difficult. They were drawn by the fertile, well-drained, and easy-to-farm soils, as well as by the variety and abundance of wild species of plants and animals.

This fundamental similarity of Mississippian groups (they all occupied river floodplain habitats) was mirrored by another: they all appear to have adapted to, or utilized, their floodplain environments in much the same way. It is thus possible to describe a general *Mississippian pattern of subsistence.* I hasten to add, however, that this apparent general uniformity in the subsistence patterns of Mississippian populations is to some extent a result of the limited information that archaeologists have to work with. The bits and pieces of animal bones and plants that are excavated from floodplain Mississippian settlements tell the same story time after time, at site after site, but as yet have not revealed very much of the variations from place to place, and through time, as populations adjusted the basic Mississippian adaptation to different conditions in the various river-valley floodplains.

What is this Mississippian pattern of subsistence, this widespread adaptation to river floodplain ecosystems? In terms of the utilization of wild species of plants and animals, Mississippian populations focused their gathering and hunting on five groups: (1) back-water species of fish, (2) migratory waterfowl, (3) the terrestrial trinity: white-tailed deer, raccoon, and turkey, (4) nuts, fruits, and berries—primarily hickory nuts, walnuts, acorns, persimmons, cherries, plums, and hackberries, and (5) seed-bearing "pioneer" plant species (what we would call weeds): primarily *Polygonum* and *Chenopodium.*

These five species groups form an interesting pattern of selectivity. Of the thousands of species in the environment that could have been exploited by these mound builder societies, they utilized the five species groups that occur in greatest abundance in Mississippian settlements. The explanation for this selective pattern of utilization can be found in a number of important attributes shared by the species listed above.

First, these species were dependable. Not only could they be counted on to be available in sufficient numbers each year, but they were relatively invulnerable to overutilization by human populations. Second, each of these species groups occurred in high density in known locales at known seasons of the year. Third, all of these species groups could be harvested easily, with fairly little effort or energy expenditure. Taken together, these three attributes describe a *subsistence strategy* of selective utilization of a limited number of species groups of wild plants and animals that represented dependable, seasonally abundant energy sources that could be exploited at a low level of energy expenditure. Keeping this underlying subsistence strategy in mind, we can turn to a brief consideration of each of these groups.

1. Back-Water Species of Fish

The species of fish which are represented in greatest numbers at Mississippian settlements are those that prefer quiet, stagnant waters (i.e., bowfin, gar, buffalo fish, bullheads, catfish, and freshwater drum). Directing their efforts toward the oxbow lakes and back swamps rather than the main channel, Mississippian groups probably obtained fish both by spearing and seining during the spring spawning season and by intensive seining or simple collecting during the low-water stage of summer, as the waters of temporary pools receded. Although wading through the mud and stagnant water of back-swamp ponds in pursuit of fish can hardly be enjoyable, it can yield large numbers of fish in a short time, and requires little expertise—as two archaeologists have recently demonstrated. Simply by rolling two logs the length of a shallow floodplain pond, then removing the "corralled" fish by hand, they obtained over 100 pounds of fish in just under two hours.[1] Although there is no direct archaeological evidence that such techniques were employed by Mississippian groups in harvesting back-water fish, analysis of seasonal growth rings on fish scales that have been recovered from a number of Mississippian sites indicates that fish were obtained primarily during the spring and early summer.[2]

2. Migratory Waterfowl

The oxbow lake and seasonally inundated shallows within meander-belt habitat zones, with their abundant aquatic vegetation, provided an excellent support base for populations of migrating waterfowl. Numerous species of ducks and geese represented, in turn, an easily accessible and virtually inexhaustible seasonal food source. The seasonal availability and the density of these migratory populations were related to the location of Mississippian communities in the Atlantic and Mississippi flyways—main north–south corridors of waterfowl movement in the Eastern United States.[3] A great volume and variety of species filled the flyways during the fall (October–November) and spring (March–April) migration peaks. Availability in winter months also depended upon the north–south location of settlements within the flyways. Moving south, from St. Louis to the Gulf, wintering populations of waterfowl increased in density, and the Gulf coastal marshes and Louisiana delta were major wintering areas. Corresponding to this pattern, the seasonality of Mississippian exploitation of waterfowl suggests a north–south gradient, with harvesting in the northern sections of the flyway more limited to fall and winter migration, while exploitation in the southern section of the flyway would have been possible throughout the winter.

3. White-tailed Deer, Raccoon, Turkey, and Other Terrestrial Species

Contributing from 50 to as high as 90 percent of the animal protein consumed by Mississippian groups, the white-tailed deer (*Odocoileus virginianus*) was far and away the most important animal species in their diet. Analysis of deer mandibles recovered from Mississippian sites indicates a fall–winter period of primary exploitation.[4]

Next in importance in providing a consistent food supply for Mississippian communities were the raccoon (*Procyon lotor*) and turkey (*Meleagris gallopavo*). Although there is little direct archaeological evidence to support the hypothesis, I think that the raccoon and turkey, as well as such less important species as opossum (*Didelphis marsupialis*), rabbits (*Sylvilagus*), and squirrels (*Sciurus*), were also exploited primarily during the fall and winter. This is not

69

to say that these species were killed only during fall and winter, but that this was the period of deliberate, concentrated harvesting of these species.

4. Nuts, Fruits, and Berries

The remains of a great variety of nuts, fruits, and berries have been recovered from Mississippian sites. The most commonly reported nuts are of the following species: oak (*Quercus* spp.), hickory (*Carya* spp.), walnut (*Juglans* spp.), and pecan (*Carya illinoensis*). All of these nuts became available for harvesting during the fall, in September and October. Fruits and berries at Mississippian sites include persimmon (*Diospyros virginiana*) and paw paw (*Asimina triloba*), both available during September and October, as well as cherry (*Prunus serotina*) and plum (*Prunus* sp.), both available in August, and hackberry (*Celtis occidentalus*), available during October and November.

The nuts could have been stored through the winter season, while the fleshy fruits and berries would (for the most part) have been consumed during the period of availability. These wild-plant food sources would have been available in greatest abundance in the vegetational associations on levee crests and immediate backslope areas.

5. Seed-bearing Pioneer Plant Species

In addition to nuts, fruits, and berries, the abundance of pioneer seed-bearing species at Mississippian sites indicates that these too were harvested during the fall. Principal among them were goosefoot (*Chenopodium*), pigweed (*Amaranthus*), and smartweed (*Polygonum*), all of which could be harvested from September to November. These seed-bearing plants would have colonized (or sprung up in) a variety of disturbed habitats, both natural and man made (mudflats, clearings, village margins, etc.), and may have been encouraged by Mississippian groups.[5]

In addition to harvesting the five species groups within the floodplain ecosystem, Mississippian populations selectively destroyed vegetation on fertile and well-drained natural-levee soils and replaced it with domesticated plant species that were dependable, seasonally abundant energy sources. Taken together, these cultigens formed a sixth species group.

6. Maize-Bean-Squash Cultivation

The garden plots of Mississippian groups were dominated by maize (Zea mays), beans (Phaseolus), and squash (Cucurbita pepo). In addition to this "horticultural trinity," three crops of secondary importance were grown: sunflower (Helianthus annuus), marsh elder (Iva), and gourd (Largenaria silceraria).

Other than the (often infrequent) presence of these cultigens in Mississippian sites, there is little direct archaeological data pertaining to Mississippian agricultural methods. Some evidence indicates that Mississippian fields, in some cases at least, consisted of small plots (separated by paths) in washboard patterns of ridges and furrows.[6] The large chert hoes, recovered from Mississippian sites, were undoubtedly used to clear vegetation from field plots and/or break the soil for planting, pulling it into parallel ridges or into the small mounds described in early historical sources.

Largely on the impressive size of many Mississippian communities, it is assumed that their agricultural efforts were intensive. It has also been suggested that Mississippian agricultural strategies were fairly complex and diversified, in that varieties of maize, having different moisture requirements and growth-to-maturity characteristics, were planted in fields that differed from one another in terms of soil fertility, probability of inundation, etc. It is also possible that Mississippian farmers may have utilized low-lying mudflats and sandbars for agricultural pursuits.[7]

Within the various river valleys, planting schedules would have varied according to the receding of spring floodwaters and the probability of killing frosts. Since a number of varieties of different ripening lengths were probably grown, corn (in different states of development) would have been available from perhaps as early as August to the first frosts of winter. Complex multiple-crop strategies would have been prevalent in regions of the longer growing seasons of the Lower Mississippi Valley and the Southeast.

Taken together, the six species groups (briefly described above) form a Mississippian pattern of subsistence: an annual cycle of selective utilization of seasonally abundant plant and animal resources. When this seasonal pattern of selective resource utilization is charted, fall stands out as a period of abundance and intense activity (figure 3-2).

During September, October, and November, the seasons of availability of nuts, fruits, and seeds would have overlapped the harvest period for fully mature domestic crops. The first southward movement of migratory waterfowl would have begun in September, with peak population movements in October and November. The primary exploitation of the white-tailed deer, raccoon, turkey, and less important species also began during September and October, and continued through the winter months. In the midst of this fall abundance, demands upon labor and time must have been intense.

After fall and the period of abundance, survival through the winter would have depended upon stored plant foods (primarily maize and nuts) and hunting, with deer, raccoon, turkey, and wintering populations of waterfowl of primary importance. The last months of winter would have been the period of greatest stress for Mississippian communities; and the spring flights of waterfowl, as well as rising floodwaters and spawning fish, must have been welcomed not only as signs of approaching spring but also as signs of abundant fresh meat.

With the receding of spring floodwaters and the departure of migratory waterfowl, attention would shift from oxbow lakes and low-lying flooded areas to the clearing and preparation of levee-crest fields for planting. Fish would have been available, in declining numbers, through the summer months, and a short summer hunt may have followed the spring planting.[8] Edible plants and berries were probably utilized through the summer, as well as corn in the green state during late summer, but little evidence of such foods would survive.

As might be expected, regional variations on this theme of Mississippian subsistence correspond to the regional differences in the abundance of preferred species of plants and animals (discussed above). For example, as one moves east from the Mississippi Valley (and the Mississippi flyway) into the river systems of the Southeast, the lower availability of migratory waterfowl is reflected in lower representation in Mississippian settlements.[9] In addition, late prehistoric groups that inhabited the Black Warrior and other river valleys of the Southeast appear to have depended less upon fish resources than those Mississippian groups that occupied the Mississippi Valley, and perhaps to have directed their efforts not so much

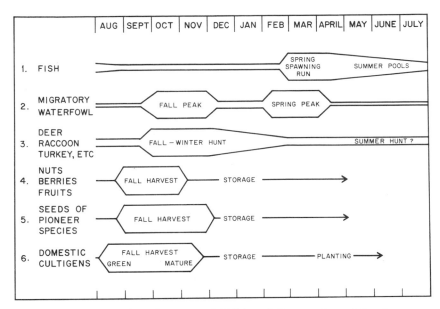

FIGURE 3-2. *Seasonal Utilization of Wild and Domesticated Food Sources by Mississippian Groups*

toward oxbow-lake–back-swamp habitats as to main-channel shoals and fish-dam and fish-weir technology.[10]

The greatest obstacle to obtaining a sharper picture of regional and temporal variations in the subsistence base of Mississippian populations continues to be the differential preservation and recovery of animal and plant remains. Besides, recognition of the importance of fish and waterfowl in the diet of some Mississippian groups is rather recent. It was only with better ways of recovering small and fragile animal bones from archaeological sites, together with selective excavation of Mississippian sites, that the full importance of these species groups has been recognized.

In addition to clarifying the dietary importance of fish and waterfowl, the great volume and variety of small bones that have been recovered from a small number of "good preservation" sites allows discussion of the Mississippian pattern of utilizing animal species and species groups with much more confidence. As more of these "good preservation" Mississippian sites throughout the river valleys of the East are located and excavated, with an eye toward

73

recovery and analysis of animal bones, our understanding of these regional and temporal differences will be refined. Unfortunately, the remains of wild and domestic plants are much more susceptible than animal bones to natural forces of deterioration, as well as more likely to be lost or fragmented during excavation and processing.

The underrepresentation of plant materials, in comparison to animal bones, at Mississippian sites is further complicated by the differential preservation of plant materials—some kinds of plant-food remains are far more likely to survive in the ground than others. Accidental carbonization (partial burning or charring) almost determines whether plant remains survive in Mississippian sites, to be eventually recovered during excavation. Some plant foods were consistently exposed to Mississippian fires (and possible carbonization), either during cooking (e.g., parching of seeds, boiling nuts to extract oil) or because they were used as fuel (e.g., corn cobs, nut hulls). The occurrence at Mississippian sites of plants in the likely-to-be-carbonized category is probably an accurate gauge of their dietary importance *in relation to each other*. At the same time, many plant foods that were no doubt utilized by Mississippian groups have *not* been preserved at their settlements, because they were not routinely exposed to carbonization or they were largely devoid of durable structure (e.g., tubers, rhizomes, stem foods, greens, and flowers).[11]

This total lack of representation of some dietary plants at Mississippian sites, combined with the underrepresentation of the carbonized category (in comparison to animal bones), makes it impossible, on the basis of plant and animal remains alone, to determine either the importance of plant versus animal resources in the diet of Mississippian groups or their dependence upon domestic crops, particularly corn.

Fortunately, it is possible to obtain information about the dietary importance of animals and wild and domestic plant foods from archaeological materials other than plant remains. Through chemical analysis of human skeletal material from Mississippian sites, it appears to be possible to compare the dietary contributions of plants versus animals and to measure the importance of maize as a Mississippian food. By measuring the trace elements (particularly strontium) in samples of human bone from Mississippian sites, the "relative importance of meat in comparison to vegetable food in the diet at any one point in time can be approached."[12] There are, however, difficulties in interpreting trace-element analysis, and the

74

technique has yet to be applied in a systematic way to Mississippian subsistence.[13]

Similarly, carbon isotope analysis ($13_c/12_c$ ratio) of human bone samples appears to provide unequivocal evidence of the importance of maize in the diet of Mississippian populations. But to date, analysis of the $13_c/12_c$ studies of human bone samples from Mississippian sites has not shown a comfortably homogeneous and straightforward picture of corn consumption within Mississippian communities. For example, of the eight burials from the Aztalan site in Wisconsin recently analyzed, corn appears to have composed almost half the diet of one individual whereas another ate almost no corn at all. Almost as great a variation in corn consumption was found in a group of five burials from Mound 72, Cahokia.[14] Thus while $13_c/12_c$ ratio analysis holds promise of providing a much clearer and more accurate picture of corn consumption by Mississippian groups, this picture is likely to be very complex and to involve much more than basic patterns of differential consumption related to sex, age, or status.

The two fundamental similarities of Mississippian groups (they occupied river floodplain habitats and adapted to them in much the same way) were, in turn, largely responsible for the similarity in the distribution of Mississippian groups. The best way for Mississippian populations to have occupied a floodplain habitat, so as to take advantage of its soils and wild foods most effectively, was in a pattern of small, dispersed settlements on preferred soil types, adjacent to channel-remnant lakes and ponds. The typical floodplain habitat is a line of small settlements along the natural levees adjacent to oxbow lakes (figure 3-3). These small-homestead settlements, representing the minimum economic unit, are occupied by a single (or perhaps several) nuclear-extended family group on a year-round basis. The garden plots of each household are located close by, minimizing the time and effort necessary for cultivation and crop protection. Each small settlement would also have easy access to the rich protein resources of the oxbow lakes.

Efficient use of environmental resources was not, however, the only concern of Mississippian populations. Each of these societies, politically independent and economically self-sufficient, typically occupied a small amount of river-valley real estate, which nonetheless was coveted by its Mississippian neighbors. Consistently, as a result, Mississippian populations had to be able to defend their slice of the meander belt. This necessitated ways to deal with both the

Bruce D. Smith

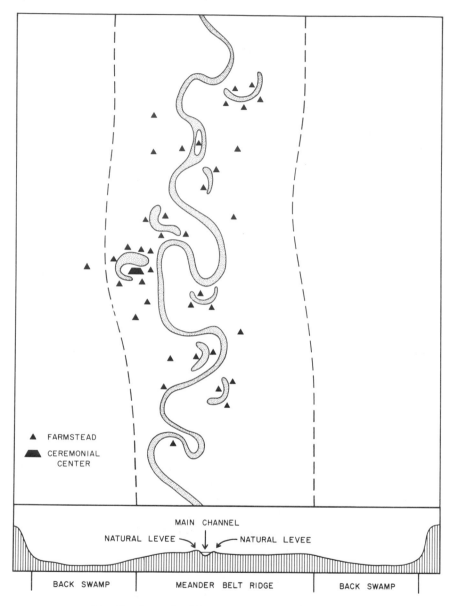

FIGURE 3-3. *Distribution of a Mississippian Population within a River-Valley Floodplain (Illustration by G. Robert Lewis)*

76

internal problems of social cohesion and cooperation and the external problems of defense of land and people, and one of the most obvious and effective solutions is nucleation into fortified villages. This is a good solution to the problems of defense, but is inefficient in utilizing meander-belt resources. Similarly, small, dispersed farmsteads are a good solution to "energy capture," but a very poor solution to problems of defense and boundary maintenance.

Many Mississippian populations appear to have developed a compromise—a settlement system that not only balanced these opposing pressures but adjusted to changing defensive needs: large, often fortified settlements in the center of a pattern of small, dispersed homesteads. Such centralized settlements (often termed "ceremonial" or "mound centers") were the political and religious focus for family homesteads, scattered across the surrounding landscape (figure 3-4). These "mound centers" would have been the locus for public activities (plazas, mounds, ceremonial structures) and the residence of individuals who held important ceremonial-political positions. Only a small segment of the local population would have lived within the walls of a mound center on a permanent basis, but the center would be capable of sheltering the total population during periods of hostility with neighboring groups.[15]

Individual family units, living in dispersed homesteads, probably visited the mound center regularly, and may have maintained a second, temporary habitation structure in the center for seasonal ceremonies of cultural integration, for group-labor projects (mound and fortification construction), and for protection during periods of hostility with neighboring groups. During peaceful times, the need for protection behind fortified walls decreased and the ceremonial centers would have been only partially occupied, as most of the population was distributed in outlying homesteads. During prolonged periods of hostilities, on the other hand, homesteads would be abandoned as the entire population took up residence close to, or within, the fortified walls of the ceremonial center. It is likely that Mississippian groups could have shifted back and forth (and probably did) between dispersed and nucleated settlements repeatedly, even within a period as short as 100 years.

This continual adjustment of location makes it difficult for archaeologists to determine which settlements were occupied at the same points in time. Working, at best, with 200-year-long segments, we can discern the pattern of a ceremonial center and outlying farmsteads, but we cannot focus on and understand the cycles of

Bruce D. Smith

FIGURE 3-4. *This painting by John Douglass shows a reconstruction of Powers Fort, a thirteenth-century Mississippian ceremonial center in southeast Missouri. Bounded on the right by a cypress swamp, the 12-acre fortified settlement contained four mounds around a central plaza. (Courtesy of Smithsonian Exposition Books)*

population expansion and contraction within the centers, as farmsteads were established, occupied for a few years, and then abandoned for any number of reasons, including withdrawal to the protection of the center. To complicate things further, the balance of power between adjacent Mississippian groups sometimes shifted enough to enable one of them to bring several neighbors under political control. The most obvious archaeological indication that this happened is the growth of the ceremonial center of a regionally dominant group and an accompanying increase in the size and/or number of its mounds, plazas, public structures, and fortifications.

The ceremonial centers of subjugated Mississippian populations, with their political and religious leaders, usually took second-level district administrative roles and owed allegiance (as well as corporate labor and agricultural "surplus") to the elite members of the dominant regional center. The Black Warrior River Valley contains archaeological evidence of the emergence and growth of one of these regional political organizations. By A.D. 1100 there were perhaps as many as ten apparently independent Mississippian societies, each with its own ceremonial center, along a 75-mile floodplain from Tuscaloosa south to the Black Belt.[16] By A.D. 1250, one of these Mississippian groups, with its ceremonial center at Moundville, had brought the other groups in the Black Warrior Valley under its control, and the expansion and elaboration of Moundville as regional center continued for another 300 years.

To no one's surprise, unraveling the developmental sequence is proving just as difficult as trying to go beyond general statements on Mississippian subsistence. Fortunately for those who have an interest in such things, Mississippian patterns of subsistence and settlement will continue to be fascinating and complex questions that hold no promise, at any time soon, of being solved to anyone's satisfaction.

II

Hernando de Soto Claiming the Mississippi (Courtesy of The Historic New Orleans Collection)

The Age of Exploration

4 Early European Penetration of Eastern North America

John H. Parry

One of the most striking features of the early exploration of the Americas is the persistent influence of the notion of Asia-in-the-West: the idea that Asia could be reached by sailing west—even that Columbus' New World *was* Asia. It is true that the more bizarre of Columbus' suggestions—that Cuba was a peninsula of China, that Hispaniola might be Japan, that Honduras might be Marco Polo's Indo-China and Paria the earthly paradise were quickly discredited or discounted. Nevertheless, for twenty or thirty years after Columbus' initial discovery, many intelligent and well-informed people continued to assume, or at least hope, that the newly discovered lands lay within striking distance of Asia, that they were connected with Asia in some way, and that they were to be valued not so much for their own sake as for the convenience they might afford as staging points on the route to richer and more civilized parts of Asia.

These assumptions and hopes affected both government policy and the course of events. The early Spanish-government-sponsored expeditions to the New World were all directed to areas south, not north, of Columbus' original island discoveries, because south was believed to be the way to Asia, whether by an eastern or a western route. Privately sponsored expeditions—more numerous though less ambitious—were less directly affected. Those who organized and conducted them were looking for precious metals, pearls, productive land, and docile inhabitants. Probably they did not much care whether the lands where they found these things were connected with Asia; but they too tended to head south rather than north. Gold, in the European mind, was associated with hot countries; so south was the direction for riches, and indeed it was on the Caribbean coasts of Colombia and the Isthmus that gold artifacts were first found, available for trade, in significant quantity.

All these considerations help to explain why the Caribbean and Atlantic coasts of South America were rapidly explored, while North America remained unknown, a vast blank on the map. Cartographers (*some* cartographers at least) were aware of the existence of the Florida peninsula from about 1503, a decade or so before the first recorded reconnaissance by Juan Ponce de León; but for all that anyone knew to the contrary, it might be only another large island. Martin Waldseemüller, it is true, in 1507 gave North America as a whole an attenuated continental shape, separate from Asia and with a western coastline; but this seems to have been an inspired guess, based on conjecture (so far as we know) rather than on the evidence of exploration.

One cannot be quite sure of this, of course. The record of early exploration is like the tip of an iceberg. There may have been early voyages, perhaps many voyages, of which no record has survived. Some may have gone even beyond Florida. All we can say with certainty is that Waldseemüller in 1507 did not represent orthodox or even generally accepted opinion. Of the surviving maps and charts drawn in the first two decades of the sixteenth century, some—the Schöner globe of 1515, Peter Apian's *Typus Orbis* of 1520—follow the general lines of the 1507 woodcut. Others show Florida attached to a fair-size stretch of territory, but avoid commitment by using an edge of the maps to cut it off on the north and west. Waldseemüller himself treated the Florida territory in this way in the 1513 Strasburg *Ptolemy*, and in his *Carta Marina* of 1516 he added a legend indicating that the territory was part of Asia: *"Terra de Cuba Asie Partis."* Whether this represented a change of mind or a slip of the pen is impossible to say.

Many maps, on the other hand, fully as authoritative as those of Waldseemüller, contradict the 1507 woodcut flatly. Examples are those of Contarini-Rosselli in 1506, Contarini in 1508, Ruysch in 1508, Vesconte Maggiolo in 1511. In all these maps the mainland of Asia stretches from west to east across the northern portion of the globe in a great peninsular extension, usually labeled "Tangut," terminating in the lands discovered by John Cabot and the brothers Corte-Real. Far to the south is the big amorphous lump of *"Terra Crucis,"* South America. In between is a great expanse of sea, broken only by the Antillean Islands. Mainland North America, in short, was not only unexplored; in the minds of many distinguished cartographers it did not even exist.

In the 1520s, all this changed abruptly—both the general European picture of the New World and the distribution of European interest within it. The invasion of Mexico revealed to Europeans a large, productive territory densely inhabited by people of sophisticated culture and formidable political organization. One might surmise—as missionaries shocked by pagan wickedness often did—that the Mexicans were the latter-day descendants of the Ten Lost Tribes and, therefore, Asian in their remote origin; but no one denied that they had traveled a long way from their original home. Nothing in their present condition suggested the East; they were a New World society, the richest and most powerful so far encountered. There was no obvious reason to assume, moreover, that they were the only such society.

In the same year that Cortés invaded Mexico, a less well-known, much less well-recorded expedition, commanded by Alonso Alvarez de Pineda, coasted the northern Gulf of Mexico and proved the coast to be continuous, all the way from the Pánuco River to the Florida peninsula. Except for a question mark over the Gulf of Honduras, this meant continuous land from Florida to southern South America. Pineda's voyage put an end to hopes of a sea passage through Central America to Asia, but at the same time it revealed a mainland of large and undefined extent between Florida and Mexico, and prompted speculation as to how many more Mexicos might await discovery there. Inevitably, these discoveries and conjectures gave great encouragement to those who were disposed to explore the New World for its own sake, rather than press beyond it to the Spicery.

In that same busy year, 1519, Ferdinand Magellan sailed from Seville to reach the Spicery by a southwest passage; three years later, the battered *Victoria*, with eighteen enfeebled survivors, limped into Seville with a cargo of cloves and with news, some good, some very bad. The passage, they said, existed. That was the good news. The bad news was that the passage was too long, too stormy, and too dangerous to serve as a regular commercial route. The South Sea that Balboa had sighted in 1513 was not a mere Ptolemaic gulf, an arm of the Indian Ocean; it was a separate ocean, terrifying in its immensity. These gloomy findings were overlooked in the euphoria of discovery, and continued to be resisted in official circles for several years, until later voyages confirmed them. But no confirmation was needed; for years, Magellan's strait was left to the penguins and seals. Exploring interest promptly shifted from the South to the North Atlantic: to the broad channel of sea which, according to many maps, passed through to the Pacific somewhere north of Florida and south of the Baccalaos, the "codfish coasts." For a few years, explorers, intent on finding a passage to the East, and *conquistadores*, weary of the Caribbean islands and looking for loot, land, and labor farther afield in the New World, concentrated on the middle latitudes of eastern North America.

Five major expeditions entered this area in the 1520s: three from the Atlantic, two from the Gulf. Of the Atlantic attempts, two were maritime expeditions in search of a sea passage to Asia, and both sailed from harbors in Europe. The other Atlantic expedition, and both of the Gulf *entradas*, were designed for conquest and settlement. All three sailed from bases in the Antilles, and all three ended in disaster, which Oviedo, in his acid way, attributed to the incompetence of the organizers.

The two maritime expeditions also failed in their purpose, because the object of their search did not exist, but both seem to have been ably planned and executed. One was French, out of Rouen in 1524, commanded by the Florentine Giovanni Verrazzano; the other was Spanish, out of Coruña in 1525, commanded by the Portuguese Estevão Gomes. Gomes had been with Magellan, but had deserted in the Strait and returned to Spain. For this action—unheroic but, in the light of later events, not unsensible—he had succeeded in exculpating himself and in blaming Magellan, whom the Spanish authorities had always regarded with suspicion. So now here he was, searching for an easier alternative to Magellan's Strait. Few details are known of his voyage; those we have come from the chronicles and from cartographical evidence.

The Verrazzano voyage is better known because a good eyewitness account survives in several manuscript copies. Verrazzano followed the coast from south to north, from Cape Hatteras to somewhere in Maine; Gomes sailed in the same direction, probably from northern Florida to Cape Cod. Gomes, probably, Verrazzano certainly, entered the Hudson River, but both, oddly, missed the entrances to Chesapeake and Delaware bays, either of which might have been a candidate for the looked-for strait. Both reported—Verrazzano in plausible detail—on the natives they encountered, and Gomes kidnapped several and brought them back to Spain. Peter Martyr commented severely on this. He and Oviedo saw the captives in Spain and remarked on their tall stature. Probably they were Algonkians from what is now southern New England.

Verrazzano's report, careful and credible in most respects, contains one oddity: he took the Outer Banks about Cape Hatteras for an isthmus, and Pamlico and Albemarle sounds, visible beyond it from the masthead, for the broad Pacific. This quaint conceit—a Panamanian "wasp waist," so to speak, in North America—appears on several Italian maps, including one by Verrazzano's brother Girolamo and another by Vesconte Maggiolo; but the supposed discovery was not followed up, and had no practical effect.

The combined result of these two voyages was to suggest that a continuous mainland coast stretched from southwest to northeast, all the way from Florida to Maine, much farther than anyone had formerly supposed; that the object of Asia-in-the-West, if it was to be pursued further, must be sought either through a passage much farther north or by building ships on the Pacific Coast, as Cortés was already doing; that the natives of the Atlantic Coast, though amiable, were primitive and possessed no gold; and that, from a Spanish point of view, attempts at settlement were likely to prove unrewarding.

One Spaniard of standing dissented from this last view, and the enterprise of Lucas Vázquez de Ayllón, abortive though it was, calls for brief mention. He was a judge in the *audiencia* of Santo Domingo, with many business interests in the island, including a sugar plantation and mill near Puerto Plata. Slavers, operating out of Puerto Plata, regularly raided the Bahamas and sometimes went farther north, up the coast of what is now Georgia. Ayllón, who invested in such an expedition, obtained as part of his dividend an Indian boy, to whom he became greatly attached. The boy was intelligent, learned Spanish, was baptized as Francisco, and entertained Ayllón with tales of his homeland, Chicora. Ayllón became obsessed by the notion of founding a settlement in Chicora. When he visited Spain on official business, he took Francisco with him, to entertain a wider audience and to support his application for a license to colonize.

Francisco rose magnificently to the occasion. Some of the features he described were real and can be identified; others proceeded from a fertile inventiveness—for example, people with short, thick tails, who had to dig holes in the ground, when they sat down, to accommodate their tails. He must have been a plausible rascal, for Peter Martyr, not usually credulous, was taken in by him. The sardonic Oviedo, however, at once suspected fraud and tried to dissuade Ayllón from his folly, but in vain. Ayllón procured his license and in 1526 sailed from Hispaniola with six ships, 500 men, and 80 horses. The small number of horses is evidence of the peaceful intentions, and humble standing, of most of those who took part. (Horses at that time were cheap and plentiful in Hispaniola; if an armed and plundering *entrada* had been intended, many more participants would have been mounted.) This was to be a genuine colony of settlement. Its character was further emphasized by its party of Dominican friars, including that veteran champion of Indian interests, Fray Antonio de Montesinos.

Virtuous intentions are rarely an adequate substitute for sound planning. The place selected for disembarkation was probably the mouth of the Waccamaw River, near modern Georgetown. Foolishly, the provisions that were to sustain the colony for the first few months had all been loaded into the largest ship, and this vessel, leading the others up Winyah Bay, was wrecked and all her cargo lost. Francisco ran away, as no doubt he had planned to all along, and the company was left without food, guides, or interpreters in a strange area of sand and swamp. They reembarked and made their dispirited way southwest, down the coast and through the sounds to a second camp, near modern Savannah, where Ayllón died. Discipline broke down. Some wandered into the bush in search of food; some starved to death or were killed by Indians. Eventually about 150 men, sick and hungry, made their way back to Hispaniola.

This was the last Spanish attempt to found a genuine colony, for settlement's sake, on the Atlantic Coast. There were several subsequent settlements, but all, including the abortive Jesuit mission to Chesapeake Bay in 1570, were governed principally by strategic considerations: to forestall French or English settlements and to protect the "silver fleets" in their passage through the Florida Strait to Spain.

The Gulf Coast seemed to offer better prospects for settlement, if only because of its proximity to Mexico. When Ponce de León reconnoitered the southwest coast of Florida in 1513, he had been driven off by the Indians; his contract, however, remained in force. In 1521, he returned in high hopes from his base in Puerto Rico, but failed to profit by his earlier experience. His people were again ambushed and defeated, and he was killed by an arrow. His death, and the subsequent death of Francisco de Garay, one of Cortés' rivals, who had a contract for the north coast of the Gulf, left the entire area, including Florida, open for settlement and conquest by any Spaniard who could procure a contract. Such a contract went to Pánfilo de Narváez in 1526.

Narváez, one of the least attractive *conquistadores*, had considerable experience in fighting Indians in the islands and a coarse *bonhomie*, which made him superficially popular, but little else. He was brutal, feckless, faithless, and is so described by chroniclers of all shades of opinion, from Oviedo to Las Casas. He had been responsible, as Diego Velázquez' lieutenant, for overrunning and devastating Cuba and Jamaica, and had become a rich man in the process. He was then sent by Velázquez to Mexico to supersede and arrest Cortés, but was outwitted and outmaneuvered. Most of his men went over to Cortés, and Narváez was captured in a skirmish in which he lost an eye. Released, he returned to Spain to press charges against Cortés. In 1526, Cortés' authority in New Spain was not fully recognized, and those in charge of the Indies administration still regarded him with deep suspicion. Narváez' chief qualification for the title of *adelantado* of the vast region north of the Gulf—apart, of course, from his persuasive wealth—seems to have been his hostility to Cortés. The purpose of his appointment was not only to search for more Mexicos but to outflank Cortés in Mexico.

Narváez, though a man of very different stamp from the gentle, conscientious, gullible Ayllón, fared no better. His ships had a slow and stormy passage from Hispaniola to Cuba and thence to Tampa Bay, where he and his men disembarked. He had not loaded enough provisions, or enough fodder for the horses, presumably expecting to commandeer Indian supplies. Over 100 horses died on the passage. When the army landed in April, no crops were ripe and Indian stores were nearly depleted. Foolishly, Narváez sent his ships to a vaguely indicated rendezvous on the northern Gulf Coast, and never saw them again.

Marching north on their rations of biscuit and bacon, his people found nothing to eat except palmetto shoots. Two months later, near modern Tallahassee, they found ripening maize and old corn in cribs, but their foraging provoked fierce retaliation and they were constantly harassed by Indians with bows and arrows. Horses, killed by these arrows, were eaten. As they moved west through the forested, sandy coastal plain, their march became a retreat. At Saint Andrew's Bay, near modern Panama City, the survivors built boats and tried to reach the Pánuco River in Mexico, but most of the company, including Narváez, were drowned in this attempt. About 90 men drifted in makeshift boats to the coast of Texas, near modern Galveston. Among them were Álvar Núñez Cabeza de Vaca and his three companions, who walked from Texas to Culiacán, passing from one Indian tribe to another; they were treated by some as harmless lunatics, by others as powerful medicine men. Their journey took eight years, so that they were treated in Mexico City (where they arrived in 1536) as though they had risen from the dead.

With the Narváez expedition, the long series of mainland ventures mounted from island bases came to an end. Almost all had been of one pattern: failures due to adverse circumstances, but also to incompetence. Oviedo, recounting the failures, thought Narváez came to the most ignoble end of all. But nearly all the leaders had sought, as Narváez did, to acquire wealth and standing by plunder, without troubling to ensure adequate provisioning, reliable intelligence, and prudent organization. The one exception was Cortés, who is often described as the archetypal *conquistador*; but he was exceptional, and would have been exceptional in any age or circumstance. Added to this, he was lucky, whereas few of the others had much luck.

But luck was not the reason why island-based ventures to North America came to an end. Rather, the islands had largely been stripped of men and news trickling through from Peru offered more tempting attractions to the few who remained. There was no disillusion, as yet, with North America; hopes, though temporarily in abeyance, still ran high. Some of the Narváez survivors, Cabeza de Vaca among them, had reported favorably on some of the territory they had traversed. Indeed, the Narváez expedition was a foreshadowing—almost a dress rehearsal—of the more ambitious venture of Hernando de Soto ten years later, but with these differences: Soto mounted his expedition from Spain, and whereas Narváez had turned to North America after failing in Mexico, Soto went there after he had been all too "successful" in Peru.

Peru introduced a new scale of dimensions, geographical and financial, into the conquest. Foot soldiers acquired more loot in one day at Cajamarca than experienced captains acquired in years of campaigning in the islands, on the Isthmus, or even in Mexico. Soto, much more than Cortés, was the archetypal *conquistador*: a *hidalgo* (a standing which many *conquistadores* claimed after the event but to which few were entitled) and a fighting man. In his teens, he went to the Indies in the train of Pedrarias, possessing, in the phrase of the time, nothing but his sword. He became rich in the free-for-all sack of Central America under Pedrarias—rich enough to raise, equip, and transport his own company of 100 men, armed and mostly mounted, to join Pizarro in the initial invasion of Peru. He was at Cajamarca and at Cuzco, and his captain's share of the loot made him immensely rich. He was a dashing leader, a superb horseman, but reckless and somewhat irresponsible. On several occasions he advanced into exposed positions and had to be extricated by the more cautious Pizarro. He protested (after the event) the murder of Atahuallpa and thereby acquired a reputation for knight-errantry that was probably undeserved. (Moreover, his conduct on that occasion was not disinterested.) He had some education and was literate, but was not a thoughtful man—nor, I think, very intelligent, though he was certainly not as stupid as Narváez.

When the conquest seemed secure, Pizarro faced the fact that his army had too many captains, too many claimants for fiefs and governorships in the conquered empire. Some of the prominent (possibly dangerous) rivals to the Pizarro clan received broad intimations that Peru held no future for them, that they should take their share of the plunder and leave. Soto, in one of the more sensible acts of a wild career, took the hint and left. He returned to Spain, where his great wealth opened many doors, and obtained the grant and title of *adelantado*, which Narváez' death had left vacant.

Soto's expedition, unlike that of Narváez, was carefully prepared and well equipped. Between 600 and 700 men left Spain, all well armed and more than half of them mounted. There were artisans, including skilled boat builders, among them (to whom the survivors would owe their lives). Soto's commission included the governorship of Cuba, where the expedition made a long pause and loaded ample provisions, including large numbers of live pigs. These were Spanish range pigs, long snouted, long legged, agile, and accustomed to foraging for mast and acorns in woodlands and to being driven in herds—very different from the heavy, short-legged breeds brought over in later centuries by north European settlers. Soto's men knew how to manage them and drove them along with the army, an ambulant and self-reproducing food supply. Some escaped or were stolen by Indians, who were quick to see the value of these novel animals. They were probably the ancestors of the feral pigs reported by European settlers in Georgia many years later, and of the characteristic rural breeds in the South today.

The army landed (almost certainly) in Tampa Bay in late spring of 1539. Soto had no knowledge of the area, and apparently no clear idea of what to do with it if his occupation were successful. His instructions required him to establish settlements on the coast, but he made no attempt to do so. Contemporary accounts—of which there are several, including three by participants—suggest that he had no specific aim, other than plunder. This perhaps explains why Cabeza de Vaca did not join the expeditions. According to some accounts, Cabeza de Vaca had been invited to join, and his experience would have been of great value, but he was a man of puritanical conscience and, presumably, would not share in such an undertaking.

Soto had amassed a fortune in Peru by extorting treasure from living Indians and by robbing the tombs of dead ones, and he proposed to do the same in North America. His curiosity about the funerary customs of the Mississippian peoples was not wholly anthropological. Soto had no evidence that the region had anything worth plundering; he assumed—and is recorded as saying—that in so large an area there must be places where treasure could be found. This attitude—predatory but vague—perhaps explains his apparently aimless wandering, over the next three years, through the territories of Florida, Georgia, North Carolina, Alabama, Tennessee, Arkansas, Mississippi, and Louisiana.

Relations with the peoples he encountered were almost uniformly bad. Even where his army was received with generous hospitality, relations were quickly soured by ruthless foraging and demands for tribute, porters, and women. No attempt was made to penetrate, even to understand, native society—to get on good terms or to form alliances. The Spaniards would occupy, temporarily, major Indian towns; they would on occasion kidnap chiefs to enforce their demands (a time-honored device). They collected enough food and firewood to live comfortably in stockaded camps through three successive winters; but when they were on the march, they suffered steady attrition from Indian retaliation and attack.

Soto died beside the Mississippi in 1542 and was buried surreptitiously in the river. He had resisted suggestions for exploring the river to its mouth—for fear, perhaps, that his men might mutiny and insist on returning to New Spain. Antonio de Mendoza, the viceroy, was no friend to Soto, and it is clear from participants' accounts that

Soto's personal magnetism had worn very thin. No surviving participant or contemporary chronicler made any attempt to defend his conduct. The picture of him as a paladin of Spanish valor and enterprise was the invention, years later, of the romanticizing Inca Garcilaso de la Vega. After Soto's death, an attempt to march the army overland to Mexico was abandoned after some months. The army returned to the river, above Natchez, and built a fleet of boats in which about 300 survivors, in rags, reached the Pánuco River, nearly five years after their departure from Spain.

The expedition had few practical results, apart from the pigs and a great deal of vague information. Europe was apprised of the great extent and varied nature of the region that had been traversed. Spaniards, the people most affected, found the information discouraging. The Mississippian peoples were granted a respite of a century or so before the next wave of European incursions.

The Soto expedition failed partly because its purposes were never clearly defined, partly because the objects it sought did not exist, partly because the experience of the leaders was not appropriate to the conditions they encountered. Soto was driven not by a rational plan nor by information, true or false, but by obsessive memories. But he was certainly an experienced fighting man, and it is curious that a force so well equipped proved relatively ineffectual in a military sense. It was not only harassed on the march but not infrequently defeated in battle (notably at the place they called Mabila) by Indian forces that outnumbered it but cannot have been numerous.

We are accustomed, as Soto was, to assume the superiority of European weapons over those of people we are pleased to consider savages. This is not necessarily true, and it was not true in the circumstances in which Soto found himself. The peoples whom the Spaniards encountered in Peru and Central Mexico were highly organized city builders. They fielded large, disciplined forces that fought in dense formation with clubs, spears, and slings. Against them the Spaniards employed armored horsemen, who used slashing swords in melee and lances in pursuit, and footmen armed with sword, pike, and crossbow or arquebus. Against organized Indian armies, these weapons had proved highly effective; in North America, on the other hand, Soto encountered skilled archery for the first time.

In the early sixteenth century the longbow, in skilled hands, was still the most efficient missile weapon known to man, more efficient than either the crossbow or arquebus. It had less stopping power at short range against a charging enemy and marginally—but only marginally—less penetrating power against armor; but it had greater accuracy, a greater lethal range, and a much more rapid rate of discharge. Against this, it had two disadvantages. The archer, in taking aim, must stand and expose himself; he could not shoot from behind the breastwork of a fortification or the gunwale of a ship; but if the archer shot from forest cover, this disadvantage did not matter. The other was more serious: effective use of the longbow required great skill and specialized muscles that could be acquired only by frequent and lifelong practice, and such practice, as a rule, came only to people who were habitual hunters. In western Europe (and for that matter in Mexico and Inca Peru), wild game was limited and hunting was the privilege of a restricted group of people. Thus the longbow had been abandoned as a military weapon in Europe because of the lack of skilled archers; nor was it effectively used by the Aztec and Inca armies. Among Europeans, the crossbow and arquebus had displaced it, not because they were more efficient but because they demanded less skill. A man could be trained to use either in a few hours on the range.

In both the Narváez and Soto narratives there are many references to Indian archery. Cabeza de Vaca told of an arrow that missed him and penetrated eight inches into the trunk of a nearby oak tree. In every part of the Americas where Spaniards encountered skilled bowmen in dispersed formation in forest cover—in Chile, Colombia, in the woodlands of the Upper Rio de la Plata drainage, and in some parts of the Amazon drainage—the story was the same: heavy losses and frequent defeats.

It is tempting to speculate on what might have happened if Soto had been a different kind of man—a Cabeza de Vaca, or perhaps a Cortés, a Valdivia or a Quesada—or if he had been interested in settling the question of the supposed "Sea of Verrazzano," with its promise of easy access to the Pacific and to the East; or if he had seriously investigated navigation of the Lower Mississippi (which was not undertaken until 100 years later). Of course, such speculations are idle. Soto was neither a planner of settlements nor a systematic explorer. He probably never heard of the "Sea of Verrazzano," though, had it existed, it would have lain across his route.

Asia-in-the-West, that seductive mirage, had no place in his plans or his instructions—nor, indeed, had geographical inquiry of any kind, except for the 200 leagues of the Gulf Coast that he was to explore and on which he was told to found three towns (but did not). His achievement must be judged in relation to what he undertook. By that criterion the expedition—so well prepared, so ill conducted—was a failure. It found no treasure, except a box of inferior fresh-water pearls, because there was none to find. More significant, it struck no roots, left no serious trace. Modern scholars cannot agree on even the exact route of his aimless, wandering army.

Soto's aimlessness was a subject of severe comment by all the contemporary chroniclers. "He went about for five years hunting mines," wrote López de Gómara, "thinking it would be like Peru. He made no settlement, and thus he died, and destroyed those who went with him. Never will conquerors do well unless they settle before they undertake anything else, especially here where the Indians are valiant bowmen and strong." Soto's failure, no doubt, is among the reasons why this symposium is conducted today in English, not Spanish.

5 The Archaeology of the Hernando de Soto Expedition

Jeffrey P. Brain

Any attempt to place the 1539–43 expedition of Hernando de Soto in historical and ethnohistorical perspective must treat the motives for the exploration against the background of European traditions, events, and mentalities, as well as both the contemporary and subsequent impact of its startling appearance among the American Indian societies. The impacts of such contact between peoples of two fundamentally different cultural traditions are of most interest and concern to anthropologists, but to pursue such studies, it is critically important to identify the archaeological contexts, which means that we must be accurate in determining points of contact between the army and the Indians. In short, we must reconstruct the route of Soto accurately. Historians, ethnographers, and geographers have worked on this problem for generations and in recent years have been joined by archaeologists as we begin to develop our discipline and data base vis-à-vis this problem.

At the outset, we must acknowledge that, at present, we cannot trace the route of Soto with precision. We can trace his movements only within a reasonable approximation. Valid theories may have been presented, but none has yet been proved. Of course, archaeologists deal in small particulars, and these must be closely correlated before we can be satisfied. It must also be noted that while historical analysis may identify a probable site, archaeological investigation is necessary to prove it.

Throughout Soto's route, considerable problems beset the coincidence of historical and archaeological data, which is not surprising when the scale of the expedition is measured against the vast area that it traversed. It is a needle-in-a-haystack problem, and although we have found the needle, we do not know exactly where it was hidden in the haystack. Apparently, as the Soto chronicler Garcilaso notes several times, the army marched without the benefit of precise "navigational" fixes, although there were sailors in its ranks.[1] Thus even the participants had little idea where they were at any time and, therefore, their geographic references in the unknown land are almost impossibly vague.

Compounding the problem is the fact that the objectives of the expedition were different from ours. They were not as interested in where they were, or had been, as in where they were going; they were not as interested in what they found (they realized practically nothing from their daring endeavors) as in what they *hoped* to find. Their directions, when given, were generally expressed in broad segments of the compass. The result is that while historical interest has raised expectations, our hope of tangible archaeological recovery from the immense landscape is all but forlorn—but not impossible.

For centuries, scholars have speculated on the expedition's route. When all serious speculations and hypotheses are amalgamated, they reduce to little more than a broad swath across the map of the Southeastern states (figure 5-1). Forty-five years ago, therefore, the United States De Soto Commission, under the chairmanship of the distinguished ethnologist and historian John R. Swanton, was formed to make the first major attempt at defining the entire route of the expedition and placing it in native contexts. Its conclusions were to be the definitive and official determination, and its final report was issued on the quadricentennial of the landing of the army.[2] It attempted to penetrate the cloud of speculation which had accumulated and, in a tour de force of analysis and interpretation, present a closely defined hypothesis. However important its research, which serves as the base for all modern Soto studies, its conclusions are not sacrosanct. It is now conceded that many of the commission's conclusions are far from final, and as new evidence accumulates, it becomes increasingly clear that many reconstructed segments (practically the whole route) are in need of revision.

The commission's interpretations were perhaps the best it could make with the evidence at hand, but the precision that it attempted was not warranted by the documents' vague information. Nor were

97

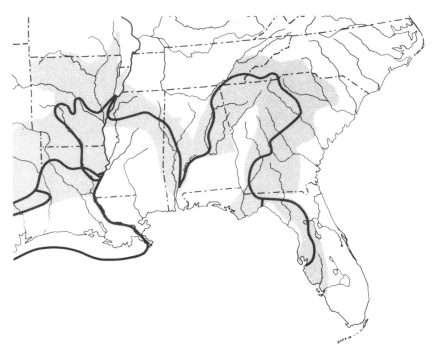

FIGURE 5-1. *Official Route of the De Soto Expedition Commission, Superimposed on an Amalgamated Field of Alternate Hypotheses*

sufficient and reliable archaeological data available at that time—or even now.[3] However, Swanton was aware of deficiencies in many reconstructions of the route and he left the door open for archaeology,[4] which has addressed itself to these problems during the intervening decades. In many instances, as we shall see, the commission's identifications of probable Soto sites have been denied, as well as many segments of the "official" route. New archaeological data have provided important evidence for major revisions and alternative identifications. Furthermore—although it may seem a step backward—scientific honesty requires that some reconstructed segments of the route be accorded broader latitude as a prerequisite for further archaeological study.

The Route and Archaeological Evidence

In tracing the route, we consider three categories of archaeological evidence: positive, negative, and suggestive. Positive evidence of the

Soto *entrada* is an encampment, burial, or other in-ground proof of the army's presence. To date, no such discovery has been authenticated, and therefore this category must be dismissed—with the hope that this primary form of evidence will yet be revealed, perhaps through refinements generated by other categories of evidence.

Negative evidence can disprove a postulated Soto site—after sufficient archaeological investigation. The ultimate benefit is that it narrows the possibilities. On the other hand, negative evidence is never final, and we must always suspect that something was over-looked—unless it is proved that chronological or cultural affiliations are impossible correlations. Archaeologically, this is a valid and pertinent approach to the problem; but traditionally, Soto studies have been based too much on negative evidence.

Suggestive evidence falls in the gray zone between the black and white of negative and positive. It consists of secondary forms of evidence which seem to prove that the army passed through a locale, without confirming its presence in a particular context. Although it may take several forms, the most important form to be considered in these pages is discovery of Soto-related artifacts in native contexts. Such artifacts attest to *passage* of the army, though not necessarily to *specific contact* with the Indians. Thus, while they may not yield precise locational evidence of the army, we have evidence of its nearby presence. This permits refinement of the route and is one of the exciting new developments in Soto studies.

The following discussion details some of the negative and suggestive archaeological evidence currently available for refining the route of the *adelantado*, Hernando de Soto, through Florida and the Southeastern United States. First, however, we will discuss the De Soto Commission route as it pertains to negative evidence, since the commission proposed the "final" conclusions that have been ac-cepted by more than a generation of historians and other re-searchers.

From the very beginning there are problems. We do not know where Soto first set foot in Florida in late May 1539, notwithstanding the fact that the exact place of landing has received more attention than any other part of the route (except, perhaps, for his discovery of the Mississippi River). The traditional consensus, accepted and given the mantle of orthodoxy by the De Soto Commission, is the vicinity of Tampa Bay. Yet when all the original narratives, secondary historical sources, archaeological evidence, and many interpretive

99

arguments have been analyzed, only one conclusion is certain: Soto and his army landed on the southwest coast of peninsular Florida. It is not yet possible to pinpoint the location within the 100-mile stretch from the Caloosahatchee River on the south to Tampa Bay on the north.

The reasons for imprecision in resolving this matter are (1) the evidence within the primary documents is not sufficient to allow more definitive answers (a problem, as already noted, that hounds the entire route of the expedition); (2) the secondary documentation—in greater profusion of historiographic and cartographic sources than for any other portion of the route—obscures, rather than clarifies, the situation; and (3) archaeology, at this writing, offers no significant evidence or proof of Soto's presence at a specific locale.

Archaeology, however, denies an identification in which the commission placed great confidence: the location of the Indian village of Ucita, in which the army is reported to have established its first headquarters. The site was investigated more than thirty years ago, with negative result.[5] This finding, alone, does not invalidate the possibility that Soto's army landed in the vicinity of Tampa Bay, but it seriously weakens the De Soto Commission's conclusions, for it based a considerable part of its argument on this identification. This is but one of the commission's "strong points" that we shall find assailable as we move along behind the army.

After consolidating his base camp near the landing (wherever it was), Soto led most of his army northward through peninsular Florida on the first leg of his exploration. He was seeking the riches of the unknown continent and hoping to find another Aztec or Inca empire (he had been with Pizarro in Peru and now sought a similar conquest of his own in this northern land). Hearing of the rich province of Apalache, he headed northwest toward the Florida panhandle. There is nearly universal agreement that Apalache was in the vicinity of modern-day Tallahassee, but despite this unusual agreement we do not have a *precise* location, although likely possibilities await archaeological investigation.[6]

After wintering at Apalache, the army headed north through Georgia and east into South Carolina in the spring of 1540. Then it turned north again, to North Carolina, then west to Tennessee and south into Alabama. Its objective was the famous town of Coosa, of which the *conquistadores* had heard since they had reached central

Georgia. The commission placed Coosa in Talladega County, Alabama—another "strong point" on which much of its determination of the route depends, both before and after. The identification seemed so certain that the commission considered it "one of the best established points along de Soto's route."[7] Alas, archaeology has also devastated this bastion: excavations reveal that the site was occupied much later.[8] Coosa is now believed to have been farther north, in northeastern Alabama or northwestern Georgia, or even southeastern Tennessee.[9]

From Coosa, Soto continued south to meet the great chief Taskalusa, and proceeded to the town of Mauvila, where the army was nearly destroyed in a great battle. Mauvila was probably considerably north of its traditional placement in Clarke County, but to date no likely sites have been authenticated.[10]

Soto turned his badly mauled army north and west from Mauvila, probably passing south and west of Tuscaloosa, Alabama. It seems certain, however, that he did not visit the great Indian site at Moundville. Again, negative evidence must be adduced: there is no mention of an extraordinary group of mounds in the narratives of the expedition, and considerable archaeological investigation over the years at this important site has failed to uncover evidence of Soto artifacts.[11] The latest archaeological opinion is that, at the time of Soto, Moundville was not the major site it had been during late prehistoric times and that political power had shifted to another, less imposing site.

The army entered Mississippi and headed for the province of Chicasa, homeland of the ancestors of the Chickasaw Indians, which they found near Tupelo (probably some miles to the south). In this part of Mississippi, archaeological investigation is still in its infancy; we have found some likely sites, but they have not yet been tested.

Soto camped in Chicasa during the winter of 1540/41. In the spring, ready to set forth, he made what the Chicasa apparently considered an outrageous demand for porters (preferably female) to accompany the army. The Chicasa responded—and it must be considered that other antipathies had developed during the long winter, in addition to those engendered by this request—by mounting a surprise night attack that almost achieved what Taskalusa had attempted at Mauvila: destruction of the army. Somehow, the army survived, and the narratives give thanks to God (as do we). If the

Chicasa had prevailed, the adventure would have been terminated; there would be no record, and little for scholars to debate or researchers to investigate.

In tatters, the army fled west, looking for the great river it had heard about and had reason to believe afforded an avenue of escape south to the Gulf and thence to Mexico. The commission concluded that Soto discovered the Mississippi River—his most enduring claim to fame—not at Memphis (one of the city's claims to fame) but much farther south, in northwestern Mississippi, where it posited the native province of Quizquiz. It is not possible, here, to consider the complex arguments concerning where Soto may have discovered the Mississippi River.[12] There have been many theories, but none has yet been proved.

Archaeologically, the evidence is mostly negative, but some suggestive evidence has also been discovered. The negative evidence is primarily due to the fact that the restless, ever-shifting Mississippi River has almost certainly destroyed any evidence of Soto along its banks during the intervening four and a half centuries. The best interpretations are that a "Memphis discovery" is illogical, as pointed out by the commission, while the commission's identification is so unconvincing that it must be dismissed as well.[13] Although we have no positive evidence, archaeology indicates that the army's discovery of the river was probably near Friars Point, Mississippi. This conjecture is based on suggestive evidence, which consists of appropriate Indian sites in the vicinity of Friars Point that were contemporary with Soto and discovery in some of these sites of sixteenth-century artifacts that, in the absence of other sixteenth-century expeditions, could only have been brought by Soto.

Thus we arrive at significant new and suggestive evidence in the archaeological record and, therefore, we shall not follow the army farther, even though we are only halfway through its four-year epic. Ill defined though the route has been to this point, we are nevertheless much closer to defining it than in the trans-Mississippi west. So we now turn back and look more closely at new, suggestive evidence that may compensate for the negative evidence presented thus far.

If there is one satisfactory contribution (as opposed to speculations) to modern Soto studies, it is that we at last have some idea of what we should be searching for artifactually. This knowledge is a major intrinsic advance, of course, and is especially important since we have not yet identified any expedition sites and so must concentrate on finding contemporary Indian settlements for evidence of Soto. In this context, we are more likely to find items that were willingly dispensed to the Indians, rather than military hardware (cannons, swords, armor, and other equipage of the well-accoutered army) that has traditionally been sought because of the nature of the expedition and the high-level recognition of such artifacts.

But there are repeated references in the chronicles to the fact that military items were carefully *conserved*, because the expedition could not replenish its stores. They were part of the advantage of the *conquistadores* and were not surrendered easily. Besides, the many dead (half the expedition, including Soto, perished) were probably stripped of all usable items, thereby denying archaeology one of its most important forms of primary evidence (and giving the lie to the many "Soto burials" discovered over the years). Of course, some of these paraphernalia would have been given away or lost, and a few good possibilities or instances have been found, though typically at undocumented locations. For example, the artifact in figure 5-2A appears to be the first sixteenth-century halberd discovered in the Southeast. Soto's private guard consisted of a company of halberdiers, and a halberd of this type is as conclusive a piece of evidence as could be wished for.[14] Unfortunately, all we know about this artifact is that it was found while someone was digging a ditch in Tupelo many years ago.[15]

Innocuous offerings of peace, not weapons of war, afford the best hope of trailing Soto. Specifically, to follow the army itself, we may still put faith in the armaments, but with little hope of tracing the path or even the general route of the expedition; we would do better to look for trinkets, which the chronicles indicate were widely distributed. But therein lies a problem. Like the ripples of a wake, such easily portable artifacts can be expected to have spread far from the source, whether as the result of far-flung scouting by the donors or as secondary transmissions by the recipients. Such items are not infallible proof of Soto's footsteps, by any means, but they are good indicators of his presence.

Some years ago, while reviewing archaeological collections from late prehistoric and historic sites along the Mississippi River, we turned up artifacts of European manufacture which, in type and context, seemed to predate European contact of the eighteenth century.[16] These artifacts are unimpressive trinkets—little brass bells and beads of glass and cut crystal—but they are distinctive and

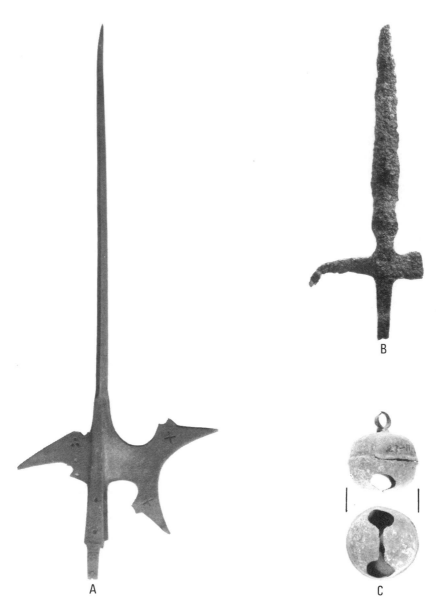

FIGURE 5-2. *Some Probable Hernando de Soto Artifacts: (A) Tupelo halberd (Courtesy of the Richard Heard Collection), (B) Halberd found near Schlater, Mississippi (Courtesy of the Cottonlandia Museum), (C) Clarksdale Bells, from Carden Bottoms, Arkansas (Courtesy of the University of Arkansas Museum). Halberds approximately ⅓ of actual size.*

A

B

C

unlike eighteenth-century artifacts in the details of manufacture.[17] The bells (named "Clarksdale bells" after the Mississippi city where the largest collection was found) are made of sheet brass and have formal characteristics which distinguish them from types traded by later Europeans (figure 5-2C). The beads, of faceted rock crystal and drawn glass, are also distinctive.[18] The question, of course, is whether these are Soto artifacts. We do not know for sure, but their distribution in the Southeast and their contextual proveniences encourage such a conclusion.

Consider the Clarksdale bells, which now number in the dozens and have been found from Florida to Arkansas (figure 5-3). All (except the Florida bell) are from sites far in the interior. They must have been introduced by an inland expedition, rather than by the many coastal explorations. It may be that the Alabama, even the Tennessee, examples could be ascribed to the slightly later Luna or Pardo expeditions: the chronologies are close enough that they may have had artifacts comparable to Soto's in their stores. But farther west, we must consider the bells a probable artifact of Soto; and overall, they closely parallel his route (that is, the best-guess route by this author in the fall of 1981). Thus, together with other types of artifacts, the bells provide clues to the route. They may not be precise indicators, but they are, to date, the most reliable evidence of the Soto presence that we have.

Given the widely varying theories for the path of the army across the vast map of the Southeastern United States (figure 5-1), an archaeologically verified set of data, which can at least describe zones of contact—if not specific sites of interaction—must be considered a significant advance toward our goal of defining the route.

Soto and the Indians

If what we have presented above approximates the route of Soto and his army, what can we say about the consequences of the expedition? We come now to the really salient point of these studies. The most important reason for tracing the route of our Spanish friend is not mere adventure, or hoary antiquarianism, or the titillation of walking in sacred footsteps, or the discovery of this or the crossing of that. The Soto *entrada* into the Southeastern United States provides a unique view of American Indians before they were overwhelmed by intensive European contact. The anthropologist is interested in where the events in the written narratives occurred so

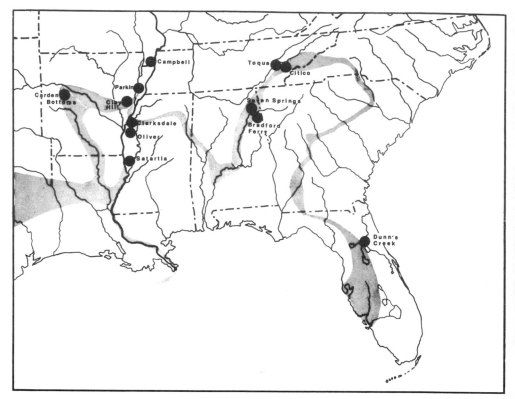

FIGURE 5-3. *Distribution of Clarksdale Bells in the Southeast and the Author's Best-Guess Route of Hernando de Soto (shows only general path of the main army; does not indicate excursions of exploring parties).*

that we can relate their ethnohistoric information to specific archaeological sites and to specific contexts within those sites, then get on with the job of more fully reconstructing those Indian contexts. And finally, we have the opportunity of correlating those contexts with others, before and after them in time, so that we can begin to evaluate the impact of this first, most dramatic contact between the European and the Indian.

Momentous changes occurred among the Indians between the time of Soto and 150 years later, when the French and English began to penetrate the Southeast. These latter explorers and settlers did not find complex and flourishing societies, as displayed in the archaeological record of the late prehistoric period and as witnessed and described by the Soto chroniclers. To the anthropologist, these changes are of great importance. Soto, then, is of more than historical interest. He is at least a datum in the native record, and maybe much more. He and his army may have been a crucial event that forced, or was a catalyst for, many of the changes.

It is not my intention to overstate the effect of the *entrada*. Many of the changes in Indian culture may have already been under way, and might have occurred in any event. But the impact of the *entrada* was considerable: whole towns were burned; large populations were enslaved as porters and taken to regions far from their homes, never to return; and biological distress was caused by diseases to which the Indians were unaccustomed. The army was surely a scourge of God, but its effects must have differed considerably from place to place. For this reason, each identified site must be excavated in order to study the details of the archaeological record. Thus we accumulate a series of closely defined contexts that may be compared to assess the impact of the *entrada* and the changes that occurred thereafter. Then we can hope to address the ultimate goal of interpreting the processes.

First, we must achieve the largely elusive goal of accurately relating archaeology to the Soto documents, and to do that we must continue the archaeological refinements discussed above. There is still much to do, but there is no cause for despair. In fact, we have come a long way since Swanton's day. If nothing else, we have reopened the inquiry. For too long, the commission's report was accepted without question. We now have more data (much of which is negative, to be sure) and important new contributions. We have a much better idea of what to look for archaeologically, as the archaeological picture comes slowly into focus.

6

The Hernando de Soto Expedition: From Chiaha to Mabila

Chester B. DePratter, Charles M. Hudson, and Marvin T. Smith

After wintering in Apalachee, in the vicinity of Talla-hassee, Florida, from October 1539 until early March 1540, Her-nando de Soto's expedition set out in a generally northeastward direction. In Apalachee Soto had met two Indian trading boys who told him he would find silver, gold, and pearls to the east, in a large town and province governed by a woman.[1] After traveling two months and passing through several provinces, the expedition reached Cofitachequi on May 1, 1540, where it found a town and province governed by a woman, and freshwater pearls, but not the silver and gold it expected—only slabs of mica and pieces of copper.[2] Perhaps more importantly, it found food, which it sorely needed after its long trek through an unpopulated area. Soto departed Cofitachequi on May 12 or 13, and on May 21 reached the town of Xuala, at the foot of some mountains. After resting here four days, the expedition again set out, crossed the mountains, and on June 5 arrived at Chiaha, a fortified town on an island in a river.

Without doubt, the most difficult problem in reconstructing Soto's movements has been establishing the locations of these towns. In the absence of one or more firmly established points of reference in the interior, it has been possible, so to speak, to route Soto and his men almost anywhere, so that many historians and anthropologists have despaired of discovering Soto's itinerary.

We believe, however, that we have precisely located two of

these towns that Soto visited in May and early June of 1540, Cofitachequi and Chiaha, and that we know the general location of the third, Xuala. We have done this after painstaking analysis of a lengthy account by Juan de la Bandera, the official notary of the Juan Pardo expedition of 1567–68, and by plotting the distribution of sixteenth-century Spanish artifacts which archaeologists have recovered in the Southeast.

Briefly, Juan Pardo and a force of just over 100 foot soldiers set out from Santa Elena, on Parris Island off the coast of South Carolina. They proceeded north to the junction of the Congaree and Wateree rivers and from there went farther north to Cofitachequi, whose old center was at or near the McDowell or Mulberry site near Camden, South Carolina, and from there they continued north to Xuala (they called it Joara), near Marion, North Carolina.[3] From Xuala, they crossed the mountains through Swannanoa Gap and picked up a trail which lay along the French Broad River. This led them to Chiaha, which we have located on Zimmerman's Island, near present-day Dandridge, Tennessee.

Using these points of reference from the Pardo expedition, it is clear that Soto crossed the mountains much farther north than the reconstruction of the route proposed by the United States De Soto Commission, which was as surprising to us as it must be to the reader.[4] Later we will discuss some of the reasons why we think other scholars did not work out this itinerary sooner, but we cannot—in this paper—discuss all our reasons for taking Pardo and his men through Swannanoa Gap and down the French Broad River, except to say that this route is most consistent with the Bandera document.[5] Instead, we want to trace Soto's movements from Chiaha to Mabila, and in so doing show that from this starting point a route can be reconstructed which is consistent with archaeological evidence, with geographical features, and with old trails and roads. Moreover, our route sometimes coincides with Indian place names, though (for reasons that will become apparent) we have given place names very low value in our reconstruction of the route.

Working with the Bandera document, we came to the conclusion that Pardo and his men ordinarily calculated distances in terms of the *legua comun* of 5.57 kilometers or 3.45 miles, and not the *legua legal* of 4.19 kilometers or 2.63 miles that was favored by the United States De Soto Commission.[6] Moreover, Pardo generally traveled 5 leagues per day, or a little over 17 miles.

In reconstructing the route of the Soto expedition, we have

generally relied on Rodrigo Ranjel for details of daily travel, while using the other accounts for supplementary information. Soto appears to have traveled a little less rapidly than Pardo. In their journey from Apalachee to Chiaha, Garcilaso says that the Soto expedition averaged 4½ leagues per day, or about 15.5 miles, using the *legua comun* as a measure.[7] And Garcilaso says that between Acoste and Coosa they traveled 4 leagues per day, more or less, or about 13.8 miles, using the *legua comun*.[8] Some evidence indicates that the Soto expedition made better distances when it traveled through "wilderness," that is, when it was short of food and when it was nearing a large Indian town where it expected to find ample food and, perhaps, precious metals. When it traveled through unpopulated areas, Elvas says, the expedition covered 5 or 6 leagues per day, or 17.25 to 20.7 miles.[9]

Let us begin with Chiaha. All the chroniclers say it was the first town that the expedition came to that was fortified by a palisade, and that it was situated on an island in a river. But only the Gentleman of Elvas describes the island:

The town was isolated between two arms of a river, and seated near one of them. Above it, at the distance of a crossbow-shot, the waters divided, and united a league below. The vale between from side to side, was the width of a crossbow-shot, and in others two. The branches were very wide, and both were fordable: along their shores were very rich meadow-lands, having many maize fields.[10]

A 1936 USGS map of Zimmerman's Island shows a mound some 550 to 600 yards from the upstream end of the island, and since a crossbow shot was on the order of 200 to 300 yards, its placement agrees with Elvas' description.[11] Likewise, Zimmerman's Island was long and narrow, measuring some 550–600 yards at the widest, and it was about 2½ miles long—somewhat less than a league. A 1925 aerial photograph of the island (in the TVA archives) shows a dark area surrounding the mound and village, which may represent a section of the palisade. (See photographs.) There are many islands in the Tennessee–French Broad River, but none matches Elvas' description as closely as Zimmerman's Island.[12]

Unfortunately, Zimmerman's Island now lies beneath the waters of Douglas Lake—behind a dam that was built very quickly during World War II—and hardly any archaeology was done before it was inundated. We know that the mound was a large one, some 30 feet high. T. M. N. Lewis and Madeline Kneberg, who excavated a 10 by 30–foot trench into the mound, recovered three burials in association with Dallas artifacts that date to the protohistoric period.[13]

Before he left Chiaha, Soto sent two of his men north to the land of the Chiscas, who were said to deal in copper (or a softer metal of that color). They were accompanied by Indians who spoke the language of the Chiscas.[14]

On Monday, June 28, Soto departed Chiaha, temporarily leaving behind several men who were too ill to travel, and crossed the northern arm of the French Broad River by fording it.[15] He traveled to the west, and passed through five or six villages. Later in the day he came to a river that had a strong current. In fact, he had again come upon the French Broad River, but at this location it was much larger, having been augmented by the waters of the Little Pigeon River. The expedition crossed the river by lining up its horses, head to tail, to break the force of the water so that the foot soldiers could wade across on the downstream side, holding to the tails, stirrups, breastpieces, and manes as they moved from horse to horse.[16] Soto and his men probably made their crossing between the mouth of Little Pigeon River and the mouth of Dumpling Creek, perhaps at Clinkingheard's Shoals.[17] They camped for the night in the vicinity of the present town of Boyd's Creek.

On Tuesday, June 29, they passed through a village, appropriated some corn, then slept in the open. They were at this time probably following a trail that paralleled the French Broad and Tennessee rivers. If they made 13 miles, they camped for the night in the vicinity of the present town of Shooks.[18]

On Wednesday, June 30, according to Ranjel, they passed over a river, through a village, and over the river again. However, this language is puzzling. The river must have been the Little River, and they may have crossed one of its tributaries, passed through a village, then crossed the river itself. Perhaps the village in question lay near the junction of Stock Creek and Little River. If they made 4 leagues on this day, they camped in the vicinity of present-day Mentor.

On Thursday, July 1, the chief of Coste (or Costehe) came to meet them. Serving as a guide, he took them to spend the night in one of his villages. If they continued along the trail they had been following, they would have reached a spot in the vicinity of the present-day village of Unitia, near the Tennessee River.

Continuing their journey the next day, they arrived at Coste,

Chester B. DePratter, Charles M. Hudson, and Marvin T. Smith

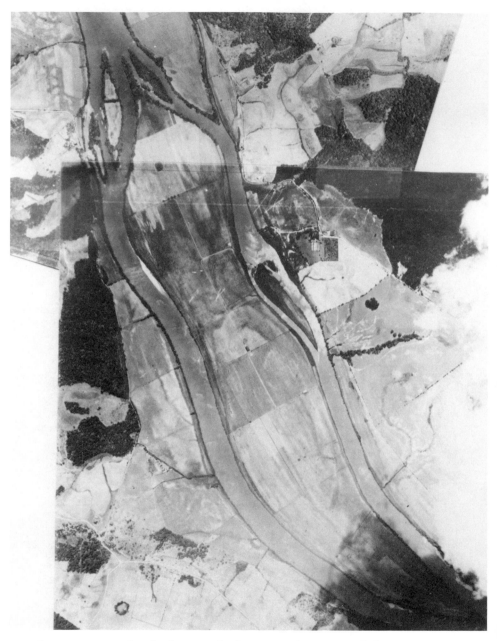

Zimmerman's Island, photographed in 1925. (Courtesy of the Tennessee Valley Authority)

Zimmerman's Island, Enlargement

situated on an island in the river where the current was swift and hard to enter.[19] This must have been Bussell Island, in the mouth of the Little Tennessee River. Cyrus Thomas, in his 1894 report on mound exploration, mentions that sixteenth-century European artifacts—an iron wedge or celt and two wire C bracelets—were found in burials in one of the mounds on Bussell Island.[20] Also, tubular copper beads, likewise sixteenth-century artifacts, have been recovered from this site.[21] Even though the branch of the river they crossed in getting to the island was the more narrow of the two, fording it was difficult.[22]

They remained in Coste for six days, during which time the men who had been left behind (ill at Chiaha) and those who had gone to the country of the Chiscas came down the Tennessee River in canoes and rejoined the expedition. On Friday, July 9, Soto and his men departed Coste, crossing the other branch of the Little Tennessee River, and from there went down the Tennessee River to a place opposite the town of Tali. We believe this was some 8 miles downstream from Bussell Island, near the present-day town of Loudon. Tali must have been the Henry site, on the north side of the Tennessee River, whose destruction began before the Civil War when a railroad bridge was built across the river.[23] At this point the Tennessee River was so deep that Soto and his men could not ford it. They forced the Indians of Tali to bring their canoes, in which Soto and some of his men crossed the river to get corn and perhaps other supplies. (It is probable that only some of his men made this crossing and that the main force remained on the south side of the river.)[24]

A problem with this interpretation of Soto's departure and direction of travel from Coste is that it has difficulty in accounting for the considerable quantity of sixteenth-century Spanish artifacts that have been found at the large mound centers on the Upper Little Tennessee River: Chilhowee, Citico, Toqua, and Tomotley. These artifacts include iron celts, iron C bracelets, Clarksdale bells, tubular copper beads, Nueva Cadiz twisted beads, Florida cut-crystal beads, and blue glass beads.[25] If Soto and his men had gone up the Little Tennessee River after they departed from Coste, they could have reached these sites in a day's travel. Also, had they done so, this would have placed the next town they encountered, Tali, near the Tellico River, whose name possibly derives from it. So far so good. But Ranjel clearly says that Tali was on the "other side of the river," and it so happens that all of the large sites just mentioned were on the same side of the river that Soto would have been on had he gone up the Little Tennessee River. Also, Ranjel makes it clear that at the place where Tali was located, the river was so "large" that they could not ford it, and this more closely fits the Tennessee River near Loudon than the Upper Little Tennessee River. By the late seventeenth century, Tali had moved southward to an island in the Tennessee River.[26]

They remained at Coste for six days under relatively peaceful circumstances, which would have allowed ample opportunity for trade between the Spaniards and the Indians from the Upper Little Tennessee River, and some of the artifacts can be accounted for in this way. In addition, some of the artifacts surely found their way there from the Juan Pardo expedition in 1567. Pardo visited the Citico site (the town which Bandera called "Satapo") and probably the Chilhowee site (the town which Bandera called "Chalahume"). To the chief of Chalahume Pardo gave an axe and a necklace. To the chief of Satapo Pardo gave an axe, a mirror, and a necklace, and to a *mandador* and two principal men of Satapo Pardo gave each a small iron wedge and a necklace.[27]

The Soto expedition stayed at Tali one day, departing on Sunday, July 11, and probably traveled along a trail that led southwest, following Sweetwater Creek. If they made 4 leagues or so, they would have spent the night in or near present-day Sweetwater, where they slept in the open.[28] Ranjel says that their travel this day was in Tali's territory and that he supplied them with food as they passed through it. Elvas, though giving fewer details than Ranjel, says that, after departing Coste, they traveled six days through towns that were subject to Coosa.[29]

On Monday, July 12, they continued, crossing a river. This was probably Oostanaula Creek, near present-day Athens, Tennessee. If they made 4 leagues or so, they spent the night just beyond Athens, sleeping in the open.

On Tuesday, July 13, they crossed another river. In all probability, they had by this time swung more directly south on a trail that led to the Upper Hiwassee River. The river they crossed was probably Chestuee Creek. If they made 4½ leagues, they probably spent the night just to the south of the present-day village of Dentville. According to Ranjel, they were still in the territory of Tali.[30] All along the way they passed villages that supplied them with corn, *mazamorras* (i.e., *sofkee*), cooked beans and other foods.

On Wednesday, July 14, they crossed a large river, the Hiwassee.[31] By nightfall they had reached the town of Tasqui.[32] If they made 4½ leagues this day, Tasqui was near present-day Old Fort or Conasauga, Tennessee. They appear, at this point, to have been in the territory of Coosa. As they marched, messengers traveled back and forth to Coosa.[33]

On Thursday, July 15, they continued, passing through a small village, and if they made 4½ leagues or so, they spent the night near the present-day town of Eton. The next day, July 16, they passed through several small villages, probably on tributaries of the Conasauga River, and finally arrived at Coosa, in the intermontane valley of the Coosawattee River, just east of the town of Carters, in northwestern Georgia.[34]

At first, we located Coosa in the vicinity of Chattanooga, but subsequently we discovered that an account of the Tristán de Luna expedition proves that Coosa could not have been at Chattanooga. We are referring to Fray Augustín Dávila Padilla's *Historia de la fundación y discurso de la provincia de Santiago de México de la Orden de Predicadores* (Brussels, 1625), in which he tells of the force of soldiers and missionaries sent into the interior from Luna's colony on the Gulf Coast in 1560. Once Luna's men arrived at Coosa, the chief of Coosa persuaded them to send a detachment of 25 cavalry and 25 foot soldiers to assist his warriors in subjugating the Napochies, who had formerly paid tribute to Coosa but had broken away and were at that time hostile.

The important thing is that Luna's men traveled 8 leagues from Coosa on their way to the Napochies before they camped for the night, where the Indians performed a military ceremony in preparation for battle. Then the next day they traveled farther and reached the first village of the Napochies, 2 leagues from a great river. Finding that the people had fled, they went to another Napochie village, on the bank of the river, which was described as very deep and the width of two harquebus shots. It could have been none other than the Tennessee River, which the Indians called Oquechiton (which means "great water" [*la grande agua*]).[35] This second Napochie town was probably at the Citico site in Chattanooga, from which sixteenth-century European artifacts have been recovered. The first town was probably on Chickamauga Creek.

A description of the lay of the land around Coosa by a member of the Luna expedition is consistent with the location at Carters. In a letter from Coosa (dated Aug. 1, 1560), Fray Domingo de la Anunciación described it as follows:

This province of Coosa is somewhat better as regards the land and the forest, and much more densely populated than any we have left behind. There is a mountain range to the north of the town, which runs east and west. It is fairly high and well-wooded, but up to this time we do not know where it begins or ends. This town is situated on the banks of two small rivers which unite within it. Around the town there are some good savannahs, and a valley well peopled with Indians where they plant all that they raise to eat. After one leaves here all the rest is forest.[36]

Anunciación wrote this letter soon after the force arrived at Coosa, before it could have done much exploring; hence it is likely that the mountains he refers to are Fort Mountain (2,835 ft.), some 12 miles north of Carters; Turniptown Mountain (2,585 ft.), some 18 miles northeast of Carters; and perhaps Bald Mountain (4,010 ft.), Cowpen Mountain (4,149 ft.), and Flattop Mountain (3,732 ft.), which are about 20 miles north-northeast of Carters. These are some of the southernmost Blue Ridge mountains, and they are significantly higher than some of the smaller mountains Luna's men saw on their way to Coosa (most of whose peaks are from 1,300 to 2,300 feet above sea level).

The two small streams that unite within the town of Coosa are the Coosawattee River and Talking Rock Creek. Here, on one side of Talking Rock Creek, the Little Egypt site has two mounds, and on the other side of Talking Rock Creek the Bell Field site has one mound.[37] At the nearby Sixtoe Field site, Arthur Kelly recovered a dirk in a Dallas burial, along with bone awls, a celt, a clay pipe, a bear mandible, a bone ornament, and a cache of fourteen projectile points.[38] Very early glass beads and iron celts and spikes were found at the Little Egypt site.[39]

Coosa was a powerful chief who had power over a vast territory, and as Soto's party approached, the chief was brought some 400 to 600 yards from the town on a litter carried by 60 or 70 "principal men," working in relays.[40] He was dressed in white and surrounded by attendants who played on flutes and sang. Soto's chroniclers, moreover, described the province of Coosa in glowing terms: very rich in food, with plums like the early plums of Seville, and small wild apples like the *canavales* of Extremadura.[41] This is Elvas' description of Coosa:

In the barbacoas was a great quantity of maize and beans: the country, thickly settled in numerous large towns, with fields between, extending from one to another, was pleasant, and had a rich soil with fair river margins. In the woods were many *amexeas*, as well as those of Spain as of the country; and wild grapes on vines up into the trees, near the streams; likewise a kind that grew on low vines elsewhere, the berry being large and sweet but, for want of hoeing and dressing, had large stones.[42]

Garcilaso adds that the chief had three dwellings, on mounds, and that the town was on the banks of a river. He says that an entire section of the town was emptied for use by the soldiers.[43]

The expedition remained in Coosa just over a month—from July 16 until August 20—and, upon departing, put the chief of Coosa and some of his principal men in chains and took them along in the direction of Tascaluza. A man named Feryada, a Levantine, abandoned the expedition and remained in Coosa, and a Negro, named Robles, was left behind because he was ill and could not walk.[44]

On the first day, the expedition went to Talimachusy, a large, abandoned village, and encamped half a league beyond it on a river bank. If it made 5 leagues, it would have got beyond present-day Fairmount, Georgia—perhaps near the present-day town of Bolivar.[45] The river was probably Pine Log Creek.

On Saturday, August 21, it traveled in heavy rain and reached the town of Itaba, a large village along a fine river. If it made 5 leagues, this would have put the expedition just beyond Cartersville, Georgia, on the Etowah River, perhaps near the junction of Pumpkinvine Creek.[46] That is, Itaba was probably at the Etowah site.[47]

The expedition remained in Itaba six days, because the river was swollen from rain,[48] and on Monday, August 30, departed. It crossed to the other side of the river and spent the night in an oak wood.

On Tuesday, August 31, it arrived at Ulibahali, a palisaded village close to a fine river. This appears to have been on the south side of the Coosa River at present-day Rome, Georgia. The chief of Ulibahali also had a village on the north side of the river,[49] where the Indians of Ulibahali, who were subject to Coosa, made a move to free him. The chief, however, induced them to lay aside their arms and to supply the Spanish with food and carriers.[50]

Two men were left behind at Ulibahali: Mansano, a gentleman of Salamanca, who either deserted or lost his way, and Johan Biscayan, a Negro slave who belonged to Captain Johan Ruiz Lo-

Chief Coosa Welcomes the Hernando de Soto Expedition. This etching, based on the narrative by Elvas, was published at Leyden, Holland, in 1706. It shows the chief of the Coosa being carried out from his principal village to welcome the expedition. The site of this historic meeting is believed to be near the present-day town of Carters in northwestern Georgia. (De Gedenkwaardige Voyagie van don Ferdinand de Soto . . . [Leyden: P. Van der Aa, 1706]. Courtesy of the W. S. Hoole Special Collections Library, The University of Alabama)

billo. At Ulibahali, Soto's men ate grapes that were said to be as good as those grown in Spanish vineyards.

    The expedition remained at Ulibahali on Wednesday, September 1, and departed the next day. It reached a pretty village near the river and here spent the night of September 2. (This was probably the Johnstone Farm site, which is located a few miles west of Rome.) The Soto chroniclers do not name this place, but it may have been Apica, visited by members of the Luna expedition just before they reached Ulibahali.[51] The next day they continued on to the town of Piachi (the same name as the town they came to just before Mabila), also on the river, where they encamped for the night of September 3. They also remained at this place on September 4, awaiting the return of Lobillo, who had gone back to Ulibahali without Soto's permission to try to find his slave.[52]

This town of Piachi was probably located at the King site, on the Coosa River a few miles west of the Johnstone Farm site. Sixteenth-century European artifacts have been recovered from the King site, including a two-edged sword that dates to the middle of the sixteenth century.[53]

On Sunday, September 5, the Spaniards resumed travel, leaving the river to go southward. If they made 5 leagues or so, they spent the night in open country near the present-day village of Tecumseh, Alabama, near the Alabama-Georgia state line. The next day, September 6, they reached the town of Tuasi.[54] This was possibly on Nance's Creek, perhaps at its junction with Terrapin Creek. Keith Little and C. B. Curren, Jr., describe an unusually large number of sixteenth-century European artifacts from a site at this location, including iron spikes, a chisel, axes, and glass beads in association with protohistoric ceramics and rattlesnake gorgets.[55]

They remained at Tuasi six days; then on September 13 they slept in open country. If they made 5 leagues, their camp would have been near the village of Jacksonville, Alabama. A similar day's travel on September 14 would have put them just southwest of Anniston, where they again slept in the open.[56] Beyond Tuasi, according to Elvas, they were in the territory of Talisi.[57]

Another day's travel took them to an abandoned town whose palisades were still standing. It is difficult to establish the location, but it was possibly just west of Talladega.

On Thursday, September 16, they came to a new village, close to a river (undoubtedly the Coosa); rested in this town the following day; and on Saturday traveled to Talisi, a large village that also was situated near the river. Several towns on the opposite side of the river were subject to it.[58] Talisi was probably near the town of Childersburg, and this, it should be noted, is near Tallasseehatchee Creek. The Baron de Crenay map of 1733 shows a "Talachys" in the same vicinity. Garcilaso says that Talisi was completely encircled on a peninsula of a large river, though he is probably not to be trusted on this.[59]

Talisi, the last town said to be subject to Coosa, was heavily fortified and it bordered on the territory of Tascaluza. The expedition rested in Talisi from September 18 until October 4, and released the chief of Coosa, who was incensed because Soto refused to release his sister and because he had been taken so far from his town.[60]

Tascaluza sent messengers to Talisi and preparations were made for Soto to continue his march to the south, after one of the messengers explained that there were two trails from Talisi to Tascaluza.[61] The route of these trails is not specified, but it is clear that one of them followed along the river and that this is the one Soto and his men took.

On Tuesday, October 5, they departed Talisi and traveled through a series of small villages along the Coosa River on their way to Tascaluza. The first night they came to Casiste, a small village near the river, possibly just west of present-day Talladega Springs. On October 6 they came to Caxa, which Ranjel describes as a "wretched village," possibly at the mouth of Weogulfka Creek. On October 7 they camped alongside the river, with the village of Humati on the other side, possibly at the mouth of Shoal Creek. On October 8 they came to Uxapita, a new town, probably near present-day Wetumpka. The Crenay map shows an "Ouchapa" near this location. Elvas implies that some or all of these towns were subject to Tascaluza.[62]

On Saturday, October 9, they encamped in open country, a league or so from the village of Tascaluza.[63] The next day, Sunday, October 10, they entered Athahachi, the town of Tascaluza, and Ranjel notes that it was a recently built village. Tascaluza, wearing a feathered cape down to his feet and a turban on his head, was on a kind of balcony atop a mound, seated on a mat on two cushions. He was surrounded by high-ranking Indians, one of whom held a circular shade to shield him from the sun.[64]

We cannot be definite about the location of Athahachi. The contingent of men whom Tristán de Luna sent to Coosa passed through an Indian town and province named Atache, which was probably the same as Athahachi.[65] The Indians had fled this town to escape Luna's men, and it is difficult to reconstruct the movement of this party of men. However, they say that the Indians of Coosa were accustomed to travel as far south as Atache and, more importantly, that goods could be taken up the Alabama River as far as Atache, which implies that it was at or near the head of navigation.[66] This would place Atache south of Wetumpka and probably to the south of the Tallapoosa and Alabama rivers near their junction with the Coosa River. The Crenay map shows "Atache" in this location, and it is not impossible that this was the town visited by Soto and Luna in the sixteenth century. It is reasonable to think that Athahachi, or Atache, was ancestral to the eighteenth-century town of Atasi.[67]

It is clear that Tascaluza wanted to hurry Soto and his men

along. Moreover, he promised Soto that, in a certain town of his, Mabila, he would give him and his men 100 women and anything else they needed.[68] So on Tuesday, October 12, the expedition departed Athahatchi and slept in open country.

The next day, October 13, they went through the town of Piachi. Ranjel says it was high above the "craggy" gorge of a river;[69] Elvas merely says the town was next to a great river, the Alabama.[70] Garcilaso may have had Piachi in mind when he described the main town of Tascaluza as well fortified on a peninsula in the river, the same river that passed by Talisi.[71]

If one were to trust Garcilaso, the most likely area for Piachi would be Durant Bend, a sharp bend in the Alabama River just east of Selma.[72] The Alabama River was 400 to 600 feet wide in this area, with steep banks on both sides but particularly on the northern side, where some bluffs were 100 feet high.

One problem with locating Piachi at Durant Bend is that this would place it 16 leagues or more from where we have located Athahachi. To have reached this place in two days would have required more than 8 leagues of travel each day—well within the army's capability, particularly if Soto was traveling with his cavalry in advance of the foot soldiers—but it is also possible, and perhaps likely, that Piachi was farther upstream, perhaps near Ivey Creek or Beaver Creek.

In 1560 Tristán de Luna sent a party of men north from Pensacola Bay to find a place for an inland settlement. These men, some of whom had been with Soto, reached "Piache" after traveling an estimated 40 or 50 leagues.[73] Measured on a map, the distance between Pensacola Bay and the section of the Alabama River just discussed is about 42 leagues. Some of Luna's people lived at "Piache" but most of them lived at Nanipacana, which was some distance away, probably downriver. The Luna documents do not make it clear whether "Piache" was a town or a province.

In Piachi, Soto learned that the Indians had killed two men from the ill-fated Pánfilo de Narváez expedition, who had put ashore in 1528 when they were skirting the Gulf Coast in crude boats, trying to reach Mexico.[74] The two men were Don Teodoro (a Greek) and a Negro who had gone ashore with some Indians in a canoe to get fresh water near Pensacola or Mobile Bay. When the Indians returned in their canoe, Teodoro and the Negro were not with them.[75] The Indians of Piachi showed Soto a dagger which had belonged to Teodoro.[76]

Soto asked for canoes at Piachi, but the Indians claimed they had none—which seems to be what Ranjel was referring to when he says that the chief of Piachi "was evil intentioned, and attempted to resist their passage."[77] Because of this, Soto and his men had to work for two days building rafts of cane.[78]

Ranjel says they departed from Piachi on October 16.[79] If all of them crossed the river on this day, they could have traveled only a short distance beyond the river. Garcilaso says they traveled only a half a league beyond and camped in a beautiful valley.[80] Again, if we are to trust Garcilaso, this may have been the valley of Mulberry or Ivey Creek. Ranjel says only that they traveled into a woods (or mountain) where they met one of the two men Soto had sent ahead to Mabila. This man reported that many Indians with arms had gathered there.[81]

On October 17 they reached a palisaded village, probably just to the west or southwest of Selma, where messengers from Mabila brought chestnut bread for Tascaluza to eat.

On Monday, October 18—St. Luke's Day—they passed through several villages and reached Mabila, a small, heavily palisaded frontier town,[82] situated on a small plain.[83] (Garcilaso says it was only a league and a half from where they had camped the night before, and they reached it at eight or nine o'clock in the morning.)[84] At Mabila, the Indians of Tascaluza launched a military offensive against Soto the likes of which would never be seen again in the Southeast.

If our reconstruction of the route is sound to this point, Mabila could not have been many miles west or southwest from Selma, and was probably on the Lower Cahaba River. Except when very high, the Cahaba is easily forded; hence Mabila could have been on either side of the river. It is clear that many smaller settlements were near Mabila, and this is consistent with the terrain, that is, dispersed villages in the rich soils of the meander zone of the Cahaba and Alabama rivers. Its fortifications indicate that Mabila was a frontier town, but between which societies? Between towns on the Upper and Lower Alabama River or between towns on the Alabama and Black Warrior rivers? Only detailed study of the archaeological evidence can answer this question.

A problem with this segment of the route is that the chroniclers failed to mention at least one river crossing where there are two possibilities. We accept Garcilaso's statement that the expedition crossed the Coosa River at Talisi, and therefore it must have followed a trail down the west bank.[85] But if this was the case, Athahachi would have been on the north side of the Alabama River and Mabila on the south side, but all of the chroniclers failed to mention recrossing the river to get back to the other side. The other possibility is that the expedition followed a trail down the east bank of the Coosa River; then, just before it came to Athahachi, it forded the Tallapoosa River (which was easily fordable in the low-water month of August) and went on to cross the Alabama River at Piachi on rafts—a crossing that *all* the chroniclers mentioned. Of the two possibilities, we prefer the second.

We have come to the end of the segment of the route with which we are concerned. As we said above, we have not used place names as evidence in reconstructing the route of Soto's explorations, because we are convinced there were widespread movements of Indians in the century and a half after the explorations of Soto, Luna, and Pardo. (For example, in 1715 Coosa was close to where Talisi was in 1540.) After we reconstructed the route, however, we were surprised to note that some of the towns visited by Soto are at or near places with similar names on maps that date to the eighteenth century and later.

On a 1715 manuscript map in the British Public Record Office, the Tennessee River is called the Cusatees River (i.e., Coste). Tali was in the vicinity of present-day Tellico, Tellico River, and Tellico Plains. Tasqui was but a few days' travel from the junction of the Tellico and Little Tennessee rivers, the eighteenth-century location of Tuskegee, a town of non-Cherokees who affiliated for a time with the Overhill Cherokees.[86] Coosa was on the Coosawattee River, a place name derived from the Cherokee word *kusawetiyi*, meaning "old Coosa place."[87] Itaba was at or near the Etowah site. Talisi was somewhere between Alabama's two Tallaseehatchee creeks, one in Calhoun County and the other in southern Talledega County. Athahachi was near the eighteenth-century town of Atasi. Piachi was just upriver from the "Panchy" bluff of the Crenay map of 1733, and Mabila was near the *Vieux Mobiliens* (the "old Mobilians") of the same map.

The key to our reconstruction of this portion of the route of Soto's expedition is our identification of French Broad River as its avenue through the mountains and our placing of Chiaha on Zimmerman's Island. Given the fact that that there were two main avenues to the Tennessee Valley from Georgia and the Carolinas,

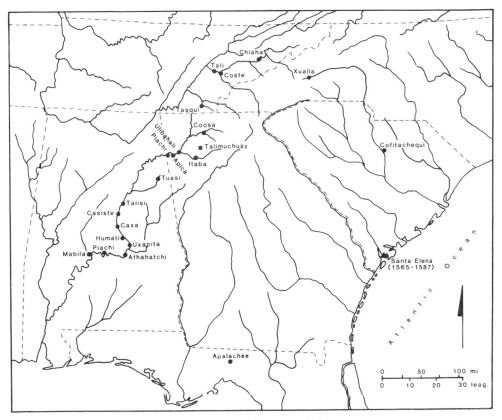

Hernando de Soto's Expedition: Chiaha to Mabila

one along the Hiwassee River and the other along the French Broad River, why have scholars consistently chosen the Hiwassee? We can think of at least four reasons.

1. From a glance at the remarkable "spaghetti map" that accompanies the United States De Soto Commission Reports, showing all major attempts at reconstructing the route, one can see that scholars have been reluctant to route Soto through the Blue Ridge Mountains, as if such a course would have been too difficult an undertaking for him. But Soto had been one of the principals in the conquest of the Incas, and after having navigated the Andes, how could he have been deterred by the Blue Ridge Mountains? Moreover, precious metals tend to occur in or near mountains, and the discovery of precious metals was one of Soto's dominant motives.

125

2. A second reason why previous scholars have not taken the expedition by way of the French Broad River is that most of them have thought that Silver Bluff, on the Savannah River below Augusta, was the most likely location for Cofitachequi. Why this location has been so appealing is not clear to us at this point, but perhaps it has been taken on the authority of Albert Pickett, who was evidently the first scholar who placed it here.[88] Analysis of the Bandera document clearly places Cofitachequi in the area of Camden, South Carolina. Moreover, in recent years archaeological research at Silver Bluff indicates that its occupation was at too early a time for it to have been Cofitachequi.

3. Previous scholars have probably undervalued Soto's compelling necessity of taking food from the Indians, and thus have neglected the fact that given the mode of food production used by the Southeastern chiefdoms, abundant food could only be had in certain places. Thus, once Soto was at Cofitachequi, a powerful reason for his going north from there was that that was where the food was. To the west lay a vast uninhabited buffer zone they had just traversed. The only source of food, and that none too abundant, lay to the north along the Wateree-Catawba River. The availability of Indian food was so compelling that Juan Pardo, who had been commanded by Pedro Menéndez de Avilés to establish a trail from Santa Elena to Zacatecas, had started out by going due *north*, instead of west, and he went pretty far to the north.

4. A fourth reason why scholars have routed Soto along the Hiwassee River, and not the French Broad, is probably an accident of cartography. A trail down the Hiwassee River to the Overhill Cherokee towns, shown on maps rather early in the eighteenth century, had long been used by traders, both on foot and on horse, but the trail down the French Broad River was apparently never used by traders (unless very early and very briefly by traders from Virginia), and it is not shown on English manuscript maps until the end of the eighteenth century. However, when this latter trail became available to American frontiersmen, it quickly became the main road between Tennessee and the Carolinas. The first horse-drawn wagon to reach Knoxville from the Carolinas came in by this road, down the French Broad River—the same road by which the first Europeans reached the Tennessee River in the sixteenth century.

We are confident that our reconstruction of this important segment of the Soto expedition is supported by all sources of evidence—historical, geographical, archaeological—better than any previous reconstruction. But this is not to say that we are equally confident of *all* parts of our reconstructed route.

For reasons we have mentioned, we have greater confidence in the route from Chiaha to Ulibahali and Tuasi than from Talisi to Mabila. Our reconstruction of this latter section of the route fits the lay of the land, but we would like to have better verification for some of the towns, particularly Talisi, Athahatchi, Piachi, and, most of all, Mabila. Also, we are puzzled why neither Ranjel nor Elvas mentioned a river crossing near Athahatchi. Some of the answers to these questions may be discoverable through extant information, and other answers should be obtainable through further archaeological research.

7

From Exploration to Settlement: Spanish Strategies for Colonization

Charles H. Fairbanks

The expedition of Hernando de Soto through considerable parts of Florida was not well recorded, at least by modern standards. While John R. Swanton and the United States De Soto Expedition Commission in 1939 settled on what they felt was his most probable route, they had little archaeological evidence on which to base their deliberations. Since then, some forty-five years of research have helped clarify some points of Indian cultural inventories and have helped to define the styles of Spanish artifacts. We should therefore be able to make more positive statements, but I must confess I am doubtful that we can do this. The documents remain "secretive" about precise places. Nevertheless, I will discuss the sorts of evidence that have been accumulated since 1939, and add a little weight to Swanton's arguments.

During those forty-odd years the objectives of archaeological and anthropological research have changed dramatically. Publication of *The Archaeology of the Florida Gulf Coast* in 1949 marked a significant synthesis and classification of cultures and periods of Florida aboriginal cultures.[1] Since then, archaeologists have managed to add only minor details to the chronology constructed by Willey. What we have done, or begun to do, is think about what happened during, and especially after, the events of 1539 and 1540. As the work of archaeologists has become more concerned with explaining past cultural events in terms of the processes at work, there has been a shift to the general from the particular. These are the explanations that seem to interest archaeologists today.

Few would dispute Swanton's assumption that Soto and his army landed on the west coast of the peninsula. As he pointed out, only two major bays could have been the ones discovered by the Spaniards. While Swanton considered Charlotte Harbor, he came out rather firmly for a landing on the shores of Tampa Bay. This is also my opinion; besides, Charlotte Harbor presents problems in its shallowness,[2] and the distance from Charlotte Harbor to Apalachee is considerable—too far to have been traversed in the time involved. Linguistic evidence of Timucuan place names in the narratives also points to the more northern location, and modern archaeology casts doubt on the Terra Caia Island aboriginal shell mound as the probable site. We now look for later cultural complexes that show strong Mississippian elements. Safety Harbor and other sites of that period on the northern and northeastern fringes of Tampa Bay fill the bill much better.

Recently, a few students have proposed that the Soto landing may have been at the mouth of the Caloosahatchee River, at the southern extremity of Charlotte Harbor. The route of the expedition is postulated to have been up that river, to the large earthwork sites near Lake Okeechobee. In my view, the Ortona Mound Group, some 40 miles inland, would serve as the likely site, as its collection of early glass beads fits the time frame very well. An argument *against* the mouth of the Caloosahatchee River is the much greater distance to Apalachee, although slow progress from the landing place to Apalachee would have allowed the Spaniards to adjust to New World conditions of march. However, the fact that place names, and primarily persons' names, between the landing place and Apalachee are clearly Timucuan—and never Calusa—supports the northern location. Also, the Charlotte Harbor or Caloosahatchee-mouth landing would have added four rivers to cross. Swanton could not fit them into the descriptions and time frame, nor can I. Further, the overt hostility of the Calusa to the earlier landing in that area by Ponce de León seems essentially different from the timorous reception that Soto received. Fifteen years later, Menéndez found the Calusa (probably at Estero) still intransigent.

Early sixteenth-century Spanish artifacts from both the Charlotte Harbor and Tampa Bay vicinities consist largely of distinctive glass beads that reflect trading activities by Soto and other members of the expedition. Columbus, on his first voyage, planned to barter for spices and other East Indian products, and this practice continued some time, especially among the various exploring expeditions. Documents and archaeological sites demonstrate that brass hawk bells, copper *maravedí* coins, and glass beads were frequent items of this barter. These, moreover, have shown up in a number of sites in the Southeast and go far to prove the presence of Spaniards in various regions. In many cases, I believe, they show that presence only by region, not at specific sites. There is good reason, therefore, to believe that Spanish gifts entered rapidly into the aboriginal trade systems, and it is worth noting that copper *maravedí* coins are found almost exclusively near the coast.

In the southern area, the Punta Rasa site, near Ft. Myers, and Ortona Mound, near the Caloosahatchee River, well in the interior, have produced this distinctive assemblage of early Spanish glass beads and metal artifacts. Neither site has been systematically excavated, and the Ortona Mound Group has been virtually destroyed by use as a sand pit, but fairly close to Ortona is the Ft. Center mound complex, where at least one early bead has been found, associated with gold and silver. The silver beads and cut-quartz crystal beads seem to be somewhat later than the early expeditions that we are considering here, but it is likely that these objects—at Ft. Center, at least—represent salvage by East Coast groups, paid as tribute to the powerful Calusa in the western Okechobee Basin and Gulf Coast. Brass hawk bells or *maravedí* coins have not been reported at any great distance from any of the southern sites. It seems likely that Ortona and Punta Rasa may represent trading contacts with one or more early sixteenth-century Spanish exploring or slaving groups. Punta Rasa also shows late sixteenth-century bead types.

In the Tampa Bay area, the Seven Oaks site also had early Spanish beads, and it is certainly in a strategic location for contacts with the Soto expedition. I hesitate to fix a town name to the find, but it does strengthen the assumption that the army landed on the shores of Tampa Bay. The site was not excavated systematically, and has now been destroyed by urban development.

Even more informative are two sand-burial mounds, north of Tampa Bay, that may be points where the northern-bound army traded with Indians. A very similar burial mound was systematically excavated on St. Simons Island, Georgia,[3] and though Lawrence Mound on St. Simons cannot be related to the Soto expedition, only early sixteenth-century groups could have been involved. Only Lawrence Mound has been systematically excavated and reported. Of the Florida examples, one was near the Withlacoochee River, the other at Weekeewatchee Springs. Inasmuch as the Soto narratives make no mention of a large spring, the army evidently did not visit the site where the materials were eventually buried. All three mounds seem to share a number of very similar characteristics.[4]

Structurally, the mounds are late Weeden Island sand-burial mounds, though none had any characteristic Weeden Island artifacts. They probably represent late St. Johns, Ft. Walton, and Sutherland Bluff periods, when burial-mound construction was still practiced. The Weekeewatchee Springs Mound contained a number of burials, pottery similar to Lake Jackson Plain (a Ft. Walton—period type), and numerous Spanish artifacts. No Spanish ceramics were found; so it is unlikely that the mound was related to a mission site or another fairly permanent station of Spaniards. Withlacoochee and Weekeewatchee Springs had many early glass beads and shell beads of late-aboriginal type, and probably both had small, 6-inch-long, thin, triangular iron celt blades. These would have been set into wooden handles, instead of the handle inserted into an iron eye. Weekeewatchee Springs Mound also had small silver beads, about the size of glass seed beads, that appear to have been cut from a uniform silver tube of small diameter.[5]

As the best excavated and reported, Lawrence Mound may be suggested as a model of the others. Again, it is a typical late-prehistoric sand-burial mound, showing elements that originated in the Southeastern Gulf Burial Mound tradition. Ceramics were of late Irene or Sutherland Bluff types. Burials had been made during several discrete mound-construction episodes in both extended and flexed positions. Glass beads were of the Nueva Cadiz Plain and Nueva Cadiz Twisted types.[6] With them were several *maravedí* coins, probably minted in Hispaniola before 1538.[7] There were also thin, triangular iron celt blades, as well as large iron ships' spikes more than 6 inches long. The latter may have been hafted as war-club heads or digging tools, but the superiority of iron may have been so apparent that the Indians were willing to purchase them even though they were not fully formed into tools. It is not clear what the Spaniards may have purchased, aside from food supplies.

An interesting aspect of Lawrence Mound is that one skeleton, probably of a male juvenile, gave evidence of a deficiency that had left him with extensive bone porosity. This type of osteoporosis is characteristic of iron-deficiency anemias, and it was considered that this might have been sickle-cell anemia or a similar form, which would indicate that he was mestizo as the anemia is confined to Mediterraneans and Negroes.[8] Of course, a corn-heavy diet might lead to similar anemias, so the question must remain open. Aside from obvious traumas and a few specific diseases, detection of illness from skeletal remains alone is often difficult.

We have learned from these three sites that the communities in which they were constructed and the individuals who were buried in them had access to early sixteenth-century goods of the types often used in trade. The assemblage of Spanish artifacts illustrates the sorts of things that might be bartered to Indians for food or other favors. Clearly, they do not imply extended European presence in the native community. It seems doubtful, therefore, that such brief visits and exotic goods had an extensive cultural effect on the local culture. Because there was little opportunity for Spaniards to attempt to change aboriginal customs or to modify behavior, the fact that such goods, in fairly impressive quantities, found their way into burial mounds suggests a special, evidently high value for these objects. In spite of their superior usefulness such objects were buried with deceased members of the elite who had been their owners. Burial practices (and presumably other ritual behavior), therefore, were not extensively modified.

I would not attempt to identify the Spanish expedition that was responsible for the St. Simons collection. The Withlacoochee River and Weekeewatchee Springs mounds, however, are close to the route Soto must have taken northward, from either Tampa Bay or Charlotte Harbor, eventually to spend the winter at the large Apalachee town now identified as the Lake Jackson site.

The requisite extensive excavations have not been made at Lake Jackson; enough research has been done, however, to demonstrate the Mississippian character of the Lake Jackson site and other mound complexes in the area. Clearly, they represent the remains of communities with a ranked social system, probably chiefdoms. This conclusion is supported by the evidence of the Spanish chronicles, with descriptions of chiefs who had power and other attributes of complex political organization. The large Apalachee population depended on hunting, along with full corn, bean, and squash horticulture, and it was this subsistence base that fed the Spaniards from October 6, 1539, until March 3, 1540, some 148 days. Most of the Soto army of nearly 500, and its many horses, remained in the town for all that period, although parts of the group made local expeditions (one of about two months, to and along the coast, i.e., westward).

This was certainly the most intensive and longest interaction between Indians and Europeans to that time in the Southeast, and its impact must have been great. However, there is little evidence that the Spaniards made intensive efforts to change Indian culture. They were not active in evangelizing the natives nor did they make systematic attempts to introduce European ways. They seized food, houses, guides, women, and possibly servants. Thus the trauma for the Indians must have been great and resulted in major changes. When Spanish missionaries entered the area about 100 years later, they found a very different cultural and demographic situation. It is these changes that I will next discuss as part of the effects of the Soto expedition. (In agreement with changing styles in archaeology, our attention shifts from description to explanation.)

Swanton and most other students have concluded that the main Apalachee town of Iniahica was the mound site of Lake Jackson, on the northwestern edge of present-day Tallahassee, where the Spaniards found maize, pumpkins, beans, and dried plums in abundance. The foods they looted from neighboring towns were collected at their winter camp, and seem to have supplied them adequately through the winter.

In the red clay hills around Tallahassee are a number of fairly large Ft. Walton–period mound sites, only slightly smaller than the Lake Jackson site, which indicates a populous, highly organized group that was able to offer considerable resistance to Soto's army. The Indians were evidently still using, and probably building, platform mounds that served as *loci* of houses for elite persons and as bases for religious structures. Thus we see a complex, class-stratified society, with elaborate ritual, supporting a redistributive economy. (Stored-food supplies, both dried venison and agricultural produce, are good indications of this complexity.) As the Indians had fled Iniahica at the approach of the Spaniards, the expedition's narratives do not give much information on the organization (including ritual) of the Apalachee. It is clear, however, that this province was the most populous and complexly organized that the army had yet encountered, and there is evidence at the Lake Jackson site of burial, in one mound, of elaborate copper insignia of the Southern Cult. The little excavation that has been done there has not yet turned up any early Spanish artifacts, although they might have been quite scarce as the Spaniards were occupying an abandoned town, not bartering for food or services. However, when we look at the Apalachee district about 100 years later, we find a situation radically altered.

The region was still fairly populous, but the Indians were found (by priests) in small, scattered hamlets. They were still agricultural, raising the typical crops of maize, beans, and pumpkins, but they were not building or using mound structures, and the major mound sites had been abandoned. In some respects the Leon-Jefferson complex, found at mission sites, shows resemblances to the earlier Lake Jackson variant of Ft. Walton. Globular jars and carenated bowls, predominantly plain, are probably derived directly from earlier styles. But there are, in addition, significant quantities of check-stamped and complicated-stamped pottery. Both represent additions to the Ft. Walton ceramic complex and are most likely representative of ideas of people who moved in from outside the immediate area. I am inclined to believe that these later pottery types represent movements *into* the Tallahassee red hills. Check-stamped types may have come from southern Alabama, the complicated-stamped forms from northern Georgia.

At any rate, the Spanish missionaries found little evidence of any organization above the village level. Towns had a functioning leadership system, but not nearly as elaborate as during the mid-sixteenth century. While some ritual patterns were retained, mound building and use had stopped. The major mound sites in the old Apalachee area were abandoned, and show no signs of reoccupation during the Leon-Jefferson period. Yet these people still spoke Apalachee. Ritual objects, such as Southern Cult paraphernalia, are totally absent from the mission sites. Ritual behavior seems to have been largely restricted to the several ballgames described in the Paiva manuscript.[9] So perhaps the collapse of organized tribal religion is an indication of the success of Spanish evangelism among the Apalachee.

I would therefore summarize events from 1539 to 1640 as a massive reduction of population, accompanied by loss of the redistributive chieftainship organization. The Indians' inability to maintain the elaborate ritual necessary for the smooth functioning of that polity is reflected in the cessation of mound building. The scattered villages of the mission period evidently held migrants from the west and north, probably refugees from similar depopula-

The Hernando de Soto Expedition Encounters Chief Tascaluza. The chief received the Spaniard's advance cavalry with, according to Elvas, apparent indifference. (De Gedenkwaardige Voyagie van don Ferdinand de Soto . . . [Leyden: P. Van der Aa, 1706]. Courtesy of the W. S. Hoole Special Collections Library, The University of Alabama)

tions. The Spanish *entrada* into Apalachee, and into much of the rest of the core Southeast, resulted in massive reorganization of the culture and major population reductions. Now it is necessary to investigate how these effects may have been initiated.

I have been able to define four mechanisms or hypotheses for the above effects (but unable to develop plausible testing procedures). The first of these which might be called the "military destruction hypothesis," argues that Spanish attacks killed sufficient numbers of Apalachee to scatter the population and destroy the chieftainship system. However, on the basis of the scanty accounts of the expedition, this seems unlikely. The Apalachee fled the Lake Jackson site and seem largely to have avoided the Spaniards during the winter and early spring of 1539/40. *Some* Indians were killed by Spanish lances, attack dogs, and crossbows; none of the accounts describes any large-scale slaughter of the natives, however. Nor did the

135

Spaniards instigate intertribal conflicts, as at later times in other areas. Thus military action seems not to account for the population loss.

The second explanation might be that the Spaniards killed key personnel. The capture and execution of chiefs in the large towns would have created great confusion in a primitive state. But again, there is no (or very little) evidence in the documents that this occurred. Soto, on a number of occasions, made efforts to placate chiefs in major towns and provinces, and experience in the Caribbean and Mesoamerica had taught the Spanish to rule through the existing political and structural mechanisms. Thus it seems unlikely that this second mechanism effected the changes we see.

My third explanation concerns the looting of stored-food supplies by the Spaniards, for the documents indicate that Apalachee had considerable amounts of stored maize, beans, pumpkins, dried venison, and dried plums. Certainly the Spaniards destroyed food supplies, in addition to what they consumed, but I find it difficult to believe that some 500 men, 250 horses, and an unknown number of swine could seriously deplete the food supplies of more than 20,000 Apalachee. We cannot know what the Spaniards took with them on their northern trek in the spring, but they could not have *moved* massive amounts of food. It is clear, however, that disruption of the social/political system would have seriously limited planting, hunting, and collecting during 1540 and subsequent years, and this disruption may well have been more serious than consumption and destruction of food supplies by the Spaniards. Malnutrition would have seriously weakened the remaining Indians and exposed them to infections.

The fourth explanation deals with infections, introduced European diseases, against which the native population had little resistance. The Spaniards in the Caribbean and on the mainland of the New World had by 1539 seen the effects of these diseases and must have been aware of the serious depopulation that followed the first contact between Native Americans and Europeans. The rapid loss of the Indian labor base on Hispaniola had led to the importation of African slave labor to the island, and soon thereafter to the rest of the New World. Thus it seems to me that death from infections, coupled with malnutrition from disruption of the system, could well account for the depopulation and break-up of the cultural pattern.

A question that both intrigues me and needs testing by documentary and archaeological research follows on this hypothesis: What effect did Spanish recognition of depopulation and deculturation, following contact, have on producing changes in Spanish settlement strategy? Florida was founded primarily as a military outpost, to protect the treasure fleets' return to Spain. But as Eugene Lyon has recently written, the Spanish also saw Florida as a source of profits from settlement.[10] I believe, however, that the early Spanish explorations had indicated that direct exploitation of the Indians was not feasible. Instead, Spain initiated a pattern of trade and tribute in skins, drugs such as sassafras, and a mission effort to convert these new people to Christian, Spanish peasantry, having underestimated the population loss from new, European diseases and the resultant disruption of stable social systems. Secondly, I think Spain also underestimated the number of Spanish settlers who could be attracted to the new colony. The result was a very attenuated Spanish presence in the Southeast for a hundred years, by which time a more vigorous British settlement process was well under way.

Even before the Soto expedition, Spain had determined that permanent settlements in Florida would not repeat the disastrous events of settlements in the Caribbean. The Ayllón expedition was especially interested in noting the fruitfulness of lands for raising crops and animals with which Spaniards were familiar, and Soto's orders from the king included the prohibition of harsh treatment of the natives.[11] Many Spaniards in positions of authority realized that only the establishment of self-sufficient colonies would be able to survive and export goods of value to the mother country. That the Soto expedition turned into an extended armed raid throughout the Southeast was not part of the plan of the court of Spain.

Again, I think the Spanish experience with the rapid loss of native populations in the Caribbean demonstrated that only peaceful coexistence with the Indians would make settlement and enterprise possible. In the sixteenth century, transport and communication were so precarious that founders of a colony could not depend on regular resupply either from home or from Caribbean ports.

Organizers of new expeditions to the Southeastern United States no doubt assembled all available information on its people, places, and resources. For example, the Luna expedition was apparently provided with extensive documents from the Soto expedition describing the area. That the surviving documents now exist only as fragments[12] may indicate how frequently the reports of earlier trips were used. It is certain that both planners in Spain and leaders of settlements acquired written and oral accounts of the lands they hoped to settle. This resulted in the first planned frontier in what is now the Southeastern United States, and took into account the realities of Spanish economic conditions, transport, and communication, as well as the results of Caribbean settlement and the new knowledge collected by expeditions into the mainland. Spaniards of the time of Pedro Menéndez de Avilés seem to have been conscious that new settlements must also take into account Indian cultures, local resources, and the Spanish culture.

I think there was general recognition that the *encomienda* system, evolved during the reconquest of Islamic Spain, had been a serious mistake. While Spaniards were not aware of all the factors in the rapid decimation of Indian populations in Hispaniola and other Caribbean islands, they learned that direct exploitation of the Indians for food and export materials was a losing venture. Certainly the preaching and writings of Bartolomé de las Casas had the effect of changing the image of Indians as savages unworthy of consideration. This set the stage for the extensive missionary effort that was to characterize the colony of Florida. That the mission system was also used to control and exploit the natives should not obscure the fact that it was regarded by many as a means of conferring souls on the Indians and thus making possible their salvation.

The other major feature of the Florida enterprise was that the colony was to be more self-sufficient, if possible, than earlier colonies had been. Crops were to be planted to supplement supplies shipped from the Caribbean or Spain; but Indians were not to be forced to labor for Spanish masters. Rather, colonists were to establish a supporting peasantry and feudal system much like those in Spain. The early expeditions, including Soto's, had demonstrated that Indians could supply the food to feed Spaniards, although this was not chosen as the way things should be in the new colony. However, the Spanish colonial concept included the idea that the land and the inhabitants, Spanish and native, were possessions of the crown.

This was the final component of the colonial system in Florida. As subjects of the king, the Indians owed tribute to the colonial government. This seems to have included small amounts of foodstuffs, but consisted mainly of exportable items. Thus we read that cassena leaves were part of the tribute from tribes near St. Augustine.[13] Deer hides and sassafras, as well as meat and fish, were also collected as tribute. It was assumed that once the Indians were converted to Christianity and settled in stable communities, they would pay taxes and tithes to church and state. This approach was quite different from the *encomienda* in Hispaniola. We cannot assume that the early explorers' knowledge of Southeastern Indians was the only cause for these changes in colonial policy. The complementary pressures of Spanish politics, economic conditions, and the writings of men like las Casas, as well as military necessity on the new frontier, made these changes expedient choices. That ultimately they were unsuccessful was due to the inability of Spaniards to balance the consequences for Indians against the consequences for the new culture. New ideas, amid cultural disruption, led to a rapid loss of population, though not as swiftly as earlier in Hispaniola.

The archaeological remains at St. Augustine and Santa Elena show that the Florida settlements depended heavily on the Indians for food-preparation ceramics.[14] Reitz, likewise, has demonstrated the extensive use of wild mammals and fish by the Spaniards at St. Augustine.[15] These data indicate how much the colonists depended on Indians for subsistence in the settlements. At St. Augustine, they could draw on the nearby missions. Santa Elena seems to have lacked that advantage, and shows more evidence of attempts to establish Spanish agriculture.

On a new frontier, a new strategy was called for. If it proved to be unsuccessful, it was not for lack of planning. The Spaniards simply failed to understand how much damage had been done to Southeastern Indian populations by the excesses of the Soto expedition.

III

Bernardo de Gálvez,
Governor of Louisiana
(Courtesy of The
Historic New Orleans
Collection)

Colonization and Conflict

The Southeast in   *Wilcomb E.*
     the Age of Conflict   *Washburn*
     and Revolution

The Southeast does not loom large in the writing of American history, but it ought to, and particularly the period of conflict in the eighteenth century. Its importance should be reflected in hundreds of scholarly works, though only a handful exist. There are many reasons why the Southeast does not loom large in American history, and one reason is that most of it was written in other parts of the country, particularly in New England, and reflects different values, different understandings, different sources, and in some cases simple ignorance.

In 1975 Michael Kammen reported on two surveys of the most significant books about American history published in the years 1960–68 and 1969–74, as selected by practicing historians. Of the thirty-two books listed, not one was by a professor in a Southern university, although three were by historians who were born in the South.[1] Charles Hudson, in a study of obituaries in the *American Anthropologist*, demonstrated a similar paucity of Southern-born and Southern-based anthropologists and archaeologists who have achieved recognition in American anthropology, even among those who dealt with the South.

As a New Englander, I am acutely aware of the intense concern with history shown by other New Englanders, from the moment William Bradford stepped off the *Mayflower* to the latest Ph.D. dissertation at Harvard. Writing history, or keeping a diary, was almost implicit in the Puritan religious outlook and the philosophical traditions that derived from it. My first venture into Southern history, with my dissertation on Bacon's Rebellion in Virginia, was undertaken in part because of the realization that, from a New England point of view, Virginia history had hardly been scratched whereas New England history was deeply plowed. But if Virginia's history has been relatively unexplored, compared with New England history, the history of the colonies farther south has been even less critically and less fully examined.

Jack Greene, in his Fleming Lectures at Louisiana State University in 1980 (to be published under the title *Southern Colonies in the Creation of American Culture*), challenged the New England–centered view of American history, in which New England is seen as the model for the development of English societies in the New World, while Southern culture is regarded as a deviant growth. In part, this view is a product of the early-established and strongly developed New England colleges and historical societies, which long produced the leading thinkers and writers in American history.

Virginians used to complain that most Americans thought the first English settlement was at Plymouth in 1620, unaware that Jamestown was founded in 1607. Now, the Virginia complaint is largely a canard of the past. Most Americans now recognize the Old Dominion's priority in providing an overseas home for English culture, but you can still fool most Americans by asking them to identify the first permanent European settlement in the United States. Thus St. Augustine has yet to take its place in the American historical consciousness. (In graduate school, Dr. Scardaville [see his essay in this volume] was discouraged from studying St. Augustine by the comment that it was *"local* history.") In part, American ignorance of the Deep South reflects the false values of an earlier period, when Florida was held to be a worthless tract of sand and swamps, Southern agricultural lowlands were malarial and pest ridden, and the Southern interior was bereft of great cities and great universities.

The historical literature on the Southeastern United States (or what is called in this book "Alabama and the Borderlands") is not only less extensive than the literature on other parts of the country, it is overrepresented by the antebellum, bellum, and postbellum South and underrepresented by the Colonial South. In college courses and in the public consciousness, the "Old South" often begins around 1820. The literature of the pre-Revolutionary South is underrepresented in the middle period, that is, the late seventeenth and early eighteenth centuries.

The fact that the History of the South series is now complete *except* for volume II epitomizes the problem. This volume, covering the period between Wesley Frank Craven's *The Southern Colonies in the Seventeenth Century* and John Alden's *The South in the Revolution, 1763–1789*, was originally assigned to Clarence Ver Steeg, but it was not completed.[2] Peter Wood, of Duke University, is now working on a manuscript to fill this major gap. In talking with Professor Wood about this "hole" he has committed himself to filling, I learned that it "keeps opening up." Professor Wood is young and vigorous, and intends to close the breach, but he warned us "not to hold our breath."

One of the major gaps in the New American Nation series is the volume for the period 1713–63, which Jack Greene of Johns Hopkins University agreed to produce. (He has since withdrawn from the project.) Though it will cover all the colonies, its most difficult portion will be the colonies of the Southeast, where documentation is most difficult. (The volume has been reassigned to Lawrence Leder of Lehigh University.)

W. Stitt Robinson produced *The Southern Colonial Frontier, 1607–1763*, which somewhat filled the gap, but again, the area and period least adequately treated are Alabama and its neighbors in the first half of the eighteenth century.[3]

The most serious problem for the student of Alabama and the Borderlands is the lack of documentary materials of the sort that provides the New Englander, the New Yorker, the Pennsylvanian, and even the Virginian with sufficient data upon which secondary works can be based. The Northern states and the Middle colonies got an early start in recovering, editing, and publishing the historical records of their Colonial forefathers through the creation of such groups as the Massachusetts Historical Society and the American Antiquarian Society (in the late eighteenth and early nineteenth centuries) and the activities of such historians and historically oriented individuals as Peter Force, Ebenezer Hazard, Jared Sparks, and Richard Bartlett.

The South, as Ernst Posner pointed out in his *American State Archives*, played an honorable role in establishing state archives in which to preserve the historical record[4] (although the weakness of private libraries and historical societies in the South made this a necessity). Thomas McAdory Owen, Sr., secretary of the Alabama

Historical Society, was influential in causing the General Assembly to create the Alabama Historical Commission in 1898—one year before the American Historical Association created a Public Archives Commission to investigate and report on the "character, contents and functions of our public repositories of manuscript records." As chairman of the Alabama Commission, Owen guided legislation through the Assembly that in 1901 established the Department of Archives and History of Alabama, of which he became director. Alabama's example was soon followed by the state of Mississippi, which established its Department of Archives and History in 1902. As the first state to establish a Department of Archives and History to serve as the official custodian of the state's archives, Alabama deserves high praise, but much of the state's, and particularly the region's, Colonial history is inadequately represented in the manuscript depositories and in the published literature.

Alden T. Vaughan, who is editing a series of documentary publications pertaining to Colonial treaties and the American Indian, under the title *Early American Indian Documents*, tells me that the Southeast volume (being edited by John Juricek of Emory University) has the highest proportion of manuscript documents— 40 percent—in his series.[5]

The state of Florida, in celebrating the United States' bicentennial, reprinted a number of primary sources on the colonial origins of the state and sponsored several conferences on Florida and the Borderlands. More recently, in 1980, a Gálvez Celebration Commission was established that is sponsoring publication of a number of works that deal with the siege of Pensacola in 1781. But these publications and events have not succeeded in focusing national attention upon the history of the Southeast in any permanent or substantial way.

William S. Coker, in his "Entrepreneurs in British and Spanish Florida, 1775–1821" (in the collection *Eighteenth-Century Florida and the Caribbean*), spoke optimistically of completion by 1978 of a project to microfilm the records of Panton, Leslie and Company and Forbes and Company, and to publish a three-to five-volume edition of selected documents.[6] Coker's optimism—like that of most editors—has been tempered by reality, but suffice it to say that this project, like others that are much needed, will eventually see the light of day and the sooner, the better.

Partly because of the weakness of the undergirding documentary structure and partly for other reasons, already alluded to or to be mentioned, there is no Francis Parkman of the South who has attempted to portray its development in the broad strokes that this Bostonian used for his history of conflict in the American forest. Yet the struggle between France and England was as much a Southern as a Northern phenomenon, and in many ways more complex and interesting in the South.

Nor has the historiography of the Lower South reached the stage of Chesapeake studies, where the techniques of quantitative history and the new "social history" (originating in New England) have begun to be extensively applied. Thad W. Tate noted this in his "The Seventeenth Century Chesapeake and Its Modern Historians," in *The Chesapeake in the Seventeenth Century: Essays on Anglo-American Society*.[7]

The South's alienation from the rest of the nation as a result of the Civil War led not only to physical disruption but to excessive concern with the lost war, lost values, lost opportunities, and lost wealth—in short, the Lost Cause. It has caused the literature about the South to be couched in overly plaintive or assertive terms: the South, whether "Old" or "New," is too often "everlasting," "struggling," "emerging," "proud of its civilization," conscious of itself as "mind," "idea," or "myth," "suffering an agony," and "carrying a burden" that other regions have no need to shoulder. Such literature emerges more from suffering hearts and minds than from the red-rimmed eyes and dust-smeared fingers of scholars who spend years in the archives of England, France, Spain, and the United States.

Not only is the history of the early Southeast less thoroughly studied than the history of other areas, it is relatively neglected in comparative history: the history of colonization by different countries, in different climes, in different periods. Michael Kammen, in his paper "The Unique and the Universal in the History of New World Colonization" (read at the First Annual Bicentennial Symposium, sponsored by the American Revolution Bicentennial Commission of Florida at the University of Florida, May 18–20, 1972), emphasized Florida's importance in the study of comparative and universal aspects of colonization.[8] But little use has been made of the early history of Alabama, Florida, and the other Gulf states in studies of colonial rivalries, imperialism, and the like.

Yet the importance of the Southeast in our early history is *primary*. The most powerful groupings of Indian nations on the continent were here: the Cherokees, Creeks, Choctaws, Chicka-

saws, and (before their destruction by the French) other great nations in the Mississippi Valley, such as the Natchez and the Tunica.
And not only did the interests of *two* great European nations
clash—as in the North—but the interests of the *three* greatest
European nations of the time came into direct conflict. If one were
to construct a model for the possible outcomes among the different
"players" in the Alabama Borderlands, one would have to devise a
three-dimensional chess game, rather than the conventional flat
board with only two opposing sides. (Perhaps our future Parkman is
a young person who now is sharpening his or her wits on Rubik's
Cube, which brings the concept of multidimensionality into special
prominence.) Any game that involves three players, as any theory of
games will note, encourages instability and movement as each
player assesses the strengths of the other two. Concern for "friend"
and "foe" becomes subservient to jockeying for the balance of
power, and anyone who looks at the relationship between the
U.S.A., the U.S.S.R., and the People's Republic of China today can
see the same principle at work. Now add to the Southeastern
"theater of operations" the native players, whose power is signified
not only in their occupation of one of the most fertile and desirable
portions of the North American continent but in their number of
warriors, normally exceeding the power that their European friends,
or enemies, could exert against them. Such a complex formula is not
associated with other parts of the continent.

Although independent and powerful in the period of conflict and
Revolution, the Indian nations of the Southeast chose to maintain
their traditional enmities and ally themselves with the European
powers. Had they chosen to unite against Europeans in general or
against one European power in particular, the outcome in the South
might have been different. By dividing their allegiance among the
contending European nations, they played the game in terms of
European interests, while believing they played it in their own
interests. Whether this policy was rational, blind, or an inevitable
concomitant of perceived or real dependence upon European trade
goods is one of many questions for sophisticated scholarly analysis.

Valuable work has been done by a number of anthropologists
who deal with individual Indian tribes of the Southeast, and John R.
Swanton's *The Indians of the Southeastern United States* and
Charles M. Hudson's *The Southeastern Indians* deal with the Indi-
ans of the Southeast collectively.[9] The work on Indian tribes of the
Southeast is excellent, and getting even better, but it tells us only a

small fraction of what we want to know, largely because it is based on the inadequate documentation of Indian history in the area. Much information has been lost forever through the disappearance of tribal memories, languages, and peoples, but "new" information continues to emerge, particularly through archaeology and anthropological theory.

Jeffrey Brain's recent *Tunica Treasure,* an example of the newly emerging data, throws light on the interaction and trade between the Tunica Indians of Louisiana and the French.[10] DePratter, Hudson, and Smith's selection (in this book) is another example. Yet the judgment of Hudson is still at least partially true: "More than any of the native people of North America, the Southeastern Indians have been victims of scholarly neglect"—despite the fact that the Southeastern Indians "possessed the richest culture of any of the native people north of Mexico." Their political organizations were highly evolved and complex, their shaping of their natural environment in towns and buildings was impressive and unusual, their art was richly expressive; yet the average American knows the Indians of Virginia or the Plains or the Southwest desert much better than the Indians of the Southeast.

This neglect of Southeastern Indians is also seen in our hazy knowledge of the historical actors in the South. Not only are Europeans (such as Christian Priber) tantalizingly insubstantial, but a number of "Indian leaders" continue to pose unanswered questions. William C. Sturtevant, for example, in his commentary on Helen Tanner's paper in *Eighteenth-Century Florida and Its Borderlands* raised doubts about some conclusions in John Walton Caughey's *McGillivray of the Creeks* and J. Leitch Wright, Jr.'s *William Augustus Bowles, Director General of the Creek Nation.*[11]

While the work of historians, like the work of anthropologists, has added to our understanding of the complex history of Alabama and its Borderlands, it poses more questions than answers. Despite the work of Arrell M. Gibson (in *The Chickasaws*) and particularly of Marcel Giraud (whose multivolume *Histoire de la Louisiane Française* carries the story from 1698 to 1723—one volume of which, *The Reign of Louis XIV, 1698–1715,* has been translated by Joseph C. Lambert), many significant and tantalizing questions remain. A more recent study by Patricia Dillon Woods, *French–Indian Relations on the Southern Frontier, 1699–1762* (a revision of a doctoral thesis), fills some of the gaps. But we are still at a loss to understand with certainty how France's Natchez controversy and ultimately war—which led to extinction of the Natchez in the 1720s—occurred.[12] Patricia Galloway may answer some of the questions in a book she is preparing.

J. Leitch Wright, Jr.'s recent *The Only Land They Knew: The Tragic Story of the American Indians of the Old South* deals with Indian affairs in geographical order, from Virginia to the Gulf of Mexico, but it fails to shape Indian history into whatever unity that history may have had.[13] (Because of the wide scope of the work, Wright must pass over problems that call for monograph-long explanations.) Perhaps there is no common history for Southeastern Indians and Southeastern whites, but they were locked into a relationship with each other that has not yet been satisfactorily defined and delineated.

The perspective of South Carolina on the Southeastern Borderlands is better than the perspective of other Southeastern Colonial centers. But despite the work of Robert L. Meriwether (*The Expansion of South Carolina, 1729–1765*), Verner W. Crane (*The Southern Frontier, 1670–1732*), David Duncan Wallace (*South Carolina, a Short History, 1510–1948*), M. Eugene Sirmans (*Colonial South Carolina: A Political History, 1663–1763*), and David H. Corkran (*The Creek Frontier, 1540–1783*), we do not have the detailed and comprehensive coverage that is available for other parts of the country.[14] The Yamassee War of 1715 and the Choctaw Revolt of 1746–50 should be as familiar to historians as King Philip's War or Bacon's Rebellion. Nevertheless, they are passed over, half in confusion and half in ignorance.

The Choctaw Revolt, beginning in 1746, is a prime example. If we are to believe James Adair, the trader who lived with the Chickasaws and was directly involved in the complex maneuvers associated with the event, the Choctaws might have sided with the English but for the bungling of the authorities at Charleston. I am inclined to accept Adair's evaluation of the affair, as I have noted in my introduction to his *History of the American Indians* (in Lawrence Leder's *The Colonial Legacy*, volume III: *Historians of Nature and Man's Nature*).[15] But the complex diplomacy of French–Choctaw, French–Chickasaw, French–English, English–Chickasaw, English–Choctaw, and English–French relations in the first half of the eighteenth century is still undetailed. Many "revolts," incipient revolts, acts of disaffection and "disloyalty," and backsliding marked Choctaw–French relations in the thirty years before the

Choctaw Revolt of 1746, yet we know virtually nothing (beyond some bare and uncertain "facts") about any of these incidents.

The American Revolution, which marked the beginning of the end of conflict and turmoil in the Southeast, started as a quarrel between Englishmen, from which the Indians were urged to remain aloof and in which Spain and France were not immediately involved. It developed into a convulsion that separated Englishmen into two nations, irreparably weakened the powerful Indian nations that were eventually drawn into the conflict, and reshuffled the interests and possessions of the Spanish and French in the area.

James H. O'Donnell III, in his *Southern Indians in the American Revolution*, dealt with the Indians' role in Revolutionary activities in the South,[16] but the subject calls for further and more detailed treatment. As a theater of war involving Indians, the Deep South was more important than any other. Large armies maneuvered and fought—Spanish as well as English, Indian, and American. Yet, despite the work of O'Donnell (and William Coker), important events, such as the capitulation of Pensacola (defended by 1,500 British soldiers, 400 Choctaws, and 100 Creeks) to a Spanish fleet and an army of 4,000 on May 8, 1781, is less well known than any Revolutionary skirmish in New England or New Jersey.

The facts of the siege of Pensacola will be better known with the circulation of William S. and Hazel P. Coker's *The Siege of Pensacola, 1781, in Maps, with Data on Troop Strength, Military Units, Ships, Casualties and Related Statistics.*[17] The Cokers, in their preface, note that they (and other scholars of the area) had been unaware of Father Manuel Ignacio Perez-Alonso's unpublished 1954 Ph.D. dissertation at Georgetown University, "War Mission in the Caribbean: The Diary of Don Francisco de Saavedra (1780–1783)." In addition, the Cokers relied on a book by Father Francisco de Borja Medina Rojas, S.J., *José de Ezpeleta: Gobernador de la Mobila, 1780–1781.*[18] The Cokers note that Father Borja Medina's 978-page volume "ranks as the best study published on the siege to date." At last, perhaps, this important military event will begin to emerge from the shadows.

When the British finally evacuated St. Augustine, in 1783, they were surprised that a great number of their Indian allies sought to go with them. As one Indian put it: "If the English mean to abandon the Land, we will accompany them—We cannot take a Virginian or Spaniard by the hand—We cannot look them in the face."[19] Can a historian of today fully explain why these Indians had decided to "abandon their country," as the British commandant noted in amazement?

To sum up. Alabama and the Borderlands, or the Southeast in general, are a vital but insufficiently recognized and exploited area of historical inquiry. This generalization applies particularly to the period of conflict and Revolution in the eighteenth century. The reasons for this scholarly neglect, though varied, are implicit in the fact that institutions that traditionally nourish the study of history in other parts of the country have been laggard in the Deep South.

This volume celebrates the 150th anniversary of the founding of The University of Alabama. In New England, we soon will celebrate the 350th anniversary of the founding of Harvard College. Yet Englishmen, Frenchmen, Spaniards, and Americans were *making history* in Alabama and the Borderlands during the *first* 100 years of Harvard's existence and during its *second* 100 years. Despite its late start, Alabama can make up for lost time by throwing off the "burden" of Southern history, by cleansing the "Southern mind" of false ideas, and by grasping—with confidence—the opportunity provided by Southern history in the unexploited terrain of the corresponding two centuries of the university's nonexistence. In practical terms, that means building support for study of Alabama and the Borderlands within the university community so that the almost unlimited research opportunities of the Southeast are available both to local scholars and "outsiders."

How can this be done? First of all, by a change of attitude toward the region in which The University of Alabama finds itself. Instead of apologizing for being regional or provincial, the university should take pride in its special, regional character. Instead of attempting to achieve excellence simultaneously on all fronts, the university should put new emphasis on the region in which it finds itself.

We have been calling that region the "Borderlands," a term that has been incorporated in the name of an association of which Dr. Scardaville is a prime mover: the Southeast Borderlands Association. However, the term is not, in my opinion, ideal. It does not specify the center or centers to which the borderlands are related. Spanish? English? French? American? It does not take into account the passage of time that changes a borderland into a *non*borderland. It does not clarify the term "border" or "borderland," which—as

John Juricek pointed out in a paper on the meaning of "frontier"—has many and even contradictory meanings.

I prefer a geographical definition that is consistent with the interests of the organization that uses the term. For The University of Alabama, I suggest that it focus upon what I call the "Gulf South." I prefer this term to "Deep South" or "Lower South" because "Gulf South" emphasizes Alabama's maritime origins and connections without ignoring its overland links to the rest of the mainland. As a focus for the university's scholarly endeavors, I prefer "Gulf South"—even to "the South" as a whole—because The University of Alabama can more readily achieve distinction by limiting its special programs to the area in which it plays a dominant role, rather than by competing with similar programs in other universities that study the South as a whole or the United States as a whole.

The University of Alabama has a Center for the Study of Southern History and Culture, and perhaps that center (or a different center) should focus more narrowly on the *Gulf* South. At the same time, it might build a broader interdisciplinary base to put greater emphasis on anthropology, archaeology, literature, geography, psychology, and folklore, thus achieving a unique distinction that would be recognized throughout the country. And can one not imagine a Gulf States Professorship, endowed by Mr. Jack Warner, president of Gulf States Corporation, to fill the gap in the university curriculum concerning the history of this region in the sixteenth, seventeenth, and eighteenth centuries?

Greatness in a university can be achieved only by natural growth, by utilizing both the resources at hand and imported materials that find fertile soil for renewed growth after transplantation. Greatness requires appropriate ideas, appropriate leadership, and appropriate organization. Paul "Bear" Bryant made Alabama No. 1 in football by utilizing such an approach. The same approach is not inappropriate for Alabama history.

9 Continuity in the Age of Conquest: The Establishment of Spanish Sovereignty in the Sixteenth Century

Eugene Lyon

The purpose of this essay is to explore threads of continuity among the several efforts of sixteenth-century Spaniards to conquer North America east of New Spain. It will also examine the culmination of these attempts, during the period of Pedro Menéndez de Avilés and his advances into Florida from 1565 to 1577.

By 1536, Spaniards had touched the East Coast of the North American continent and traversed its Gulf shoreline, and the crown had parceled out vast areas to successive would-be conquerors, from Juan Ponce de León to Pánfilo de Narváez. Tales told by the few survivors of Narváez' expedition, who straggled into Mexico City, sparked a rivalry of exploration and a lawsuit between Hernando Cortés, Viceroy Antonio de Mendozo, Hernando de Soto, and Pedro de Alvarado.[1] After Soto landed in Florida, the viceroy sent Francisco Vázquez de Coronado northward and eastward to the pueblos of Arizona and New Mexico and thence to the plains of Kansas, the fabled Cíbola and Quivira. Coronado, of course, sought more than fertile land and mineral riches, and Baltasar de Obregon, a sixteenth-century commentator on his expedition, states that Coronado's captains were bitterly disappointed at what they considered his premature return to New Spain. They felt they had been drawing near to "the great salt river and the Sea of the North, where they were certain would be the Strait of Newfoundland, which opens toward Ireland."[2] This rumored transcontinental waterway (the

154

famed but elusive Northwest Passage) was a preoccupation of six-teenth-century Spanish explorers.

Reports of expedition survivors, royal and viceregal letters, and accounts of friars and soldiers added to Spain's knowledge about the continent. Some explorers found remnants of previous Spanish explorations; Indians described direct or traditional recollections of contacts with Europeans; and the most important result of the lengthy journeys of Hernando de Soto was their contribution to the body of continental knowledge. The several narratives of Soto's expeditions furnished some understanding of major rivers, natural roadways, and the quality and products of the land. Areas rich in promise, such as Coosa, were noted.

Tristán de Luna y Arrellano, who had served Coronado as major lieutenant, was named by Viceroy Velasco to command the next effort to dominate Florida, in 1559. The viceroy provided Luna with a map of the lands the Soto expedition had traversed and with a copy of a relation of the journey.[3] The Luna and the later Villafañe expeditions failed, but the Spanish efforts in Florida—considered to be all of Eastern North America—had not ended.

On Tuesday, August 14, 1565, the ships of Pedro Menéndez de Avilés arrived in San Juan, Puerto Rico, on their way to Florida. Menéndez, an Asturian shipowner who had served as general of the royal ships in the Indies trade, had just been appointed the latest *adelantado* and captain-general of Florida. In another instance of continuity in the Spanish crown's approach to the settlement of North America, the king again chose the instrument of *adelanta-miento*—the licensing of quasi-private-conquest entrepreneurs. In a time when the resources of the crown were often insufficient to compass the reach of policy, the resources of the *adelantados* could underwrite conquest.[4]

A typical "contractor in conquest," Menéndez received govern-mental control for a season, revenues, a personal land grant (25 square leagues) and the title of marquis to go with it, tax exemp-tions, and ship and slave licenses. In return, he was obliged—at his expense—to populate and pacify all the lands under his control, stretching from the Gulf Coast to Newfoundland. Philip II signed Menéndez' *asiento* before he learned of the French incursion at Fort Caroline in Florida; thereafter, the king added crown aid, in the form of royal soldiers and supplies, to the resources of the *adelantado*.

At San Juan on that day, a copy of the Florida contract was made, and a marginal note indicates it was for the *adelantado*'s personal

use. There followed a note and two narratives, first located in the
Archive of the Indies in 1975. The note read:

In most parts of Florida there is much worked copper. . . . In the inland
mountains are great veins of silver, very concentrated ore. Those who
entered from Mexico by way of Copala toward Florida discovered great
things and found a place with more than 20,000 inhabitants, and strong and
high houses of seven stories and very strong enclosures. They found dies
with which they worked silver and many jewels of it and of gold; they had
word of Kings crowned with golden crowns, far inland. . . .

At the end was a cynical statement, to the effect that the note was
prepared at the request of Spaniards in Menéndez' entourage, but
"without hope of it."[5]

In the same hand follows a one-page summary of a relation of
Fray Sebastián de Cañete, a participant in the earlier expedition of
Hernando de Soto. This summary, of interest for both its content
and its inclusion in the document bundle, describes the fruits, birds,
bison and other mammals, the Indian peoples, their dress, social and
religious customs, and the terrain of Florida. Also, it mentions the
heavily populated region of Coosa. The fact that the documents
were appended to Pedro Menéndez' contract shows he was an
inheritor of the knowledge of previous Spanish explorers.

As this last, most ambitious, and most costly of Spain's sixteenth-century efforts to master the vastness of Florida began, what
were the views and plans of its would-be conqueror? Before his
asiento (or contract) was issued, Pedro Menéndez told Philip II that
he believed North America was divided by two waterways. One,
arising in Newfoundland, joined the second, which led to New
Spain and thence to the South Sea. In March 1565 he told the head of
the Jesuit order that Florida adjoined New Spain, and Tartary and
China might possibly be reached through "an arm of the sea,"
through which, he was certain, one could go to the Spice Islands,
then back to Florida and Spain.[6]

Although Pedro Menéndez de Avilés is known to history as the
avenging arm of the Spanish Counter Reformation, who expelled
French intruders from his sovereign's North American lands, there
was more to his conquest of Florida than this. Menéndez had
developed a coherent schema for the exploitation, conversion, and
settlement of the whole continent. As a mariner—and a consum-
mate maritime strategist—he planned to consolidate his Florida
conquest by using its ports and waterways. But first he would secure

the coasts. His major cities, St. Augustine and Santa Elena, were set on the Atlantic to guard the Bahama Channel, lifeline of Spain's Indies commerce. After he discovered the Cuchiago Passage, shortening New Spain's voyages around the Dry Tortugas to Havana, he sought to avoid the dangerous Keys altogether by finding a cross-peninsular-Florida water route. Menéndez hoped to employ a fleet of *fragatas* on the St. Johns River, utilizing the great lake and exiting by the Caloosahatchee into the Gulf.[7] Through the sea-to-sea waterway, he could also reach the mines of Zacatecas and Guanajuato. Thus Menéndez hoped to engross the New Spain trade, in which he had a vested interest in his ships and licenses. As the *adelantado* stated, his purpose in Florida was "to fix our frontier lines here, gain the waterway of the Bahamas, and work the mines of New Spain."[8]

Pedro Menéndez also told his king of a plan to control the Newfoundland Banks by the use of twelve fast oar-sail craft and to levy tribute on foreigners who fished there, in waters he believed belonged to the Spanish crown. Later, probably in 1571, Menéndez sent his nephew, Pedro Menéndez Márquez, to Newfoundland.[9]

The Florida *adelantado* had a definite plan for evangelization of the Florida aboriginals. Years earlier, in Peru and New Spain, friars had perfected the *reducción* and *doctrina* for wholesale conversion of Indians to the Catholic faith, and Menéndez intended that the newly founded Jesuit order, fervent and increasingly influential, begin its New World mission in Florida. Moreover, regional centers would be established for Christianization of the children of Indian elites. At the same time, he signed tribute treaties with friendly Indian groups, attempting to substitute overall fealty to Philip II for local rivalries and thus pacify the land.

Both policies were challenged by the Indians' prior loyalties to the French and by the nature of many Indian cultures. Besides, many Indian groupings were more scattered in Florida than in other areas, which made them even more resistant to mass governance and reduction to settled units. In areas with greater populations, such as those of the eastern Timucua, rivalries among the major entities inhibited Spanish efforts.[10]

When his peninsular forts and missions (except that at St. Augustine) failed, the *adelantado* shifted his emphasis to the north. After the first expedition to the Carolina Banks came to naught, the Chesapeake (known to Spaniards as the Bay of the Mother of God) and a settlement within it (known as the Bay of Santa María) were chosen for a Jesuit mission. The entire territory (called the Land of

Santiago) was abandoned, however, when Indians murdered most of the missionaries. After the journeys of Juan Pardo into South Carolina, the city of Santa Elena became the "anchor port" of the inland northern effort.[11]

From 1568 to 1570, Pedro Menéndez de Avilés spent heavily of his substance to provide settlers for Santa Elena. The king had promised that an armed force of 150 soldiers would be underwritten by the crown, but his promise did not immediately materialize. Facing financial stress, Menéndez nevertheless gathered, supplied, and dispatched 273 settlers; he also sent hundreds of hogs, calves, and chickens to the settlers and provided seeds, tools, and vine shoots. By October of 1569, 327 persons were crowded into the little town of Santa Elena (now being excavated by archaeologist Stanley South, of the University of South Carolina, on Parris Island). From Pardo's reports, the *adelantado* knew there was good land in the interior, where, toward Guatari, he would build his estate, to justify the title of marquis of Oristán. Perhaps he could even equal Cortés in rich holdings and revenues.[12]

Pedro Menéndez was a visionary but, paradoxically, he was also practical. For years, with his associate Castillo in Cádiz, he had been in the sugar and hide trade with Hispaniola and Cuba. He had gained his income from freighting fees and the sale of ship licenses. But Menéndez and his followers also desired land: for gardens and for commercial agriculture. Although he erred in attempting sugar-cane culture in areas too far northward, vineyards apparently thrived in Santa Elena. (Archaeologist South has found what he believes to be evidence of vineyard ditches in the city.)

In the sixteenth century, cedar and other woods, and pitch and sassafras and furs were exported from Spanish Florida. In the seventeenth century, Spaniards in the Alachua savannah fulfilled Menéndez' vision by building and operating large cattle ranches on which beef, hides, and tallow were produced both for local consumption and export.[13]

In 1569, before the Council of the Indies, Pedro Menéndez argued for support of Florida by continuing the royal subsidy. That aid, he said, would encourage merchants to invest heavily in the land. Livestock would increase; he would plant mulberries for silk culture; and the area could be expected to produce naval stores. There was lumber ample for shipbuilding and for export, and inland settlements would utilize the fertile land for agriculture. When the Council approved the Florida subsidy in 1570, one, and possibly two, of eight *fragatas* Menéndez built for the royal armada were made in Florida.[14]

Captain Juan Pardo's explorations reached beyond the Appalachian Mountains, into the rich piedmont of northern Georgia and Alabama to areas that offered good settlement possibilities, and Pedro Menéndez, with news of the Pardo journeys and new resources in hand, planned to reach even farther. He pressed for and obtained (from Philip II) another "conquest contract," this time for Pánuco, the empty area between Florida and New Spain. He computed the distance from Santa Elena to the boundaries of New Spain at 500 leagues (not an altogether inaccurate estimate; a Spanish league of the sixteenth century was approximately 3 miles), and suggested to the Jesuits that they establish two missions along the overland route at a 200-league interval. After he obtained the Pánuco privilege in 1573, Menéndez settled its boundaries with the authorities of New Spain and New Galicia. According to a document found in the Notary's Archive of Madrid, Menéndez arranged for Luis de Velasco to handle details of the conquest from New Spain. In the meantime, to establish his cities (as at Santa Elena and St. Augustine), Menéndez utilized another long-established institution, the *consejo,* with its governing *cabildo.* This was the basic instrument for administering local justice and bringing order to conquered areas. It also governed the parceling out of land to Menéndez' associates (fellow Asturians who shared power in Spanish Florida) and to the settlers he had recruited in Estremadura and from nearby Toledo.[15]

To Santa Elena, which became the capital of Spanish Florida in the 1570s, Menéndez sent his wife, relatives, servants, and extensive household goods. After Menéndez became general of the new Royal Armada, his son-in-law, Diego de Velasco, served as lieutenant governor of Florida with headquarters in Santa Elena.[16]

After his death in 1574, a tangled inheritance was left to the children and associates of Pedro Menéndez and to the Spanish crown. Then, in 1587, with the final withdrawal of the Spaniards from their northern outpost at Santa Elena, his heirs claimed expenses of 949,000 ducats for the conquest of Florida. These claims were certainly extravagant (possibly in the order of two or three), but it is also clear that the Florida *adelantado* had incurred substantial expenses, and in the accounting of funds due or payable between the crown and Menéndez, the crown was in debt to the *adelantado*—even though the crown had spent some 350,000 ducats between

1565 and 1575 on the Florida conquest. Its most important expenditure over those ten years had been for defense in the Caribbean and the Caribbean area.[17]

Having considered the continuity in Spain's sixteenth-century North America conquest, let us examine the ways in which the last effort, of 1565 to 1577, was distinctive. For one, Pedro Menéndez, as a mariner, saw the large strategic value of the connection between the Bahama Channel passage, the Atlantic crossing, and the supposed "Strait to India." He understood the value of a shortcut across the Florida peninsula and interdiction of the Newfoundland fishing banks.

Secondly, he enjoyed the unusually long and close patronage of his king, which aided greatly in obtaining patents for settlement, ship licenses, and continued royal commitment. In spite of chronic problems with a mounting debt, Philip II spent heavily in Florida, and in 1570 he authorized a regular subsidy to support Pedro Menéndez' private efforts.

Menéndez put greater effort into settlement than his predecessors, and one of his cities, St. Augustine, has endured until today. In making his establishments, Menéndez had the advantage of the knowledge of all who had gone before him. In 1602, a visionary new governor of Florida, Gonzalo Méndez Canzo, projected expansions of Spanish Florida to the interior of Georgia and thence to New Spain. But as Philip II was dead, Méndez Canzo lacked the royal confidence that Menéndez had enjoyed, and times had changed. Spanish outreach was now discouraged. The reports of the *arbitristas* generally counseled retrenchment, not expenditure. Those who sought ways out of Spain's fiscal morass were in the ascendancy.[18]

This change in attitude is seen in a discourse by an unknown writer just after the close of the great century of Spanish enterprise. The *arbitrista* discussed the journeys of Cabeza de Vaca, Fray Marcos, Coronado, and the recent expeditions of Chamuscada, Antón de Espejo, and Juan de Oñate. The writer displays the growing knowledge of the North America continent, mixed with geographic ignorance, but his attitude is clear: he belittled the qualities of land in Florida. Speaking of the continent, he observed that "one may always justly say that a great part of it is unknown land, from the Cape of Labrador to that of Anian, but the southern half, of which . . . there is notice of old . . . does not offer great hopes of

160

riches or of greatness of empire." He recommended against a contract with anyone for its conquest, since "it seems that little will be gained."[19]

Spain's sixteenth-century attempted conquest of North America had featured intelligence gathering and long-continuing effort, but it fell short of full realization. Neither sea-to-sea waterways nor connecting lines of forts, missions, and cities spanned the North America continent. All the conquest entrepreneurs' costs, all the spending of the crown—possibly 1 million ducats for all parties— had gone for naught. Spanish sovereignty would be expunged by later events. But during this adventurous time, the North America enterprise was not an imperial sideshow in a scruffy borderland. It was a contest in a major arena for the conquest of a continent and was linked, across an exciting century, by substantial cultural and institutional bonds with the glories garnered in Peru and Mexico— lands where Spanish expectations were magnificently realized.

10 The Siege of Mobile, 1780, in Maps

William S. Coker and Hazel P. Coker

There are a number of excellent accounts of the Spanish siege of British Mobile in 1780.[1] The purpose of this study, therefore, is not to retell that familiar story but to provide a new dimension. Some histories of the siege include a map or two of Mobile Bay and its environs, showing the general location of Fort Charlotte and a few other principal landmarks, such as Dauphin Island, Mobile Point, and the major rivers that flow into the bay. Until 1981, no one had attempted a detailed presentation of the siege in maps, although the authors had used this approach with good results in studying the 1781 siege of Pensacola. They elected, therefore, in their reconsideration of the Anglo-Spanish confrontation at Mobile in 1780, to apply the same technique.[2]

With the end of the French and Indian War, Great Britain had eliminated France as a colonial power in North America. Spain lost Florida but received French Louisiana west of the Mississippi River, including the Isle of Orleans and the city of New Orleans, which lay south of the lakes (Borgne, Ponchartrain, and Maurepas and the Iberville River) and east of the Mississippi. Britain acquired everything else east of the Mississippi and north of the lakes. The British occupied Florida in 1763.

In 1764 Britain divided Florida into two colonies, East Florida and West Florida. East Florida, with its capital at St. Augustine, included all territory east of the Apalachicola River and south of the colony of Georgia. West Florida extended from the Apalachicola-Chattachoochee rivers to the Mississippi. The Gulf of Mexico and the line of lakes that separated the Isle of Orleans from British territory were its southern boundary. The northern boundary was set at 32°28' north latitude, or a line from the mouth of the Yazoo River to the Chattachoochee. West Florida included Pensacola, the capital; Manchac, Baton Rouge, Natchez, and Mobile were its principal towns or villages.[3] Campbell Town, a village about 10 miles north of Pensacola, founded by French Huguenots, existed briefly (from 1766 to 1770).[4]

British (mostly Scottish) merchants and traders along the east bank of the Mississippi and from Mobile and Pensacola, built a lucrative trade with the former French subjects of Louisiana and the few Spaniards and Anglos who came to the colony after 1763. For the most part, Spanish officials ignored this illegal British trade, but occasionally confiscated goods and ships and sold them at auction, much to the dismay of the merchants involved.[5] At the same time, Spaniards from Cuba fished and traded with the Indians in the Florida keys and along the Gulf Coast as far north as the Apalachicola River. British officials were not happy with the arrangement, but did little to interfere since British merchants were also trading in Havana and other Spanish Gulf and Caribbean ports.[6]

A series of military officers and civil officials governed West Florida between 1763 and 1770. Controversy and turmoil often marred their rule. One of these governors, John Eliot, committed suicide just one month after he arrived in Pensacola. Peter Chester, who reached the capital in August of 1770, remained in office for nearly eleven years, and was West Florida's last British governor. Parliamentary appropriations paid the cost of government in West Florida, and thus this province, as well as East Florida, escaped most of the problems that confronted the Northern colonies. In fact, East and West Florida became havens for loyalists who fled the thirteen colonies after the outbreak of the American Revolution in 1775.[7]

At first, the rebellious English colonies had to go it alone. But in 1778 France joined the Americans in the war against Britain and recognized the independence of the thirteen colonies. France wanted revenge for her losses to the British in 1763. Spain also wanted revenge, not only for her losses in 1763 but for those in 1713 as well, when Britain acquired Gibraltar. As early as 1776, moreover, both France and Spain had advanced funds for the manufacture of arms and ammunition for the colonies. The money was funneled through a fictitious French firm. Later, Spain used the commercial house of Diego de Gardoqui and Sons (of Bilbao) to ship materiel to Havana and New Orleans for the Americans. Nevertheless, for fear of the precedent it would set for her own American colonies, Spain was reluctant officially to recognize American independence. However, after efforts to negotiate a settlement of grievances with Great Britain failed, Spain declared war in 1779.[8]

As these events unfolded, Spanish Louisiana was experiencing difficulties of its own. Antonio de Ulloa first occupied the territory in 1766, but his stay was short lived when the former French subjects rebelled, forcing him to quit the colony. The arrival of General Alejandro O'Reilly in 1769 restored order, although the general's summary execution of five of the leaders of the rebellion earned him the sobriquet "Bloody O'Reilly."[9] In 1776, young Colonel Bernardo de Gálvez came to Louisiana as commander of the Louisiana Infantry Regiment. On January 1, 1777, he replaced O'Reilly's successor, Luis de Unzaga, as governor of Spanish Louisiana. Gálvez did not endear himself to the British when, a few months later, he seized 11 boats engaged in contraband trade and ordered the expulsion of all English subjects from Louisiana within two weeks.[10] The following year, 1778, after an American, Captain James Willing, raided British settlements on the east bank of the Mississippi, Gálvez opened New Orleans to Willing and permitted him to dispose of his plunder, mostly Negro slaves.

Gálvez anticipated that Spain would soon enter the war against Great Britain. In early 1778, he sent Captain Jacinto Panis to Mobile and Pensacola, ostensibly to assure the English of Spain's neutrality in the war between Britain and her American colonies, but in reality to report on military preparedness and fortifications there. Panis' report gave Gálvez confidence that Spanish arms would prevail, and word reached him in August of 1779 that Spain had declared war against Great Britain.[11]

Even before his British rival, General John Campbell, at Pensacola, received the news of the outbreak of war, Gálvez, on August 27, 1779, led an expedition from New Orleans against the British at Fort Bute on Bayou Manchac, just south of Baton Rouge. In a campaign notable for its brevity, Gálvez' forces captured Fort Bute and the fort at Baton Rouge. When Lieutenant Colonel Alexander Dickson surrendered Baton Rouge, he gratuitously included Fort Panmure at Natchez. In less than a month the Lower Mississippi Valley was in Spanish hands.[12]

Questions arose whether Mobile or Pensacola should be the next target. A victory at Pensacola might also deliver Mobile to the Spaniards. On the other hand, the Spaniards recognized that an attack upon Pensacola presented several difficulties: (1) the British had naval vessels at Pensacola with which to oppose an attack by sea; (2) the entrance to Pensacola Bay was defended by the British naval redoubt at Red Cliffs and, supposedly, by a battery on *Punta de Sigüenza*; (3) Pensacola might be able to secure assistance from Jamaica, and perhaps from Admiral John Byron's West Indies squadron.[13]

It is worth observing that Spanish planners consistently overestimated the British capability of defending Mobile and Pensacola. In reality, the British position at Pensacola in the fall of 1779 was far more vulnerable than indicated, and in view of Panis' intelligence report, it is surprising that Gálvez did not decide to attack Pensacola first.[14]

On the other hand, the capture of Mobile would bring several advantages:

1. Mobile was in a strategic position, only 50 miles or so from Pensacola and within 12 hours by boat—assuming favorable winds. After the fall of the posts on the Mississippi, Fort Charlotte (at Mobile) was the fort nearest Spanish Louisiana and a natural site from which to launch an attack upon the Spanish settlements on the Mississippi
2. Mobile supplied Pensacola with meat and provisions. Mobile, Gálvez said, did not need Pensacola, but Pensacola could hardly exist without supplies from Mobile. The capture of Mobile would also mean fresh meat for the Spanish troops.
3. The conquest of Mobile would interfere with—if not cut—communications between the British and the Choctaw and Chickasaw nations. Possession of Mobile would put the Spaniards in a better position to contact these Indians as possible allies.
4. The Spaniards believed that the French inhabitants of Mobile would welcome the Spanish presence. The French would also be a good source of information about the size of the garrison and the British defenses at Pensacola.

The principal objection to attacking Mobile centered on the strength of Fort Charlotte and its ability to resist the Spanish attack. Constructed of brick, Fort Charlotte was considered second only to Fort *San Juan de Ulúa* (at Veracruz) as the most formidable fort on the Gulf Coast.[15] (This was a gross overestimate of the fort's defensive capability; Panis' report in the previous year had described the fort as virtually in ruins.)[16] However, General Campbell had sent Captain Elias Durnford to Mobile in 1779 with orders to reconstruct Fort Charlotte, and Durnford had restored the fort's walls, replaced the rotted artillery platforms, and otherwise put the fort in the best condition that time and materials permitted.[17] (Later, Gálvez credited the fort's stout defense to the work completed under Durnford's supervision.) In any event, Fort Charlotte would have to be attacked at its most vulnerable point. Then, with Fort Charlotte in Spanish hands, the Spaniards could fall back upon Mobile if an attack upon Pensacola failed. Their forces could reach Mobile from Pensacola in three or four days, and the Spaniards believed they could defend Fort Charlotte against a force three times as great.

Since the pluses outnumbered the minuses, Gálvez decided upon Mobile, and from late September through December of 1779 the Spanish busily prepared their forces at New Orleans for the Siege of Mobile.[18] For the purpose of organizing the siege in maps, the period has been divided into seven phases:

1. Preparations for Mobile Campaign, August 17, 1779–January 11, 1780.
2. Expedition Sails from New Orleans to Mobile, January 12–February 9, 1780.
3. Expedition Puts In at Mobile Pass, February 9–17, 1780.
4. Reinforcements from Havana and Move to First Spanish Encampment, February 18–25, 1780.
5. Preliminary Negotiations with British and Move to Second Spanish Encampment, February 26–March 5, 1780.
6. Reinforcements from Pensacola and Construction of Spanish Battery, March 5–11, 1780.
7. Bombardment and Surrender of Fort Charlotte and Arrival and Departure of Spanish Fleet, March 12–May 20, 1780.[19]

One map, with accompanying legend, was selected for each of the seven phases of the siege.

Several anonymous contemporary maps served as guides for the location of the ships and fortifications on the maps presented here, but since the old maps contain obvious discrepancies, they were not followed in every detail. Two of the maps show a river, the Spanish River, some 2,000 Spanish *varas* (ca. 1,850 yards) south of Fort Charlotte.[20] A river never existed at that point, but, according to local tradition, a small bayou-like ravine had often filled with water in that area in years past. (Today, Spanish River is an eastern branch of the Lower Mobile River.) Occasionally, it proved impossible to pinpoint where some events occurred. Thus the authors selected the most probable sites for those events, based upon careful consideration of the evidence.

Finally, a word or two about the legends that accompany the maps. The letters *A, B, C,* etc. correspond to the letters on the page that follows the map. For the most part, the text was drawn from the diary of the siege prepared under the direction of Don Bernardo de Gálvez. There are several variant copies of the diary, and discrepancies have been indicated when appropriate.

Preparations for the Mobile Campaign,
August 17, 1779–January 11, 1780

January 10–11, 1780

A

On January 10, Gálvez appointed Colonel Gerónimo Girón commander of
the division and second in command of the expedition.

B

On the afternoon of January 11, Gálvez reviewed the troops as they boarded
ship at New Orleans.[21] (There were 754 troops, including regular military;
white, mulatto, and Negro militia; slaves; and Anglo-American auxiliaries.
The fleet consisted of a merchant frigate, four galleys, a packet boat, four
brigantines, a frigate of war, and a galliot.)[22]

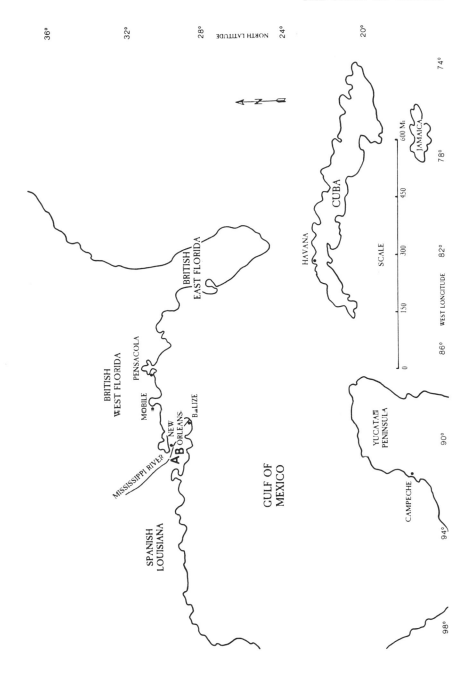

Expedition Sails from New Orleans to Mobile, January 12–February 9, 1780

January 20, 1780

A

In consultation with Lt. (Sr. Grade) Don Luis Lorenzo de Terrazas, the convoy officer, Gálvez decided to use the East Pass, which required that some ships be lightened to draw less than 12 feet of water.[23]

B

On the 20th, Oliver Pollock, agent of the Continental Congress in New Orleans, appointed Navy Capt. William Pickles to command the U.S. sloop *West Florida*, which mounted four 6 pounders and twelve swivel guns. It was provisioned for 60 days and had a crew of 58. Pollock directed Pickles to proceed to Ship Island and to join the Spanish fleet already en route to Mobile. Pickles was to assist Gálvez in the campaigns against Mobile and Pensacola for a period of 20 days, or longer if necessary. After he completed this assignment, Pickles was to go to Havana for a cargo of taffia and sugar (for use by the Continental Army), then convey it to Philadelphia—or another port that was safe from the enemy. Because Pickles had already distinguished himself in service on Lake Pontchartrain, the British subjects on the north shore of the lake had signed a capitulation that, Pollock believed, gave the Continental Congress a claim to that part of British West Florida. In sending Pickles to assist in the Pensacola campaign, Pollock reasoned that it would give the Continental Congress additional claims to territory in West Florida, and since Britain and Spain both considered Pensacola a prize, the Continental Congress might trade its claims at Pensacola for "some other valuable acquisiton."[24]

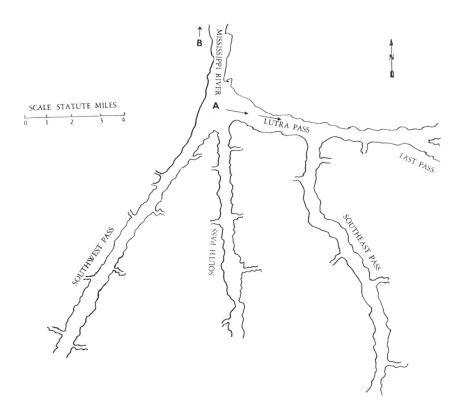

SCALE STATUTE MILES

0   1   2   3   4

B

MISSISSIPPI RIVER

A

LUTRA PASS

EAST PASS

N

SOUTHWEST PASS

SOUTH PASS

SOUTHEAST PASS

GULF OF MEXICO

William S. Coker and Hazel P. Coker

Expedition Puts In at Mobile Pass,
February 9–17, 1780

February 10–11, 1780

A

By 10:00 A.M. on the 10th, a hard southwest wind and heavy seas induced Gálvez to seek shelter in the bay.

B

With the *Volante* leading the way, followed by the *Gálvez*, the Spaniards entered the pass, intending also to capture the British ship. When the British crew recognized the Spaniards, it abandoned ship.

C

The *Volante* and *Gálvez* and four of the other ships ran aground on sandbars as they entered the pass.[25] All efforts failed to free the

D

Volante and two other ships; by 1:00 A.M. on the 11th the Spaniards had freed the *Gálvez*, which had suffered damage and was taking 9 inches of water an hour. Two of the other ships had also cleared the bar.[26]

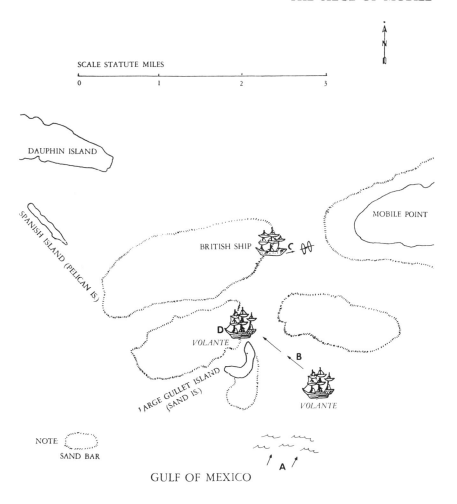

SCALE STATUTE MILES

0   1   2   3

DAUPHIN ISLAND

SPANISH ISLAND (PELICAN IS.)

MOBILE POINT

BRITISH SHIP   C

D

VOLANTE

B

VOLANTE

LARGE GULLET ISLAND
(SAND IS.)

NOTE:
SAND BAR

GULF OF MEXICO

A

173

Reinforcements from Havana and Move to First
Spanish Encampment, February 18–25, 1780

February 23–25, 1780

A

Preparations for the move continued on the 23d. The 24th and 25th were spent completing transfer of troops and supplies to Dog River, first of the Spanish encampments, 3 leagues south of Fort Charlotte.

B

Col. Girón and the engineer, Navas, reconnoitered and selected a site for the camp on the south bank of Dog River (in a clearing near the house of M. Orbanne de Mouy.)

C

Gálvez learned, on the 23d, that Charles Stuart,[27] the British Deputy Indian Commissary, had traveled with a party of Indians throughout the area, removing all the inhabitants' small craft. Another party had withdrawn all whites and Negroes, who were obliged to take up arms against the invaders. The British had been encouraged by false reports from two Spanish deserters that the Spaniards had lost 700 men.

D

The British burned and destroyed the houses, buildings, and livestock in the immediate vicinity of Fort Charlotte.

E

At midnight of the 25th, a Negro, who had escaped from the fort, went to the Spanish camp and confirmed the foregoing. He said there were only 300 men in Fort Charlotte.[28]

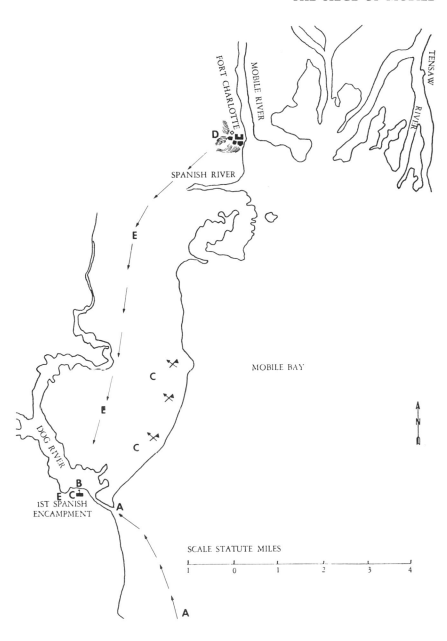

FORT CHARLOTTE

MOBILE RIVER

TENSAW RIVER

D

SPANISH RIVER

E

C

MOBILE BAY

E

C

N

DOG RIVER

B
E C
A
1ST SPANISH
ENCAMPMENT

SCALE STATUTE MILES

| 1 | | 0 | | 1 | | 2 | | 3 | | 4 |

A

A

William S. Coker and Hazel P. Coker

Preliminary Negotiations with British and Move to Second Spanish Encampment, February 26–March 5, 1780

March 2–3, 1780

A

Spanish troops were prepared to march on the 2nd, but a lookout reported that a force of 60 armed men had left the British fort. Gálvez ordered Col. Girón, with 200 men, to oppose the British troops, but Girón returned at 1:00 P.M. and reported that as soon as they were observed, the fort had sounded an alarm and the British had retired within Charlotte. Girón's force, however, captured the deputy Indian commissary, Charles Stuart.[29]

B

On the 2nd, the Spaniards moved to their new location, only 2,000 Spanish yards from Fort Charlotte.[30] The rest of the day, they transferred ammunition, provisions, and other materials from the old camp.

C

Several parties were sent out that night to cut off any troops that might be dispatched from the fort and to salvage everything possible from the abandoned houses (but since most of the houses had been burned, little was found).[31]

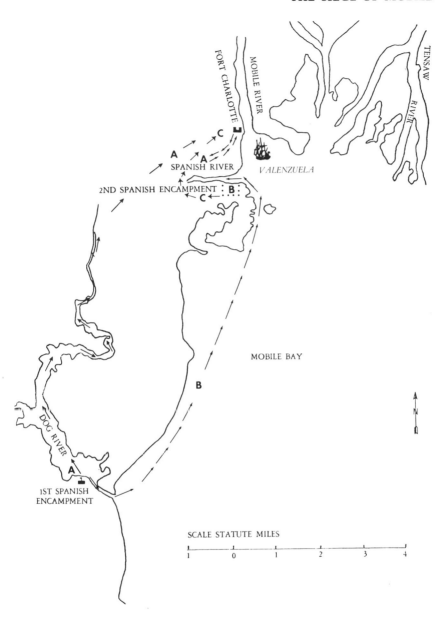

FORT CHARLOTTE

MOBILE RIVER

TENSAW RIVER

C

A A

SPANISH RIVER

VALENZUELA

2ND SPANISH ENCAMPMENT ∶ B ∶

C

MOBILE BAY

B

DOG RIVER

A

1ST SPANISH
ENCAMPMENT

N

SCALE STATUTE MILES

1   0   1   2   3   4

177

Reinforcements from Pensacola and Construction of Spanish Battery, March 5–11, 1780

March 9–10, 1780

A

Gálvez ordered 300 workmen (protected by 200 soldiers) to open the trench previously marked by Navas, and the work went so well that by 10:00 P.M. the men were under cover. They also erected a shoulder of fascines to conceal the yet-to-be-completed battery. Apparently the British did not observe all this activity, as they made no move to oppose the Spanish workforce.

B

Work on the battery proceeded rapidly on the morning of March 10. The British opened heavy fire from the fort, with cannon, carbines, and muskets, which lasted until 11:00 A.M. The Spaniards suffered 6 killed and 5 wounded, and suspended work until darkness fell.

C

That night, rain prevented the Spaniards from making much progress. Fire from the fort had decreased so noticeably that Gálvez feared the British were planning an assault on several fronts; but no assaults were launched.[32]

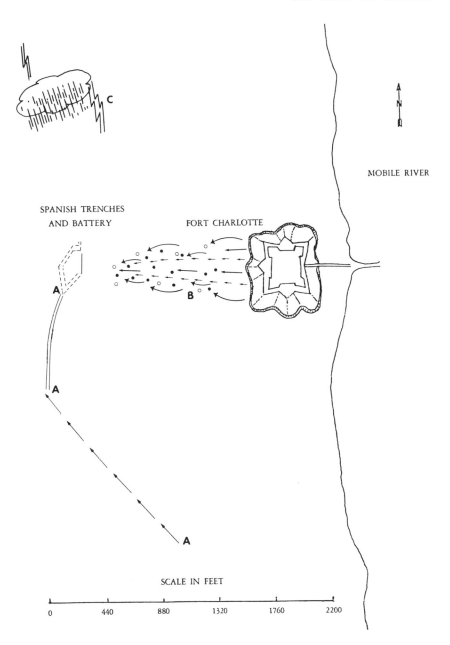

SPANISH TRENCHES
AND BATTERY

FORT CHARLOTTE

MOBILE RIVER

SCALE IN FEET

0   440   880   1320   1760   2200

Bombardment and Surrender of Fort Charlotte and Arrival and Departure of Spanish Fleet, March 12–May 20, 1780

March 15–19, 1780

A

On the 15th, scouts confirmed that General Campbell had been advancing to reinforce the fort when he heard of its surrender and returned to Pensacola.

B

Before he returned to Pensacola, Campbell left Capt. Patrick Strachan and his company of West Florida Royal Foresters behind to protect the British settlers in the area and to gather and drive cattle to Pensacola.

C

On the 17th, the Spaniards surprised and captured Strachan and 16 Royal Foresters.[33]

D

Campbell's troops reached Pensacola by March 19. In addition to Strachan's company and 4 men drowned at the Perdido, 3 of Campbell's men had deserted.[34]

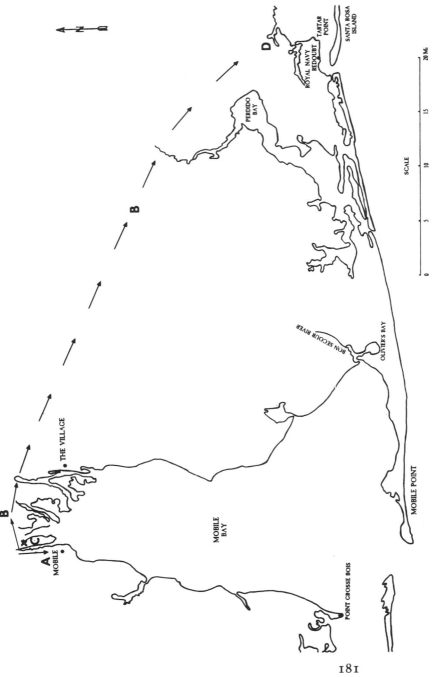

THE SIEGE OF MOBILE

MOBILE

THE VILLAGE

MOBILE BAY

POINT GROSSE BOIS

BON SECOUR RIVER

OLIVER'S BAY

MOBILE POINT

PERDIDO BAY

ROYAL NAVY REDOUBT

TARTAR POINT

SANTA ROSA ISLAND

SCALE

0   5   10   15   20 Mi.

The subsequent history of Mobile—after it fell to the Spaniards in 1780 until it became a part of the state of Alabama in 1819—represents in microcosm the transition of the Southeastern Borderlands from an area in dispute to incorporation into the new United States.

East and West Florida were ceded to Spain in 1783 at the Paris Peace Conference, but the treaty was silent on the boundaries of those colonies. The British, anticipating that they might retain West Florida, inserted a secret article in the treaty with the United States that the northern boundary would remain at 32°28' north latitude. If, however, Britain lost West Florida, the southern boundary would be at 31° north latitude, or about 100 miles farther south. Spain, believing Great Britain could hardly give away territory it did not possess (after the fall of Pensacola in 1781, Spain occupied all of West Florida), did not protest the boundary provisions between the British and the Americans. As a result, this area was claimed both by Spain and the United States from 1783 until 1795. Finally, in the Treaty of San Lorenzo in 1795, Spain waived its claim to this strip of land, which in 1798 became part of the Mississippi Territory.[35] The area south of the 31st parallel, including Mobile, remained a part of Spanish West Florida until 1810.

In 1803 the United States argued that everything west of the Perdido River and Perdido Bay was included in the Louisiana Purchase. Of course, the basis for this claim rested upon the belief that the United States had purchased French Louisiana as it existed prior to 1763. Whether the claim was valid was immaterial, because no amount of Socratic dialogue could long impede the march of American "Manifest Destiny." In the Proclamation of 1810 President James Madison stated that the territory between the Perdido and the Mississippi had been considered part of the colony of Louisiana ever since 1803.

In the same proclamation, Madison ordered Governor W. C. C. Claiborne of the Orleans Territory to occupy the area, and this was accomplished by the brief but successful revolution of 1810 at Baton Rouge, which created the short-lived Republic of West Florida. Until 1812, this area was part of the Territory of Orleans. The United States resisted the temptation of occupying Mobile between 1810 and 1812, although filibusterers nearly accomplished the occupation without official sanction. In spite of efforts by the Louisiana constitutional convention to include everything west of the Perdido in the new state of Louisiana, only that portion west of the Pearl River was made part of the state in 1812. (This section of Louisiana is still known as the "Florida parishes.") Mobile was incorporated into the Mississippi Territory in the same year.[36]

The War of 1812 finally gave the United States the excuse it needed to wrest Mobile from Spain. General James Wilkinson arrived at Mobile in April 1813 with forces far superior to those of his Spanish rival, Captain Cayetano Pérez. Unfortunately for the captain, and Spain, *Fuerte Carlota* (as the Spaniards called old Fort Charlotte) was in ruinous condition. With neither the manpower nor the gunpower to defend his command, Cayetano Pérez surrendered the fort and Mobile without firing a shot.[37] Soon afterward, Colonel John Bowyer erected a fort on Mobile Point to guard the entrance to the bay, and this little bastion saved the day for Mobile when it turned back British efforts to capture the point in September 1814. Fort Bowyer resisted the British again in early February 1815, after the Battle of New Orleans, but it capitulated on February 11. Two days after the British were victorious at Mobile Point, they learned that the treaty ending the War of 1812 had been signed. Thus Fort Bowyer protected Mobile on two occasions during the war.[38]

Mobile remained part of the Mississippi Territory until 1817, when the United States created the Alabama Territory. Two years later, Mobile became the principal seaport of the new state of Alabama.[39]

11 Approaches to the Study of the Southeastern Borderlands

Michael C. Scardaville

It is significant, and perhaps not entirely accidental, that this book on Alabama and the Borderlands deals with the least-studied area of all the former Spanish colonies in today's Sunbelt.[1] Many of us hope this signals a reawakening of interest in Alabama's Hispanic past, a story still locked up in the archives and still buried below ground.[2]

It also is appropriate to review the study of the Borderlands, since The University of Alabama Sesquicentennial coincided with the sixtieth anniversary of Herbert E. Bolton's seminal work, appropriately titled *The Spanish Borderlands: A Chronicle of Old Florida and the Southwest.*[3] Bolton, the eminent historian at Berkeley for over thirty years, is considered the father of Borderlands studies.[4] Although other late nineteenth- and early twentieth-century historians, such as Bernard Moses and William R. Shepherd, wrote sympathetically about Spanish settlement in the New World, Bolton became the foremost promoter in making North Americans aware of their Hispanic past.[5] He established the unofficial School of Borderland Studies and provided the concept, synthesis, and inspiration to generate research in this virgin field. Bolton and his disciples have produced an impressive amount of Borderland scholarship in the last six decades, and, in the process, effectively outlined the major thrust of Spain's role in what is now the United States. What Frederick Jackson Turner had done for the history of the West,

184

Bolton, a Turner student, did for the Spanish Borderlands, a frontier neglected by the Anglo-oriented Wisconsin historian.[6] All of us are indebted to Bolton and his followers for their pioneering studies.

Why have the Borderlands been treated as a separate field of historical investigation? What factors have motivated historians over the last sixty years to write about the role of Spain in what is today the United States? I would suggest at least three reasons. First and foremost is that Borderland historians have endeavored to document an unknown side of American history. To date their greatest contribution has been to offer a broader approach to the study of this country's past. Bolton and his successors intended to show that American history did not consist merely of the establishment and expansion of English settlements along the eastern seaboard of North America. Bolton deplored the fact that United States history "is written almost solely from the standpoint of the East and of the English colonies" and that "the importance of the Spanish period in American history has not yet been duly recognized."[7] Bolton was concerned that even the French received greater emphasis in American textbooks than the Spanish. He argued that "much more is known, for example, both to scholars and to the general public, of French rather than of Spanish activities in North America, and it is consequently assumed that the French influence was the more important of the two; but the reverse is true . . . (France's activities are more known) for the reason that France in America had a Parkman, while Spain in America had none."[8]

Bolton fully intended to correct this imbalance, and to publicize Spain's role in the Borderlands he devoted one-third of his 1920 textbook on the colonization of North America to the period before Jamestown.[9] Over the years, influenced by Bolton's missionary zeal, Borderlands historians have diligently attempted to offer a balanced view of Spain's contribution to the exploration and settlement of the continent.

The romance and excitement of Borderlands history also have attracted scholars and readers for decades. Historians have documented the exploits of discoverers, conquerors, missionaries, and other "colorful characters,"[10] and Bolton himself was captivated by Borderlands history, which he regarded as a "wonderland of romance, filled with figments of imagination" and wondrous stories about the Fountain of Youth, the Chicora Legend, Diamond Mountain, Gran Quivira, and the Seven Cities of Cíbola.[11] Ray Allen Billington, general editor of the Histories of the American Frontier

185

series, promoted John Francis Bannon's new synthesis on the Spanish Borderlands by describing the area as "rich with color and brimming with excitement (as must be any well-told tale of the *conquistadores* and mission fathers)."[12] And William Coker presented an enticing preview of Borderlands research a decade ago when he discussed the exploits of such frontier "schemers" as General James Wilkinson and Alexander McGillivray, who often "combined the qualities of heroes and villains" and, accordingly, appeal to our imagination and sense of adventure.[13]

A third (but least compelling) reason for study of the Borderlands is that Latin American historians wish to know more about the periphery or frontier of the larger Spanish-American empire. Although a number of prominent Latin Americanists, such as Arthur P. Whitaker and John Tate Lanning, wrote on Borderlands topics before the Second World War, most now view the Borderlands apart from Latin American history—as a subfield within United States history.[14] Until recently, with a few exceptions (such as John Te-Paske of Duke University), most historians of Latin America have ignored the Borderlands as an area of serious historical inquiry.[15] However, this rejection of Borderlands history by Latin American historians is not surprising, given Borderlands historians' avowed purpose of telling a neglected part of United States history. They even dismiss the potential contribution of Latin American historians in writing this history. For example, in attempting to explain the dearth of studies on Spanish Mississippi, one noted Borderlands scholar placed the blame not on Latin American historians but on American historians, who have focused their attention on the Civil War and prominent Mississippi authors.[16]

The three motivating factors, particularly the first two, for writing Borderlands history can easily be seen in the major themes of Borderlands research. Most Borderlands history is concentrated in three areas of study. The most-written-about and best-known era is the period of exploration and conquest. A multitude of studies, including those by Fanny and Adolph Bandelier, Arthur Aiton, Edward Bourne, F. W. Hodge and T. H. Lewis, Woodbury Lowery, Jeanette Thurber Connor, and Herbert I. Priestley, serve the dual purpose of documenting the role of Spain in exploring and establishing settlements in what is now the United States and of appealing to the imagination of the reader.[17] Several generations of schoolchildren have been told of the courageous exploits of Hernando de Soto and Cabeza de Vaca and of the founding (in 1565) of the oldest city in the United States, St. Augustine.

Another major Borderlands theme centers on the missionaries and their efforts to neutralize or control the frontier Indians, and historians such as Maynard Geiger and Michael Gannon have stressed the heroic deeds of early Catholic pioneers, paying particular attention to martyrs for the cause.[18]

As a group, international rivalry, diplomacy, and military affairs form the third principal theme, and have been warmly embraced by Borderlands historians. Studies by John Tate Lanning, Charles W. Arnade, Jack D. L. Holmes, Robert L. Gold, and many others document the diplomatic struggle for control of the "Debatable Land," as Bolton once called it.[19]

Borderlands historiography also has its share—perhaps a disproportionate one—of biographical studies on key figures in the Colonial Southeast. This technique has been unevenly used to examine such prominent historical characters as Pedro Menéndez de Avilés and other conquerors, as well as a number of Spanish governors, including Manuel Zéspedes in East Florida, Manuel Gayoso in the Mississippi Valley, and Bernardo de Gálvez in Louisiana. Although too many biographies border on hero worship, the better biographical accounts have been used to study a wide range of topics, including administrative, religious, military, and diplomatic history.[20]

These major areas or approaches to Southeastern Borderlands studies by no means exhaust all the topics examined by Borderlands historians. Research has been conducted on trade, immigration, medicine, drinking, and legal history, to name a few. However, such studies usually appear as articles, and generally represent isolated ventures into the archives.[21] They have not received the benefit of long-term, systematic research, necessary to present a better and more complete understanding of the topics. Occasionally, a book appears, such as Holmes's study of Governor Gayoso, which, through its life-and-times approach to biography, sheds light on political, economic, and social conditions in a frontier colony.[22] Such studies, however, are not common.

Despite the numerous histories of great men, major diplomatic and military events, and the advance into Indian territory, Borderlands scholarship suffers from traditionalist approaches to its subject matter. Contrary to Bolton's intentions, the nature and thrust of

Borderlands studies have contributed, though not intentionally, to an unbalanced approach to the study of Spain in America and thus to a misunderstanding of Hispanic society and its contribution to the development of this country.

To a certain extent, Borderlands historiography has contributed to the anti-Spanish "Black Legend" that permeated older historical works. By placing disproportionate attention on the exciting phase of exploration and conquest, with its romance and high adventure, Borderlands historians have left the impression that the Spanish came only for quick and greedy enrichment. Such emphasis on the early years in the Borderlands denigrates the Spaniards, who often are charged with cruelty, absence of morality, and indolence and basely contrasted with thrifty, moral, and hard-working English colonists. This stress on the exploits of the conquerors has ingrained certain Spanish stereotypes in the collective mind of North Americans, stereotypes that ignore the fact that such conquerors as Menéndez and Vázquez de Ayllón journeyed to the Borderlands to colonize and that most Hispanics worked diligently to survive on the fringes of the Spanish-American empire.

Disproportionate attention also has been given to missionaries, who are perceived as the principal social group on the expanding frontier. The Spanish friars *did* play a crucial role in certain colonies at different times, but they were not major characters *throughout* Southeastern Borderlands history. In Spanish Florida, for example, the so-called Golden Age of the missions lasted for only a half-century, out of 235 years of Spanish rule, although the amount of literature produced on the subject is impressive. We really do not know how the church and its officials were occupied during the other 185 years.

Diplomacy and military affairs also have received a disproportionate amount of attention by Borderlands scholars. Although international rivalry and armed conflicts are an important part of the Borderlands story, a great deal else was happening. We do not know what the soldiers were doing in the many years of peace.

Concentration on the traditional and romantic Borderlands themes has done an injustice to Bolton's goal of making North Americans aware of Spain's contribution to the settlement of this country, and, as we see in several college textbooks that are popular today, Borderlands historiography has reinforced the long-held stereotypes of Spanish cruelty, greediness, bigotry, and depravity. In general, the leading American history textbooks, assigned to millions of college students, dismiss the Spanish in a few paragraphs, before moving on to Jamestown and Plymouth Rock. Moreover, one gets the distinct impression that the English and Americans expanded west and south into vacant lands, except for those held by a few wild aboriginals.

In John A. Garraty's *The American Nation: A History of the United States*, the second most popular college-level textbook, the Spanish are portrayed—and briefly at that—as *conquistadores* and exploiters of Indians. Garraty attributes the Spanish drive to explore and settle to "greed for power, a sense of adventure, [and] the desire to Christianize the Indians." The graphics that accompany his text illustrate this anti-Spanish bias. Two watercolors depict "Spanish mistreatment of the Indians," and a map of North America makes no mention of St. Augustine, Pensacola, Mobile, New Orleans, Santa Fe, and other Spanish urban centers. Only Mexico City merits a black dot.[23]

The best-selling college textbook, *The National Experience: A History of the United States* (by John M. Blum, Edmund S. Morgan, Willie Lee Rose, Arthur M. Schlesinger, Jr., Kenneth M. Stampp, and C. Vann Woodward), is equally derelict in presenting a balanced view of Spain's role in the New World and the Borderlands.[24] Morgan, the author of the opening section, wrote that the

Spanish, who were the first on the scene, were also the first to see and seize the opportunities. They had happened on the most thickly populated areas, located in the tropics, and they soon put the masses of people there to work for them, digging out the things that Europeans valued most: gold, silver, pearls, and precious stones. For more than a century hardly anyone paid much attention to the most northerly lands that were to become the United States. The Spanish looked them over and could have taken them but did not bother. It was left to the English to plant themselves and begin to feel out the possibilities of life in the outsized forests and meadows along the Atlantic from present-day Maine to Georgia.[25]

Morgan, a revisionist historian, "revised" the Spanish out of United States history.

One last example of this insensitivity to Hispanics in the early Sunbelt is Henry F. Graff and John A. Krout's *The Adventure of the American People*. Summarizing the role of Spain in America, the authors conclude that

at the time only gold seemed worthwhile. In fact, the Spanish conquerors never took on the tasks of taming the forests and rivers of America and colonizing the land. Finding gold so easily and so early drove them madly on to look for more. They never found it, but the search left its mark on Spanish culture in the New World, and in its turn it also affected the mother country. . . . At home, the Spaniards failed to reinvest the gold and silver drawn from the mines of the New World. When they had used it up, Spain lived only on memories of its past. Gambling, always "hitting the jackpot," it left to others the richest prize of all—what later became the United States. How different our history might have been if our own abundant gold and silver deposits had been found first by the Spaniards![26]

This statement, by noted historians, is not merely an oversimplification and depreciation of Hispanic contributions to the New World but, frankly, an insult to people of Hispanic descent and to historians who have toiled long and hard to present the Spanish side of the story. In his study of Hispanophobia, Philip Wayne Powell correctly concludes that the

jaundiced views of the Hispanic world are taught very early in our schools and they are thoroughly inculcated by the time we enter college and university. If our students know any history at all when they reach college . . . , it is apt to be a naive, parochial version of United States development, in which Spain is honored by brief glimpses of Columbus, Balboa, Magellan, Cortés, Pizarro, De Soto, Coronado—interjected with Menéndez de Avilés butchering those virtuous French Huguenots in Florida.[27]

After this glance at leading American history textbooks, we, as students of the Borderlands, must ask ourselves if we have accomplished Bolton's goals of laying the basis for understanding between Anglo and Hispanic Americans, and of making North Americans aware of and sensitive to Hispanic culture and the participation of Hispanics in settling this land. If we conclude that we have failed, which I believe we have, we must ask what can be done to correct such deficiencies in the study of the Borderlands.

One possibility is to refocus Borderlands studies and strike out in new directions of scholarship. I question whether emphasis on great men and events has given us a better understanding of the nature and evolution of Hispanic American society in the United States. Surely Spain's contribution to North America was more than roving explorers, daring missionaries, brave soldiers, and conspiring diplomats. The major themes of exploration and conquest, conversion and pacification of Indians, and international rivalry certainly are major and legitimate themes in the history of the Borderlands, but, in their attempt to document these principal topics, historians generally have ignored the people who comprised the bulk of frontier society. What do we know about the countless thousands of Hispanics who migrated to the Borderlands, not for gold and Indian souls but to improve their lot? What do we know about the generations of Hispanics who built their homes on the frontier, raised families, tilled the soil, herded cattle, fished the seas, and in the process laid up an enduring cultural legacy? As Frances FitzGerald wrote in her study of American history textbooks, "the real distortion of the texts lay less in what they said about the Spanish than in what they did not say."[28] I believe Borderlands historiography is guilty of similar sins of omission.

A broader approach to the study of the Borderlands would balance our knowledge of this important aspect of history. Consciously, we should avoid the ways in which traditional Borderlands themes have been written, reinterpret them without the romance, and concentrate on more penetrating and longer-term analysis of Colonial frontier society and society as a whole. As a noted Southwestern Borderlands scholar realized, only through "the results of painstaking research [can we] enable our own people to understand other cultures better and to improve our knowledge of the enduring Spanish civilization as it actually was and still is in large part."[29] Only through such research can Borderlands historians provide scholarly refutation of Hispanic stereotypes and document the true nature of Hispanic society.

After sixty years, it is time to look beyond the standard themes and to examine the substance of society in the Borderlands. Numerous untouched or neglected topics are worthy of scholarly investigation that can provide deeper and better understanding of the role of Hispanics in the Colonial Southeast. Many of these topics have been suggested before, but I believe they bear repeating in the context of this essay.[30]

Despite studies on Southeastern Borderlands political institutions and officials, we do not have a comprehensive understanding of the frontier political structure, from local government to the governor's office. A model for such an approach is John J. TePaske's study of the governorship of Florida in the first half of the eighteenth century, in which he demonstrates considerable flexibility in the Colonial bureaucracy.[31] Similar studies in other colonies, and for other periods in Florida history, might indicate other examples of political latitude. Such research should correct the prevailing

"Anglo" misunderstanding of a monolithic bureaucracy that controlled the daily lives of frontier settlers.

After sixty years of research, historians know very little about the economic development of the Southeastern Borderlands. Studies of frontier economies might show that the Spanish were motivated by more than greed for gold, and that the peripheral colonies were not as unexploited as is often assumed. For example, oranges, a staple of the Florida economy in the twentieth century, were exported from that Spanish colony as early as the 1720s, and livestock and timber products, two other mainstays of the state's modern economy, were exported as early as the mid-seventeenth and eighteenth centuries, respectively. Systematic studies are needed on such topics as trade and commerce, agriculture, ranching, and (for Louisiana) industrial development. Other areas of study that would yield greater insight into the nature of the Colonial economies are taxation and tribute, the *situado* or subsidy system, labor (free, convict, and slave), wages, public works projects, the plantation system, and land tenure. Contrary to statements of the eminent historian Edmund Morgan, the English and Americans did *not* find a virgin wilderness when they gained control of the Spanish Borderlands.

The social history of the Southeastern Borderlands also awaits the attention of historians. We still are largely unaware of how people survived on the frontier from day to day. Topics that would better document the life of the common settler include subsistence patterns, medical practices, recreation, education, and social customs. To gain a clearer understanding of the composition of frontier society, studies are needed on demography, ethnicity, family patterns, social status, and social mobility. Research on crime and social unrest would offer better insight into the problems and stability of frontier life.

Two other fruitful topics await study that embodies political and economic, as well as social, history. Urban studies, of growing concern for historians of Latin America and the United States, have been neglected in the Borderlands. Hamilton's study of colonial Mobile is woefully inadequate since it largely ignored Spanish source materials; and other settlements, such as Natchez, have received only cursory treatment in the form of articles.[32] In the 125 years since Buckingham Smith first studied Spanish Florida, not one historian has attempted a comprehensive analysis of the nation's oldest city. St. Augustine generally merits attention only for when it was founded, attacked, or abandoned.[33] We have no idea how this largest and most strategically important Borderlands community evolved through time.[34]

Another broad topic that is worthy of investigation is adaptation to the frontier environment. It would be interesting to know how Spanish and Spanish-American institutions and practices, such as the family, local government, subsistence patterns, and ideas of social mobility, evolved and became transformed on the periphery of the New World empire. Given the interplay of Indians, Hispanics, French, and English in the Colonial Southeast, cultural change offers a fascinating topic of study.

In short, Borderlands historians need to study not merely the great men of the frontier but the common man as well, just as United States historians have given more attention to the common settler in the English colonies. One Southwestern historian to realize this is Oakah L. Jones of Purdue University, who recently wrote that

few historians have studied the role of the settlers in these frontier provinces. Instead, they have contributed important works on government officials and institutions of the presidial system and military affairs, and the work of the Church and its missionaries. I have chosen to concentrate on the civilian settler—the farmer, day laborer, stockman, and artisan—to depict his importance in the frontier expansion of New Spain.[35]

The Southeastern Borderlands is still waiting for its Jones—for a study of the frontierman and family, for an analysis of the true nature of Hispanic society on the periphery of the empire.

However, there is hope. Factors are at work that will encourage and facilitate new directions and approaches to study of the Southeastern Borderlands. Within the last five years there has been a growing tendency to include this area within the mainstream history of the Spanish-American empire, treating it not as a borderland between several cultures but as a frontier region in the overall plans and needs of the Spanish imperial system. Bolton saw the validity of studying the Borderlands as part of Spanish America. In his famous address to the American Historical Association in 1932, he stated that

many of the new discoveries [in research] do not fit into the nationalistic pattern. In the old synthesis their significance is lost. In a larger framework,

193

on the other hand, many things which have seemed obscure and secondary become outstanding and primary. This applies especially to borderland researches.[36]

Two recent studies merit special attention. Eugene Lyon's outstanding account of the conquest of Florida downplays the story of heroic exploits in favor of better understanding of the nature of Spanish expansion and Spanish attitudes toward the colonies. In his book on defense policies in the West Indies in the sixteenth century, Paul Hoffman (of Louisiana State University) puts the defensive posture of sixteenth-century Florida in a larger and more proper international and imperial perspective. He avoids the mistake of isolating military topics from the larger patterns in Caribbean, North American, and European events.[37] Moreover, a new generation of Spanish historians, not moved to treat the Borderlands as part of United States history, recently published some pioneering works on Borderlands topics. Pablo Tornero and Antonio Acosta, both of the University of Seville, have examined (1) the economic dependency of Florida in the late Colonial period and (2) the demography of Louisiana in the eighteenth century.[38] There is little doubt that these four North American and Spanish historians have contributed to making the Borderlands again "respectable" for historians of Latin America.

Another factor that should encourage a broader approach to study of the Southeastern Borderlands is the growing accessibility of documentary sources. One axiom of historical scholarship is that research is molded by the extent and nature of source materials, and the Stetson Collection at the P. K. Yonge Library of Florida History, at the University of Florida—150,000 photostats of documents from Spanish archives—is strong in the early years of settlements, missionary activities, catastrophes, and administrative matters. Yet this highly selective collection contains little information on the daily life of the common settler on the Florida frontier. Broader study of the Borderlands requires that new and unused sources be more systematically consulted, such as parish registers, notary and chancery records, slave papers, land-grant and survey records, criminal and civil suits, and ship and estate inventories—among others.

A series of calendar and acquisition projects of Spanish Borderlands documents at several institutions, including P. K. Yonge, the University of West Florida, Loyola University, and Louisiana State

Museum, should encourage and greatly facilitate use of these important records. Currently, P. K. Yonge is preparing an index for 1 million frames of microfilm from such important collections as the East Florida Papers and the Papeles Procedentes de Cuba, and the number of catalog cards will increase as the library acquires microfilm from Spanish archives.[39] Research on Colonial Louisiana will be greatly aided by the indexing of a half-million original manuscript pages stored in the Louisiana Historical Center at Louisiana State Museum.[40] These acquisitions and calendar projects, combined with the increased cost of international travel, might induce scholars to use these important, locally available sources, which have been overlooked. As one historian said, "There is a sense in which archives are not discovered or organized until there is a compulsion to do so."[41]

Despite my pleas to delve into archives with renewed vigor, I must temper my comments in the realization that traditional archival research alone cannot provide the data to study the nature of Hispanic society in the Borderlands adequately. What is needed most is a multidisciplinary approach to examining the frontier, relying particularly on historical archaeology. Historians must admit the limitations of their sources and realize that historical archaeology is essential where documentation is weak or absent. Also, it allows greater insight than written records alone. In the last decade, archaeologists, such as Charles Fairbanks and Kathleen Deagan of the University of Florida, have pioneered studies on such topics as diet, acculturation, racial interaction, recreation, clothing, and even mortuary practices.[42] Bolton himself, a supporter of archaeological research, would chastise historians who choose to ignore the work of historical archaeologists in the Southeast.[43]

A recently formed organization, the Southeast Borderlands Association, is attempting to dissolve disciplinary barriers that have hampered a broader and more complete treatment of Borderlands history. Its purpose is to promote study of the Southeastern Borderlands by encouraging multidisciplinary approaches and greater regional cooperation and awareness of documentary sources. To date, the organizers of the association have identified at least 400 historians, archaeologists, geographers, ethnohistorians, architects, archivists, librarians, and others who are interested in the Colonial Southeast.

One last factor that I hope will encourage Borderlands studies is

Michael C. Scardaville

the Columbus celebration in 1992. As evidenced by the popularity of the Bicentennial and the Gálvez exposition in Pensacola, North Americans are a "commemorative people." Major historical events spark popular interest, popular interest generates funding, and funding encourages research on themes that center on major events. Combined with growing awareness among Hispanics of this country's heritage, I believe the 1992 celebration can serve as a catalyst to a renaissance of solid Borderlands studies.

Notes

Chapter 1
"Trends and Trajectories in American Archaeology" by Richard A. Krause

1. James J. F. Deetz, *Invitation to Archaeology* (New York: Natural History Press, 1967), 3ff.
2. Brian M. Fagan, *People of the Earth* (3d ed.; Boston: Little, Brown, 1980); James J. Hester and James Grady, *Introduction to Archaeology* (2d ed.; New York: Holt, Rinehart and Winston, 1982), 321–422.
3. See Jane E. Buikstra, *Hopewell in the Lower Illinois Valley: A Regional Study of Human Biological Variability and Prehistoric Mortuary Behavior*, Northwestern Archaeological Program Scientific Papers, 2 (Evanston: Northwestern University Press, 1976).
4. Gordon R. Willey and Philip Phillips, *Method and Theory in American Archaeology* (Chicago: Phoenix Books, 1958), 1–7.
5. Ibid., 200–05.
6. Lynne G. Goldstein, *Mississippian Mortuary Practices: A Case Study of Two Cemeteries in the Lower Illinois Valley*, Northwestern University Archaeological Program Scientific Papers, 4 (Evanston: Northwestern University Press, 1980), 13.
7. Willey and Phillips, *Method and Theory*, 183.
8. See William T. Sanders and Barbara J. Price, *Mesoamerica: The Evolution of a Civilization* (New York: Random House, 1968).
9. Joseph R. Caldwell, *Trend and Tradition in the Prehistory of the Eastern United States*, Illinois State Museum Scientific Papers, 10, and American Anthropological Association Memoirs, 88 (Menasha, 1958), iv.
10. Guy Gibbon, "A Model of Mississippian Development and Its Implications

for the Red Wing Area," in *Aspects of Upper Great Lakes Anthropology*, ed. Elden Johnson (Duluth: Minnesota Historical Society, 1974).

11. Caldwell, *Trend and Tradition.*

12. See James B. Griffin, "Changing Concepts of the Prehistoric Mississippian Cultures of the Eastern United States," in this volume.

13. R. Bonnichesen, "Critical Arguments for Pleistocene Artifacts from the Old Crow Basin, Yukon: A Preliminary Statement," and R. Berger, "Thoughts on the First Peopling of America and Australia," in *Early Man in America from a Circum-Pacific Perspective*, ed. Alan L. Bryan (Edmonton: University of Alberta Press, 1978); Emerson Greenman, "The Upper Paleolithic of the New World," *Current Anthropology*, 4, no. 1 (1963), 41–91; Kobayashi Hayashi, "The Fukui Microblade Technology and Its Relationship in Northeast Asia and North America," *Arctic Anthropology*, 5, no. 1 (1968), 128–90; Richard S. MacNeish, "Early Man in the Andes," *Scientific American*, 224, no. 4 (1971), 36–46; Paul S. Martin, "The Discovery of America," *Science*, 79 (1973), 969–74; David M. Hopkins, "The Cenozoic History of Beringia—A Synthesis," and Hansjurgen Muller-Beck, "On Migrations of Hunters across the Bering Land Bridge in the Upper Pleistocene," both in *The Bering Land Bridge*, ed. David M. Hopkins (Stanford: Stanford University Press, 1967).

14. See Hester and Grady, *Introduction to Archaeology*, 328–42.

15. Ibid., 338–41.

16. MacNeish, "Early Man in the Andes," 36–46; Gordon Willey, *An Introduction to American Archeology*, vol. 2 (Englewood Cliffs, N.J.: Prentice-Hall, 1971).

17. MacNeish, "Early Man in the Andes," 36–46.

18. Willey, *An Introduction to American Archeology*, vol. 1 (Englewood Cliffs, N.J.: Prentice-Hall, 1966).

19. Hannah M. Wormington, *The Ancient Hunters and Gatherers of the Americas* (New York: Academic Press, n.d.).

20. John Cotter, "The Occurrence of Flints and Extinct Animals in Pluvial Deposits near Clovis, New Mexico," *Proceedings of the Academy of Natural Sciences of Philadelphia*, 89 (1937), 2–16; Elias H. Sellards, "Early Man in America: Index to Localities and Selected Bibliography," *Bulletin of the Geological Society of America*, 51 (1940), 29–31; Hannah M. Wormington, *Ancient Man in North America* (4th ed.; Denver: Denver Museum of Natural History, 1957).

21. Waldo R. Wedel, *Prehistoric Man on the Great Plains* (Norman: University of Oklahoma Press, 1961), 58–59.

22. Emil W. Haury, "Artifacts with Mammoth Remains, Naco, Arizona," *American Antiquity*, 19, no. 1 (1953), 1–4; Emil W. Haury, E. B. Sayles, and William W. Wasley, "The Lehner Mammoth Site, Southeastern Arizona," *American Antiquity*, 25, no. 1 (1959), 2–39; Wedel, *Prehistoric Man on the Great Plains*, 58–59.

23. Morris F. Skinner and O. C. Kaiser, "The Fossil Bison of Alaska and Preliminary Revision of the Genus," *Bulletin of the American Museum of Natural History*, 39 (1947), 171.

24. Wedel, *Prehistoric Man on the Great Plains*, 60–65.

25. Ernest Antevs, "Geologic-Climatic Dating in the West," *American Antiquity*, 20, no. 4 (1955), 317–35; E. Deevey and Richard Flint, "Postglacial

Hypsithemal Interval," *Science*, 125 (1957), 3240; Richard Flint, *Glacial Geology and the Pleistocene Epoch* (New York: John Wiley, 1947); George I. Quimby, "Cultural and Natural Areas before Kroeber," *American Antiquity*, 19, no. 4 (1954), 318–19.

26. Michael D. Coe, *Mexico* (New York: Praeger, 1962), 43–45.

27. Bryan O. K. Reeves, "The Concept of an Altithermal Cultural Hiatus in Northern Plains Prehistory," *American Anthropologist*, 75, no. 5 (1973), 1227; Waldo R. Wedel, "The Prehistoric Plains," in *Ancient Native Americans*, ed. Jesse D. Jennings (San Francisco: W. H. Freeman, 1978), 196.

28. W. Raymond Wood and R. Bruce McMillan, eds., *Prehistoric Man and His Environments: A Case Study in the Ozark Highland* (New York: Academic Press, 1976).

29. Thomas M. N. Lewis, *A Suggested Basis for Paleo-Indian Chronology in Tennessee and the Eastern United States*, Southern Indian Studies, 5 (Chapel Hill: University of North Carolina Press, 1934), 11–13.

30. See Richard S. MacNeish, *The Nonceramic Artifacts*, vol. 2 of *The Prehistory of the Tehuacan Valley* (Austin: University of Texas Press, 1967); MacNeish, "The Origins of New World Civilization," *Scientific American*, 211, no. 5 (1964), 29–37; MacNeish, "Ancient Mesoamerican Civilization," *Science*, 143 (1964), 531–37.

31. Michael D. Coe, *The Maya* (New York: Praeger, 1966), 42; Norman Hammond, "The Earliest Maya," *Scientific American*, 236 (1977), 116–23.

32. Ibid., 42–46.

33. Robert Carneiro, "A Theory of the Origin of the State," *Science*, 169, no. 3947 (1970), 733–38.

34. Kent V. Flannery, "The Olmec and the Valley of Oaxaca," in *Dumbarton Oaks Conference on the Olmec* (Washington, D.C.: Dumbarton Oaks Research Library and Collection, Harvard University, 1968); William J. Rathje, "The Origin and Development of Lowland Classic Maya Civilization," *American Antiquity*, 36, no. 3 (1971), 275–85; William T. Sanders, "Hydraulic Agriculture, Economic Symbiosis, and the Evolution of States in Central Mexico," in *Anthropological Archaeology in the Americas*, ed. Betty J. Meggers (Washington, D.C.: Anthropological Society of Washington, 1968).

35. Philip Drucker, Robert F. Heizer, and Robert J. Squier, *Excavations at La Venta Tabasco*, Bureau of American Ethnology Bulletin 170 (Washington, D.C.: G.P.O., 1959); Mathew W. Stirling, *An Initial Series from Tres Zapotes, Vera Cruz, Mexico*, National Geographic Society Contributed Technical Papers, 1 (Washington, D.C.: National Geographic Society, 1940).

36. Roman Piña Chan, *Tlatilco*, 2 vols. (Mexico City: Instituto Nacional de Anthropologia e Historia, 1958); Sigvald Linne, *Archaeological Researches at Teotihuacan, Mexico* (Stockholm: Ethnographical Museum of Sweden, 1934); Eric R. Wolf, *Sons of the Shaking Earth* (Chicago: Phoenix Books, 1959); Coe, *The Maya*.

37. René Millon, "Teotihuacan: Completion of Map of Giant Ancient City in the Valley of Mexico," *Science*, 170 (1970), 1077–82.

38. Coe, *Mexico*, 115.

39. Hester and Grady, *Introduction to Archaeology*, 357–62.

40. Julian B. Steward, *Basin-Plateau Aboriginal Socio-Political Groups*, Bureau of American Ethnology Bulletin, 120 (Washington, D.C.: G.P.O., 1938);

David H. Thomas, "An Empirical Test for Steward's Model of Great Basin Settlement Patterns," *American Antiquity*, 38 (1973), 155–76.

41. Alfred Kidder, *An Introduction to the Study of Southwestern Archaeology with a Preliminary Account of the Excavations at Pecos* (New Haven: Yale University Press, 1968).

42. Waldo R. Wedel, "The Great Plains," in *Prehistoric Man in the New World*, ed. Jesse D. Jennings and E. Norbeck (Chicago: University of Chicago Press, 1964).

43. See ibid., 88–94.

44. Ibid., 94ff.

45. See Donald J. Lehmer, "Climate and Culture History in the Middle Missouri Valley," in *Pleistocene and Recent Environments of the Central Great Plains*, ed. Wakefield Dort, Jr. and J. Knox Jones, University of Kansas Special Publication 3 (Lawrence: University of Kansas Press, 1970), and *Introduction to Middle Missouri Archaeology*, National Park Service Anthropological Papers, 1 (Washington, D.C.: G.P.O., 1971).

46. George I. Quimby, "Cultural and Natural Areas before Kroeber," *American Antiquity*, 19, no. 4 (1954), 318–19.

47. Lewis, *A Suggested Basis for Paleo-Indian Chronology in Tennessee and the Eastern United States*.

48. Caldwell, *Trend and Tradition in the Prehistory of the Eastern United States*, vii.

49. See ibid., 23–59.

50. Ibid., 64, and Griffin, "Changing Concepts of the Prehistoric Mississippian Cultures of the Eastern United States."

51. Irving B. Rouse, "The Inference of Migrations from Anthropological Evidence," in *Migrations in New World Culture History*, ed. Raymond H. Thompson (Tucson: University of Arizona Press, 1958), 63–68.

52. Rouse, "The Inference of Migrations from Anthropological Evidence."

53. Bruce D. Smith, ed., *Mississippian Settlement Patterns* (New York: Academic Press, 1978), 486. See also chapter 3, this volume.

54. See R. Lewis, *Mississippian Exploitative Strategies: A Southeast Missouri Example*, Missouri Archaeological Society Research Series, 11 (Columbia: Missouri Archeological Society, 1974).

55. Robert H. Lafferty III, "An Analysis of Prehistoric Southeastern Fortifications" (thesis, Southern Illinois University, 1973).

56. Lewis H. Larson, Jr., "Functional Considerations of Warfare in the Southeast during the Mississippian Period," *American Antiquity*, 37, no. 3 (1972), 383–92.

57. Lehmer, *Introduction to Middle Missouri Archaeology*.

58. Kidder, *An Introduction to the Study of Southwestern Archaeology with a Preliminary Account of the Excavations at Pecos*.

59. Griffin, "Changing Concepts of the Prehistoric Mississippian Cultures of the Eastern United States."

60. See Caldwell, *Trend and Tradition*.

61. See James A. Brown, ed., *Approaches to the Social Dimensions of Mortuary Practices*, Memoirs of the Society of American Archaeology, 25 (Washington, D.C.: Society of American Archaeology, 1971).

62. Christopher S. Peebles, "Moundville: The Social Organization of a Prehis-

toric Community and Culture" (Dissertation, University of California at Santa Barbara, 1974).
63. Charles Hudson, *The Southeastern Indians* (Knoxville: University of Tennessee Press, 1976); Christopher S. Peebles and Susan Kus, "Some Archaeological Correlates of Ranked Societies," *American Antiquity,* 42, no. 3 (1977), 421–48.
64. Peebles, "Moundville: The Social Organization of a Prehistoric Community and Culture."
65. Frank T. Schnell, Vernon J. Knight Jr., and Gail S. Schnell, *Cemochechobee: Archaeology of a Mississippian Ceremonial Center on the Chattahoochee River* (Gainesville: University Presses of Florida, 1981).
66. Elman R. Service, *The Origins of the State and Civilization: The Process of Cultural Evolution* (New York: Norton, 1975), 78.
67. See Smith, *Mississippian Settlement Patterns.*
68. Craig Sheldon, "The Mississippian-Historic Transition in Central Alabama" (Dissertation, University of Oregon, 1974).
69. Christopher S. Peebles, "Moundville and Beyond: Some Observations on the Changing Social Organization in the Southeastern United States," 69th Annual Meeting of the American Anthropological Association, 1970.

Chapter 2
"Changing Concepts of the Prehistoric Mississippian Cultures" by James B. Griffin

1. Thomas Maxwell, "Tuskaloosa, the Origin of Its Name, Its History, etc." (paper presented before Alabama Historical Society, Tuscaloosa, 1876).
2. *Proceedings of the National Research Council Conference on Southeastern Pre-History, December 1932* (Washington, D.C.: N.R.C., 1933).
3. David L. DeJarnette and Steven B. Wimberly, *The Bessemer Site: Excavation of Three Mounds and Surrounding Village Areas near Bessemer, Alabama,* Geological Survey of Alabama Museum, Paper 17 (University: Geological Survey of Alabama, 1941).
4. Robert Wauchope, *Lost Tribes and Sunken Continents* (Chicago: University of Chicago Press, 1962), 3.
5. See David M. Hopkins, *The Bering Land Bridge* (Palo Alto: Stanford University Press, 1967).
6. Henry M. Brackenridge, *Views of Louisiana Together with a Journal of a Voyage up the Missouri River in 1811* (1814; rtp., Chicago: Quadrangle Books, 1962).
7. Ibid., 188.
8. Ibid., 184.
9. Frederick Ward Putnam, *Archaeological Explorations in Tennessee,* Eleventh Annual Report of the Peabody Museum, 2, no. 2 (1878), 305–60.
10. Cyrus Thomas, *The Mound Explorations of the Bureau of American Ethnology, Twelfth Annual Report, 1890–91* (Washington, D.C.: G.P.O., 1891), 3–730.
11. Ibid., 596.
12. William H. Holmes, *Ancient Pottery of the Mississippi Valley,* 4th Annual Report, 1882–83 (Washington, D.C.: G.P.O., 1886), 367–436.

13. Holmes, *Ancient Pottery of the Mississippi Valley.*
14. William H. Holmes, *Aboriginal Pottery of the Eastern United States,* Bureau of American Ethnology, 20th Annual Report, 1898–99 (Washington, D.C.: G.P.O., 1903), 1–237.
15. William H. Holmes, "Areas of American Culture Characterization Tentatively Outlined as an Aid in the Study of Antiquities," *American Anthropologist,* 16, no. 3 (1914), 413–46.
16. Gates P. Thruston, *The Antiquities of Tennessee and the Adjacent States* (Cincinnati: Robert Clarke, 1890).
17. Ibid., 357.
18. Clarence B. Moore, "The Antiquities of the Ouachita Valley," *Journal of the Academy of Natural Sciences of Philadelphia,* 14 (1909), 13.
19. Moore, "Antiquities of the St. Francis, White and Black Rivers, Arkansas," *Journal of the Academy of Natural Sciences of Philadelphia,* 14 (1910), 259.
20. Moore, "Some Aboriginal Sites on the Mississippi River," *Journal of the Academy of Natural Sciences of Philadelphia,* 14 (1911), 370–71.
21. Henry C. Shetrone, *The Mound Builders* (New York: D. Appleton, 1931), 354.
22. *Proceedings of the National Research Council Conference on Southeastern Pre-history* (1933).
23. James E. Pearce, "The Significance of the East Texas Archaeological Field," in *Proceedings of the National Research Council Conference on Southeastern Pre-history* (1933).
24. *Proceedings of the National Research Council Conference on Southeastern Pre-history* (1933), fig. 7.
25. James A. Ford and Gordon Willey, "An Interpretation of the Prehistory of the Eastern United States," *American Anthropologist,* 43, no. 3 (1941), 325–63.
26. Thorne Deuel, "Basic Cultures of the Mississippi Valley," *American Anthropologist,* 37 (1935), 429–45; Anson Simpson, "Kingston (Illinois) Focus of the Mississippi Culture," *Papers in Anthropology, Transactions of the Illinois Academy of Science,* 27, no. 2 (1934), 25.
27. William C. McKern, "The Midwestern Taxonomic Method as an Aid to Archaeological Culture Study," *American Antiquity,* III, no. 4 (1939), 301–14.
28. *Proceedings of the Indianapolis Archaeological Conference,* Committee on State Archaeological Surveys, Division of Anthropology and Psychology (Washington, D.C: N.R.C., 1936).
29. Thorne Deuel, "The Application of a Classificatory Method to Mississippi Valley Archaeology," in *Rediscovering Illinois,* by Fay Cooper Cole and Thorne Deuel (Chicago: University of Chicago Press, 1937).
30. James B. Griffin, "A Commentary on Some Archaeological Activities in the Mid-Continent, 1925–1975," *Midcontinental Journal of Archaeology,* 1, no. 1 (1976), 27–30.
31. Griffin, "Culture Periods in Eastern United States Archeology," in *Archeology of Eastern United States,* ed. J. B. Griffin, (Chicago: University of Chicago Press, 1952).
32. Ford and Willey, "An Interpretation of the Prehistory of the Eastern United States."

33. James B. Griffin, "Culture Change and Continuity in Eastern United States," in *Man in Northeastern North America*, ed. Frederick Johnson and Robert S. Peabody (Andover: Phillips Academy Foundation, 1946), 75–76.
34. Griffin, "Culture Change and Continuity in Eastern United States," 91.
35. Philip Phillips, "Introduction to the Archaeology of the Mississippi Valley" (dissertation, Harvard University, 1939).
36. Phillips, "Middle American Influences on the Archaeology of the Southeastern United States," in *The Maya and their Neighbors* (New York: Appleton-Century, 1940), 349–67.
37. Ibid., 366.
38. Ford and Willey, "An Interpretation of the Prehistory of the Eastern United States."
39. Philip Phillips, James A. Ford, and James B. Griffin, *Archaeological Survey in the Lower Mississippi Alluvial Valley, 1940–1947*, Papers of the Peabody Museum of American Archaeology and Ethnology, 25 (Cambridge, Mass.: Peabody Museum, 1952), 452–57.
40. Alex D. Krieger, "Culture Complexes and Chronology in Northern Texas with Extension of Puebloan Datings to the Mississippi Valley," *University of Texas Publication No. 4640* (Austin: 1946), "The Eastward Extension of Puebloan Datings Toward Cultures of the Mississippi Valley," *American Antiquity*, 12, no. 3 (1947), 141–48; Phillips, Ford, and Griffin *Archaeological Survey . . . 1940–1947*, 453–457.
41. Griffin, "Culture Periods in Eastern United States Archeology"; Joseph R. Caldwell, *Trend and Tradition in the Prehistory of the Eastern United States*, Illinois State Museum Scientific Papers, 10, and American Anthropological Association Memoirs, 88 (Springfield, 1958); William H. Sears, "The Study of Social and Religious Systems in North American Archaeology," *Current Anthropology*, 2, no. 3 (1961), 223–46; Griffin, "The Northeast Woodlands Area," in *Prehistoric Man in the New World*, ed. Jesse D. Jennings and Edward Norbeck (Chicago: University of Chicago Press, 1964), 223–58; Gordon R. Willey, *An Introduction to American Archeology*, vol. 1 (Englewood Cliffs, N.J.: Prentice-Hall, 1966); James B. Griffin, "Eastern North American Archaeology: A Summary," *Science*, 156, no. 3772 (1967), 175–91; Jesse D. Jennings, *Prehistory of North America* (New York: McGraw-Hill, 1968).
42. Gordon R. Willey and Philip Phillips, *Method and Theory in American Archaeology* (Chicago: University of Chicago Press, 1958), 146.
43. Ibid., 163–64.
44. Willey, *An Introduction to American Archeology*, 292–310.
45. See Griffin, "Eastern North American Archeology," fig. 5 and p. 15.
46. James A. Brown, *Approaches to the Social Dimensions of Mortuary Practices*, Memoirs of the Society for American Archaeology, 25 (Washington, D.C.: Society of American Archaeology, 1971).
47. Don G. Wycoff and Timothy G. Baugh, "Early Historic Hasenai Elites: A Model for the Material Culture of Governing Elites," *Midcontinental Journal of Archaeology*, 5, no. 2 (1980), 225–88.
48. Bruce D. Smith, ed., *Mississippian Settlement Patterns* (New York: Academic Press, 1978).

49. James A. Brown, Robert E. Bell, and Don G. Wycoff, "Caddoan Settlement Patterns in the Arkansas River Drainage," in *Mississippian Settlement Patterns,* 170.
50. Ibid., 194–95.
51. Roy S. Dickens, Jr., "Mississippian Settlement Patterns in the Appalachian Summit Area: The Pisgah and Qualla Phases," in *Mississippian Settlement Patterns,* 115–39.
52. Jeffrey P. Brain, "Late Prehistoric Settlement Patterning in the Yazoo Basin and Natchez Bluffs Regions of the Lower Mississippi Valley," in *Mississippian Settlement Patterns,* 331–68.
53. Bruce D. Smith, "Variation in Mississippian Settlement Patterns," in *Mississippian Settlement Patterns,* 480.
54. Ibid., 486.
55. Charles Hudson, *The Southeastern Indians* (Knoxville: University of Tennessee Press, 1976), 97–119.
56. Lynne G. Goldstein, *Mississippian Mortuary Practices: A Case Study of Two Cemeteries in the Lower Illinois Valley,* Northwestern University Archaeological Program, Scientific Papers, no. 4 (Evanston: Northwestern University Archaeological Program, 1980), 13–16.
57. See Jesse D. Jennings, *Prehistory of North America* (New York: McGraw-Hill, 1968), 227.
58. Jon D. Muller, "The Southeast," in *Ancient Native Americans,* ed. Jesse D. Jennings (San Francisco: W. H. Freeman, 1978), 312.

Chapter 3
"Mississippian Patterns of Subsistence and Settlement" by Bruce D. Smith

1. W. Frederick Limp and Van A. Reidhead, "An Economic Evaluation of the Potential of Fish Utilization in Riverine Environments," *American Antiquity,* 44, no. 1 (1979), 70–78.
2. Richard Yerkes, "The Potential of Fish Utilization in Riverine Environments," *Midcontinental Journal of Archaeology,* 6, no. 2 (1981), 207–17.
3. Bruce D. Smith, *Middle Mississippi Exploitation of Animal Populations,* University of Michigan Museum of Anthropology, Anthropological Papers, 57 (Ann Arbor: University of Michigan Press, 1975), and Joseph Linduska, *Waterfowl Tomorrow,* U.S. Department of the Interior (Washington, D.C.: G.P.O., 1964).
4. Smith, *Middle Mississippi Exploitation of Animal Populations.*
5. David L. Asch and Nancy B. Asch, "Chenopod as Cultigen: A Re-evaluation of Some Prehistoric Collections from Eastern North America," *Midcontinental Journal of Archaeology,* 2, no. 1 (1977), 3–45.
6. Melvin L. Fowler, "Middle Mississippian Agricultural Fields," *American Antiquity,* 34, no. 4 (1969), 365–75.
7. Ibid., 374.
8. Richard Yerkes and John R. Swanton, *The Indians of the Southeastern United States,* Bureau of American Ethnology Bulletin, 137 (Washington, D.C.: G.P.O., 1946), 246.
9. Lauren Michals, "The Exploitation of Fauna during the Moundville I Phase

at Moundville," 37th Southeastern Archaeological Conference, New Orleans, 1980; Susan L. Scott, "Chapter 4: Analysis, Synthesis, and Interpretation of Fauna from the Lubbub Creek Archaeological Locality," in *Agricultural Communities in West Alabama*, vol. 2, ed. Christopher S. Peebles (forthcoming).

10. Scott, "Chapter 4"; and Gary Shapiro, "Lamar Period Economic Strategy in Piedmont Georgia: The Role of an Extractive Site," 36th Southeastern Archaeological Conference, Atlanta, Georgia, November 8–10, 1979.

11. Richard A. Yarnell, "Interpretation of Archaeological Plant Remains of the Eastern Woodlands," 38th Southeastern Archaeological Conference, 1981.

12. Elizabeth S. Wing and Antoinette B. Brown, *Paleonutrition: Method and Theory in Prehistoric Food Ways* (New York: Academic Press, 1979), 80.

13. A. B. Brown, "Bone Strontium as a Dietary Indicator in Human Skeletal Populations," *Contributions to Geology*, 13 (1974), 47–48; R. I. Gilbert, "Applications of Trace Element Research to Problems in Archaeology," in *Biocultural Adaptation in Prehistoric America*, ed. Robert L. Blakely (Athens: University of Georgia Press, 1977); and M. J. Schoeninger, *Dietary Reconstruction at Chalcatzingo, a Formative Period Site in Morelos, Mexico*, Museum of Anthropology, University of Michigan, Technical Reports No. 9 (1979).

14. Margaret M. Bender, David A. Baerreis, and Raymond L. Steventon, "Further Light on Carbon Isotopes and Hopewell Agriculture," *American Antiquity*, 46, no. 2 (1981), 346–53.

15. "Variation in Mississippian Settlement Patterns," in *Mississippian Settlement Patterns*, ed. Bruce D. Smith (New York: Academic Press, 1978).

16. See Christopher S. Peebles, "Determinants of Settlement Size and Location in the Moundville Phase," in *Mississippian Settlement Patterns*, 369–414.

Chapter 5
"The Archaeology of the Hernando de Soto Expedition" by Jeffrey P. Brain

1. Garcilaso de la Vega, *The Florida of the Inca*, trans. and ed. John G. Varner and Jeannette J. Varner (Austin: University of Texas Press, 1962).

2. John R. Swanton, *Final Report of the United States De Soto Expedition Commission*, 76th Cong., 1st sess., H.Doc. 71 (Washington, D.C.: G.P.O., 1939).

3. Jean Delanglez, "El Rio del Espíritu Santo," *Mid-America*, 25, no. 4 (1943), 231–49.

4. Swanton, *Final Report of the United States De Soto Expedition Commission*, 296.

5. Ripley P. Bullen, *The Terra Ceia Site, Manatee County, Florida*, Florida Anthropological Society Publications, 3 (Gainesville: University of Florida, 1951), and "De Soto's Ucita and the Terra Ceia Site," *Florida Historical Quarterly*, 30, no. 4 (1952), 317–23.

6. Louis D. Tesar, "The Leon County Bicentennial Survey Report: An Archaeological Survey of Selected Portions of Leon County, Florida," Bureau of Historic Sites and Properties, Division of Archives, History and Records Management, Florida Department of State, Tallahassee (1980).

7. Swanton, *Final Report of the United States De Soto Expedition Commission*, 206.
8. David L. DeJarnette and Asael T. Hansen, *The Archeology of the Childersburg Site, Alabama*, Department of Anthropology, Florida State University, Notes in Anthropology, 6 (Tallahassee: Florida State University Press, 1960).
9. See DePratter, Hudson, and Smith, this volume.
10. George E. Lankford III, " A New Look at De Soto's Route through Alabama," *Journal of Alabama Archaeology*, 23, no. 1 (1977), 10–36.
11. Christopher S. Peebles, *Excavations at Moundville, 1905–1951* (Ann Arbor: University Microfilms, 1979); Vincas P. Steponaitis, "Ceramics, Chronology, and Community Patterns at Moundville, A Late Prehistoric Site in Alabama" (dissertation, University of Michigan, 1980).
12. See Jeffrey P. Brain, Alan Toth, and Antonio Rodriguez-Buckingham, "Ethnohistoric Archaeology and the De Soto Entrada into the Lower Mississippi Valley," *Conference on Historic Site Archaeology Papers*, 7, ed. Stanley South (Columbia: Institute of Archeology and Anthropology, University of South Carolina, 1974), 232–89.
13. Swanton, *Final Report of the United States De Soto Commission*, 234–38, and Brain et al., "Ethnohistoric Archaeology and the De Soto Entrada into the Lower Mississippi Valley."
14. See Harold L. Peterson, *Arms and Armor in Colonial America, 1526–1783* (Harrisburg: Stackpole Co., 1956), pl. 103.
15. My thanks to John Stubbs of the Mississippi Department of Archives and History's Chickasaw Archaeological Survey for bringing this artifact to my attention, and to Richard Heard of Tupelo who owns it and graciously consented to its publication. The halberd is surprisingly rust-free, which gives rise to suspicions about its heritage, especially in the absence of good provenience data. It is possible that it was brought to Tupelo more recently than the Soto *entrada*; yet, in this instance, there is no hint of chicanery, and it is an appropriate artifact from an appropriate locale. It thus remains a tantalizing bit of evidence, which, however, does little to help resolve the details of the route. Other possible halberds have also been found. Figure 2B is an example that was discovered in the vicinity of Schlater, Mississippi, near the hypothesized route from Chicasa to the Mississippi River (see Brain et al., "Ethnohistoric Archaeology and the De Soto Entrada"). It is badly corroded, and not diagnostic in formal characteristics. If authentic, its differences from the Tupelo halberd might be explained by the fact that it was a crudely reforged specimen, resurrected from the disaster at Chicasa.
16. See Brain et al., "Ethnohistoric Archaeology and the De Soto Entrada into the Lower Mississippi Valley."
17. See Brain, "Artifacts of the Adelantado," *Conference on Historic Site Archaeology Papers*, 8 (Columbia: Institute of Archeology and Anthropology, University of South Carolina, 1975), 129–38.
18. See Brain, "Artifacts of the Adelantado," and Charles H. Fairbanks, "Early Spanish Colonial Beads," *Conference on Historic Site Archaeology Papers*, 2, part 1 (Raleigh, 1968), 3–22; Timothy Klinger, "Parkin Archeology: A Report on the 1966 Field School Test Excavations at the Parkin Site," *Arkansas Archeologist*, 16–18 (1975–77), 45–80; Marvin T. Smith, "The Route of De Soto through Tennessee, Georgia and Alabama: The Evidence

from Material Culture," *Early Georgia,* 4, nos. 1 and 2 (1976), 27–48; and Smith, "The Early Historic Period (1540–1670) on the Upper Coosa River Drainage of Alabama and Georgia," *Conference on Historic Site Archaeology Papers,* 10 (Columbia: Institute of Archeology and Anthropology, University of South Carolina, 1977), 151–67.

Chapter 6
"The Hernando de Soto Expedition" by Chester B. DePratter, Charles M. Hudson, and Marvin T. Smith

For help, advice, and criticism we are grateful to David Chase, Richard Polhemus, J. Bennett Graham, David Hally, Ned Jenkins, Vernon J. Knight, Jr., and Craig Sheldon, Jr.

1. Rodrigo Ranjel, "A Narrative of De Soto's Expedition," in *Narratives of the Career of Hernando de Soto,* trans. Buckingham Smith, ed. Edward G. Bourne (New York: Allerton, 1922), 86; Gentleman of Elvas, "Relation of a Gentleman of Elvas," in *Narratives of De Soto in the Conquest of Florida,* trans. Buckingham Smith (Gainesville: Palmetto Books, 1968), 49–50; Garcilaso de la Vega, *The Florida of the Inca,* ed. John G. Varner and Jeannette J. Varner (Austin: University of Texas Press, 1962), 252–54.
2. Garcilaso, *Florida of the Inca,* 311.
3. George E. Stuart, "The Post-Archaic Occupation of Central South Carolina" (dissertation, University of North Carolina at Chapel Hill, 1975) 98–128; see also Steven G. Baker, "Cofitachique: Fair Province of Carolina" (thesis, University of South Carolina, 1974).
4. John R. Swanton, *Final Report of the United States De Soto Expedition Commission,* 76th Cong., 1st sess., H. Doc. 71 (Washington, D.C.: G.P.O., 1939).
5. A full presentation of our evidence may be seen in Chester DePratter, Charles Hudson, and Marvin Smith, "The Route of Juan Pardo's Explorations in the Interior Southeast, 1566–1568," *Florida Historical Quarterly* (October 1983), 125–58.
6. Roland Chardon, "The Elusive Spanish League: A Problem of Measurement in Sixteenth Century New Spain," *Hispanic American Historical Review,* 60 (1980), 294–302.
7. Garcilaso, *Florida of the Inca,* 329.
8. Ibid., 342.
9. Elvas, "Relation of a Gentleman of Elvas," 79.
10. Ibid., 70.
11. Shady Grove, Tenn., Quad, USGS 7.5 min series; Swanton, *Final Report of the United States De Soto Expedition Commission,* 107–08.
12. Richard Polhemus, personal communication.
13. Polhemus informed us that before the island was flooded, a local collector gathered additional materials.
14. Elvas, "Relation of a Gentleman of Elvas," 72; Garcilaso, *The Florida of the Inca,* 337.
15. Garcilaso contradicts Ranjel by saying that they crossed in canoes and rafts (p. 342).
16. Ranjel, "A Narrative of De Soto's Expedition," 108–09.

17. "Letter from the Secretary of War Relative to the Improvement of the Holston and Tennessee Rivers." 42nd Cong., 2nd sess., Exec. Doc. 167. Also see the map accompanying Eastin Morris's *Tennessee Gazetteer* (1834).
18. Ranjel, "A Narrative of De Soto's Expedition," 198.
19. Ranjel, "A Narrative of De Soto's Expedition," 109. The people of Coste were perhaps ancestors of the Koasati.
20. Cited in Marvin Smith, "The Route of De Soto through Tennessee, Georgia, and Alabama: The Evidence from Material Culture," *Early Georgia*, 4 (1976), 32.
21. Richard Polhemus, "The Early Historic Period in the East Tennessee Valley," 37th Southeastern Archaeological Conference, New Orleans, 1980.
22. Ranjel, "A Narrative of De Soto's Expedition," 109.
23. Richard Polhemus, personal communication.
24. Ranjel, "A Narrative of De Soto's Expedition," 111.
25. Polhemus, "The Early Historic Period in the East Tennessee Valley," 5–9.
26. John R. Swanton, *Early History of the Creek Indians and Their Neighbors*, Bureau of American Ethnology Bulletin, 73 (Washington, D.C.: G.P.O., 1922), 212.
27. Charles Hudson, Marvin Smith, David Hally, Richard Polhemus, and Chester DePratter, "Coosa," paper presented at the 1983 Southeastern Archaeological Conference, November 3, 1983, Columbia, S.C.; Juan de la Bandera, "Proceeding of the account which Captain Juan Pardo gave of the entrance which he made into the land of the Floridas," April 1, 1569, Herbert Ketcham translator, North Carolina Department of Cultural Resources, Division of Archives and History; Chester DePratter and Marvin Smith, "Sixteenth Century European Trade in the Southeastern United States: Evidence from the Juan Pardo Expeditions (1566–1568)," in Henry F. Dobyns, ed., *Spanish Colonial Frontier Research* (Albuquerque: Center for Anthropological Studies, 1980), 67–77.
28. Ranjel, "A Narrative of De Soto's Expedition," 111.
29. Elvas, "Relation of a Gentleman of Elvas," 75.
30. Ranjel, "A Narrative of De Soto's Expedition," 111. This trail is shown on the U.S. Coast Survey Map of 1865.
31. Had they departed from the Upper Little Tennessee River, their travel time to the Hiwassee River would have been approximately the same.
32. Juan de la Vandera, scribe of the Pardo expedition, mentions both Tasqui and Tasquiqui. See Herbert E. Ketcham, trans. and ed., "Three Sixteenth Century Spanish Chronicles Relating to Georgia," *Georgia Historical Quarterly*, 38 (1954), 81.
33. Elvas, "Relation of a Gentleman of Elvas," 75.
34. George Lankford III was correct in surmising that Coosa was farther up the Coosa River than scholars have traditionally placed it. See George E. Lankford III, "A New Look at de Soto's Route through Alabama," *Journal of Alabama Archaeology*, 23, no. 1 (1977), 23–24.
35. Swanton, *Early History of the Creek Indians and Their Neighbors*, 231–39.
36. Herbert I. Priestley, *The Luna Papers* (De Land: Florida State Historical Society, 1928), 1:241.
37. David J. Hally, *Archaeological Investigations of the Little Egypt Site*

(9Mu102), *Murray County, Ga., 1969 Season*, University of Georgia Laboratory of Archaeology Series, 18 (Athens: University of Georgia, 1979); Arthur R. Kelly, "Explorations at Bell Field Mound and Village: Seasons 1965, 1966, 1967, 1968," report on file in the University of Georgia Laboratory of Archaeology.

38. Arthur R. Kelly, Frank T. Schnell, Donald F. Smith, and Ann L. Schlosser, "Explorations in Sixtoe Field, Carter's Dam, Murray County, Georgia, Seasons of 1962, 1963, 1964," report on file in the University of Georgia Laboratory of Archaeology, 176–77.

39. Smith, "The Route of De Soto through Tennessee, Georgia, and Alabama: The Evidence from Material Culture," 29–31.

40. Ranjel, "A Narrative of De Soto's Expedition," 112.

41. Typically, Garcilaso exaggerates by saying that the chief of Coosa was carried a full league, accompanied by more than 1,000 noblemen (p. 343).

42. Elvas, "Relation of a Gentleman of Elvas," 76–77.

43. Garcilaso, *Florida of the Inca*, 343–44.

44. Ibid., 347.

45. Ranjel, "A Narrative of De Soto's Expedition," 113; Elvas, "Relation of a Gentleman of Elvas," 78.

46. Ranjel, "A Narrative of De Soto's Expedition," 113.

47. W. K. Moorehead, *Etowah Papers* (New Haven: Yale University Press, 1932); L. H. Larson, Jr., *Archaeological Implications of Social Stratification at the Etowah Site, Georgia*, Society for American Archaeology Memoir, 25 (1971), 58–67.

48. Elvas, "Relation of a Gentleman of Elvas," 78.

49. A large but little-known Lamar site is within the city limits of Rome.

50. Ranjel, "A Narrative of De Soto's Expedition," 113; Elvas, "Relation of a Gentleman of Elvas," 78. We are grateful to Marion Hemperly for pointing out that Euharlee, the name of a creek near Rome, may be derived from *Ulibahali*.

51. Priestley, *Luna Papers*, 219–29.

52. Gonzalo Fernández de Oviedo, *Historia General y Natural de las Indias* (Madrid: Ediciones Atlas, 1959), 171. We are grateful to Vernon J. Knight, Jr., for pointing out that this town of Piachi is omitted in the Buckingham Smith translation of Ranjel as edited by Edward Gaylord Bourne (p. 114).

53. Smith, "The Route of De Soto through Tennessee, Georgia, and Alabama: The Evidence from Material Culture," 30–31; Chester B. DePratter and Marvin T. Smith, "Sixteenth Century European Trade in the Southeastern United States: Evidence from the Juan Pardo Expeditions (1566–1568)," in *Spanish Colonial Frontier Research*, ed. Henry F. Dobyns (Albuquerque: Center for Anthropological Studies, 1980), 75. The sword was found by an amateur, and is being studied by Keith Little (personal communication).

54. Elvas says they were making 5 or 6 leagues per day at this point (p. 79).

55. Keith J. Little and Cailup B. Curren, Jr., "Site I Ce 308: A Protohistoric Site on the Upper Coosa River in Alabama," *Journal of Alabama Archaeology*, 27 (1981), 117–40.

56. Ranjel, "A Narrative of De Soto's Expedition," 115.

57. Elvas, "Relation of a Gentleman of Elvas," 79.

58. Ibid.; Ranjel, "A Narrative of De Soto's Expedition," 115.
59. Garcilaso, *Florida of the Inca*, 346.
60. Ranjel, "A Narrative of De Soto's Expedition," 116.
61. Garcilaso, *Florida of the Inca*, 348.
62. Elvas, "Relation of a Gentleman of Elvas," 80.
63. Ranjel says 1 league (p. 120); Elvas says 2 (p. 82).
64. Ranjel, "A Narrative of De Soto's Expedition," 121; Elvas, "Relation of a Gentleman of Elvas," 81.
65. Priestley, *Luna Papers*, 1:207, 219, 221.
66. Ibid., 227.
67. Swanton, *Early History of the Creek Indians and Their Neighbors*, 265–66. It is possible that Athahachi was at the Charlotte Thompson site, near present-day Montgomery. See Clarence B. Moore, "Certain Aboriginal Remains of the Alabama River," *Journal of the Academy of Natural Sciences of Philadelphia*, 11 (1899): 320–28. For a different interpretation of the identity of the Charlotte Thompson site, see C. B. Curren, Jr., Keith J. Little, and George B. Lankford III, "The Route of the Expedition of Hernando de Soto through Alabama," paper presented at the Southeastern Archaeological Conference (November 12–14, 1981, Asheville, N.C.).
68. Ranjel, "A Narrative of De Soto's Expedition," 122.
69. Ibid., 122. Bourne has this as "high above the gorge of a mountain stream"; but the Spanish reads: *"alto, sobre un barranco de un rio, enriscado."*
70. Elvas, "Relation of a Gentleman of Elvas," 82.
71. Garcilaso, *Florida of the Inca*, 351.
72. C. Roger Nance, *The Archaeological Sequence at Durant Bend, Dallas County, Alabama*, Special Publication of the Alabama Archaeological Society, 2 (Orange Beach: Alabama Archaeological Society, 1976).
73. Priestley, *Luna Papers*, 1:7.
74. Ranjel, "A Narrative of De Soto's Expedition," 123.
75. Alvar Nuñez Cabeza de Vaca, *Narrative*, trans. Fanny Bandelier (Barre: The Imprint Society, 1972), 38–40.
76. Luys Hernández de Biedma, "Relation of the Conquest of Florida," in *Narratives of the Career of Hernando de Soto in the Conquest of Florida*, ed. Edward G. Bourne (New York: A. S. Barnes, 1904), 17.
77. Ranjel, "A Narrative of De Soto's Expedition," 122–23.
78. Biedma, "Relation of the Conquest of Florida," 17.
79. Ranjel, "A Narrative of De Soto's Expedition," 123.
80. Garcilaso, *Florida of the Inca*, 351.
81. Ranjel, "A Narrative of De Soto's Expedition," 123.
82. Elvas, "Relation of a Gentleman of Elvas," 83.
83. Garcilaso, *Florida of the Inca*, 353; Biedma, "Relation of the Conquest of Florida," 18.
84. Garcilaso says eight o'clock; Biedma says nine o'clock (p. 18).
85. Garcilaso, *Florida of the Inca*, 349.
86. James Mooney, *Myths of the Cherokee*, Bureau of American Ethnology, 19th Annual Report (Washington, D.C.: G.P.O., 1900), 534.
87. Ibid., 526.
88. Albert T. Pickett, *History of Alabama* (Charleston: Walker and James, 1851),

1:6–7, 310. Pickett claims that George Galphin, a trader who established himself at Silver Bluff in 1736, learned this from "the most ancient Indians" and that the tradition was preserved by other old traders, who passed it on to him.

Chapter 7
"From Exploration to Settlement" by Charles H. Fairbanks

1. Gordon R. Willey, *Archeology of the Florida Gulf Coast*, Smithsonian Miscellaneous Collections, vol. 113 (Washington, D.C.: Smithsonian Institution, 1949).
2. John R. Swanton, *Final Report of the United States De Soto Expedition Commission*, 76th Cong., 1st sess. H. Doc. 71 (Washington, D.C.: G.P.O., 1939), 117–38.
3. Charles Pearson, "Evidence of Early Spanish Contact on the Georgia Coast," *Historical Archaeology*, 11 (1977), 74–83; Carlos A. Martinez, "Culture Sequence on the Central Georgia Coast, 1000 B.C.–1650 A.D" (thesis, University of Florida, 1975), and James W. Zahler, Jr., "A Morphological Analysis of a Protohistoric-Historic Skeletal Population from St. Simons Island, Georgia" (thesis, University of Florida, 1976).
4. Albert C. Goodyear (personal communication), July 20, 1978.
5. Robert Allen (personal communication), September 23, 1970.
6. Charles H. Fairbanks, "Early Spanish Colonial Beads," *Conference on Historic Site Archaeology Papers, 1967*, 2, pt. 1 (Raleigh, 1968): 3–22.
7. William C. Lazarus, "A Sixteenth Century Spanish Coin from a Fort Walton Burial," *Florida Anthropologist*, 17, no. 2 (1964), 134–37; William C. Lazarus, "Coin Dating in the Fort Walton Period," *Florida Anthropologist*, 18, no. 4 (1965), 221–24; and Aloiss Heiss, *Descripción General de las Monedas Hispano-Christianas desde la Invasión de los Arabes* (Madrid: R. N. Milagro, 1865), plate 28.2.
8. James W. Zahler, Jr. "A Morphological Analysis of a Protohistoric-Historic Skeletal Population from St. Simons Island, Georgia."
9. Amy Bushnell, " 'That Demonic Game': The Campaign to Stop Indian Pelota Playing in Spanish Florida, 1675–1684," *The Americas*, 35, no. 1 (1978), 1–19.
10. Eugene Lyon, "Spain's Sixteenth-Century, North American Settlement Attempt: A Neglected Aspect," *Florida Historical Quarterly*, 59, no. 3 (January 1981), 275–92.
11. Ibid., 279.
12. Ibid.
13. William C. Sturtevant, "Black Drink and Other Caffeine-containing Beverages among Non-Indians," in *Black Drink, a Native American Tea*, ed. Charles M. Hudson (Athens: University of Georgia Press, 1979), 150–52.
14. Kathleen Deagan, "The Material Assemblage of 16th Century Spanish Florida," *Historical Archaeology*, 12 (1978), 25–50; Stanley South, *The Search for Santa Elena on Parris Island, South Carolina*, introduction by Robert L. Stephenson, Research Manuscript Series, no. 150 (Columbia: Institute of Archeology and Anthropology, University of South Carolina,

1979); and Stanley South, *The Discovery of Santa Elena*, preface by Robert L. Stephenson, Research Manuscript Series, no. 165 (Columbia: Institute of Archeology and Anthropology, University of South Carolina, 1980).

15. Elizabeth J. Reitz, "Spanish and British Subsistence Strategies at St. Augustine, Florida, and Frederica, Georgia, between 1565 and 1783" (dissertation, University of Florida, 1979).

Chapter 8
"The Southeast in the Age of Conflict and Revolution" by Wilcomb E. Washburn

1. Michael Kammen, "Clio and the Changing Fashions: Some Patterns in Current American Historiography," *American Scholar*, 44 (3) (1975), 484–96.
2. Wesley Frank Craven, *The Southern Colonies in the Seventeenth Century, 1607–1689* (vol. 1; Baton Rouge: Louisiana State Press, 1949); John Alden, *The South in the Revolution, 1763–1789*, vol. 3 of *A History of the South* (Baton Rouge: Louisiana State Press, 1957).
3. W. Stitt Robinson, *The Southern Colonial Frontier, 1607–1763*, Histories of the American Frontier series. (Albuquerque: University of New Mexico Press, 1979).
4. Ernst Posner, *American State Archives* (Chicago: University of Chicago Press, 1964).
5. Alden T. Vaughan, *Early American Indian Documents* (Washington, D.C.: University Publications of America, 1979).
6. William S. Coker, "Entrepreneurs in British and Spanish Florida, 1775–1821," in *Eighteenth-Century Florida and the Caribbean*, ed. Samuel Proctor (Gainesville: University Presses of Florida, 1976).
7. "The Seventeenth Century Chesapeake and Its Modern Historians," *The Chesapeake in the Seventeenth Century: Essays on Anglo-American Society*, ed. Thad W. Tate and David L. Ammerman (Chapel Hill: University of North Carolina Press, 1979).
8. Michael Kammen, "The Unique and the Universal in the History of New World Colonization," *Eighteenth-Century Florida and Its Borderlands*, ed. Samuel Proctor (Gainesville: University Presses of Florida, 1975).
9. John R. Swanton, *The Indians of the Southeastern United States*, Bureau of American Ethnology Bulletin, no. 137 (Washington, D.C.: G.P.O., 1946); Charles M. Hudson, *The Southeastern Indians* (Knoxville: University of Tennessee Press, 1976).
10. Jeffrey Brain, *Tunica Treasure* (Cambridge and Salem, Mass.: Peabody Museum of Archaeology and Ethnology, Harvard University, 1979).
11. William C. Sturtevant, *Eighteenth-Century Florida and Its Borderlands*, ed. Samuel Proctor (Gainesville: University Presses of Florida, 1975), 44–47; John Walton Caughey, *McGillivray of the Creeks* (Norman: University of Oklahoma Press, 1938); J. Leitch Wright, Jr., *William Augustus Bowles, Director General of the Creek Nation* (Athens: University of Georgia Press, 1967).
12. Arrell M. Gibson, *The Chickasaws* (Norman: University of Oklahoma Press,

1971); Marcel Giraud, *Histoire de la Louisiane française* (Paris: Presses Universitaires de France, 1953–74); Joseph C. Lambert, trans., *The Reign of Louis XIV, 1698–1715*, vol. 1 of Giraud, *Histoire de la Louisiane française* (Baton Rouge: Louisiana State University Press); Patricia Dillon Woods, *French-Indian Relations on the Southern Frontier, 1699–1762*, Studies in American History and Culture, no. 18 (Ann Arbor: UMI Research Press, 1980).

13. J. Leitch Wright, Jr., *The Only Land They Knew: The Tragic Story of the American Indians of the Old South* (New York: The Free Press, 1981).

14. Robert L. Meriwether, *The Expansion of South Carolina, 1729–1765* (Kingsport, Tenn.: Southern, 1940); Verner W. Crane, *The Southern Frontier, 1670–1732* (Durham: Duke University Press, 1928); David Duncan Wallace, *South Carolina: A Short History, 1520–1948* (Chapel Hill: University of North Carolina Press, 1951); M. Eugene Sirmans, *Colonial South Carolina: A Political History, 1663–1763* (Chapel Hill: University of North Carolina Press, 1966); David H. Corkran, *The Creek Frontier, 1540–1783* (Norman: University of Oklahoma Press, 1967).

15. James Adair, "History of the American Indians," in Lawrence H. Leder, *The Colonial Legacy*, vol. 3: *Historians of Nature and Man's Nature* (New York: Harper & Row, 1973), 91–120.

16. James H. O'Donnell III, *Southern Indians in the American Revolution* (Knoxville: University of Tennessee Press, 1973).

17. William S. Coker and Hazel P. Coker, *The Siege of Pensacola, 1781, in Maps, with Data on Troop Strength, Military Units, Ships, Casualties and Related Statistics* (Pensacola: Perdido Bay Press, 1981).

18. Francisco de Borja Medina Rojas, *José de Ezpeleta: Gobernador de la Mobila, 1780–1781* (Seville: Escuela de Estudios Hispano-americanos, 1980).

19. O'Donnell, *Southern Indians in the American Revolution*, 131.

Chapter 9
"Continuity in the Age of Conquest" by Eugene Lyon

1. The lawsuit is found in Archivo General de Indias (hereafter AGI) *Patronato* (hereafter *Pat*) 21, no. 2, ramo 4.

2. Baltasar de Obregón, "Historia de los descubrimientos antiguos y modernos de la Nueva España y Nuevo Méjico . . . ," Mexico City, April 24, 1584, AGI *Pat* 22, ramo 7.

3. See Viceroy Velasco to Tristán de Luna, Mexico City, September 15, 1560, AGI *Justicia* (hereafter *Ju*) 1013, no. 2, ramo 1, fols. 170–73.

4. For an analysis of the uses of *adelantamiento* in Spain and the New World, see Eugene Lyon, *The Enterprise of Florida: Pedro Menéndez de Avilés and the Spanish Conquest* (Gainesville: University Presses of Florida, 1976), 2–18, 24–25, 43–55. See also Roscoe R. Hill, "The Office of Adelantado," *Political Science Quarterly*, 21, no. 4 (December 1913), 646–68. Pedro Menéndez' *asiento* as Florida *adelantado* is found in many Spanish archives: in the Archivo del Conde de Revillagigedo, Madrid (*Legajo* 2, no. 5), and in the AGI (a signed copy is in *Escribanía de Cámara* [hereafter *EC*], 1024-A);

additional copies are (among other places) in AGI *Pat* 19, ramo 15; AGI *Contratación* (hereafter *Ct*) 3309, 1; AGI *Ju* 918, no. 3; AGI *Indiferente General* (hereafter *IG*) 4154 and 2673.

5. AGI *Pat* 19, ramo 15.

6. Menéndez memorial, describing the "arm of the sea," is undated, but internal evidence indicates a date between February 1 and March 15, 1565; it also is from AGI *Pat* 19. Louis-André Vigneras discusses the geographic ideas of Pedro Menéndez de Avilés in "A Spanish Discovery of North Carolina," *North Carolina Historical Review*, 46, no. 4 (October 1969), 398–414. The *adelantado's* letter to the Jesuit leader, Francisco Borgia, was sent from Madrid, and has been reprinted in Felix Zubillaga's *Monumenta Antiquae Floridae 1566–1572* (Rome: Monumenta Historica Societatis Iesu, 1956), 1–4.

7. Menéndez' first plan was found in letters to his king, sent from St. Augustine on October 15, 1565 (AGI *Santo Domingo* [hereafter *SD*] 231) and on October 20, 1566, (AGI *SD* 115).

8. Pedro Menéndez to the Crown, St. Augustine, October 15, 1565 (AGI *SD* 115).

9. Pedro Menéndez to the Crown, October 20, 1566 (AGI *SD* 115). For the Newfoundland voyage, see certification of Pedro Menéndez Marquez, Madrid, January 29, 1573 (AGI *EC* 1024-A, piece 1, fol. 127).

10. First notice of Menéndez' preference for the Jesuit order was given in the memorial mentioned in note 6, above. Borgia replied favorably to the 1565 request on May 12, 1565; see *Monumenta* (pp. 6–8). Philip II approved the mission in a letter printed in *Monumenta* (pp. 42–44). Menéndez outlined his Indian policies in his letters to Philip II on October 20, 1566. Examples of Spanish treaties with Florida Indians in 1579 and 1580 are in the "Quiros papers" (from AGI *SD* 125, no. 150-D). Descriptions of the cultures of the Timicuans and other Florida Indian groupings may be found in *Tacachale, Essays on the Indians of Florida and Southeastern Georgia during the Historic Period*, edited by Jerald T. Milanich and Samuel Proctor (Gainesville: University Presses of Florida, 1978), and *Francisco Pareja's 1613 Confesionario*, edited by Jerald T. Milanich and William C. Sturtevant, translated by Emilio Moran (Tallahassee: Florida Division of Archives, History and Records Management, 1972).

11. The first expedition is described in Professor Vigneras' article, "A Spanish Discovery of North Carolina," and the Jesuit missions in "Martirio de los Padres y Hermanos de la Compañia de Jesus," by Bartolomé Martínez (Potosí, October 4, 1616; *Monumenta*, 570–604), and by Clifford M. Lewis and Albert J. Loomie in *The Spanish Jesuit Missions in Virginia* (Chapel Hill: University of North Carolina Press, 1953).

12. Philip II's promised subsidy was discussed in an order of July 15, 1568, described in a later order of June 17, 1570 (AGI *Contaduría* 548). Colonists for Florida assembled in Cádiz in July 1568 (see "Información ante Abalia," Cádiz, AGI *IG* 2673), and their arrival in Florida was noted by Estéban de las Alas in a certificate dated, at Seville, January 1, 1573 (AGI *EC* 1024-A). The Santa Elena population was sworn to by Pedro Menéndez Márquez in AGI *Ju* 980 (no. 3, ramo 1). For the modern excavations at Santa Elena, see Paul E. Hoffman, "Sixteenth Century Fortifications on Parris Island, South Caro-

lina" (typescript, National Geographic Society, 1978), and Stanley South, "The Discovery of Santa Elena" (Columbia: Institute of Archeology and Anthropology, University of South Carolina, 1980 [Research Manuscript Series, 165]).

13. Menéndez' and Castillo's commercial dealings in the 1562–63 fleets, for example, are shown in the *fés de registro* from Archivo General de Simancas *Consejo de Hacienda 64*. The sale of Menéndez' ship licenses, handled for him by Castillo, is recorded in entries in the Archivo de Protocolos de Cádiz for the years 1568 to 1570. The *adelantado* promised his soldiers land in Florida for planting and for raising stock in their enlistment agreements; see the document, dated (at Seville) May 25, 1565 (AGI *Ju* 879, no. 3, piece 1). Captain Gregorio de Ugarte shipped 36 oak logs from Florida on his ship *Los Tres Reyes* in 1566 (see AGI *Ct* 204, no. 1, ramo 2, fols. 64–64vo). Estéban de las Alas' export of juniper, oak, laurel, and ship masts is mentioned in testimony (AGI *Ju* 1001, no. 2, ramo 1). After trial cargos of sassafras root were sent by Pedro del Castillo, larger shipments were made; see Bernardo de Valdés et al. *v.* Luis Hernández (*protocolo* of Martin Calvo de la Puerta, Archivo de Protocolos de la Havana, August 9, 1585). The cattle ranching is described by Amy Bushnell in "The Menéndez Márquez Cattle Barony at La Chua and the Determinants of Economic Expansion in Seventeenth-Century Florida," *Florida Historical Quarterly*, 56 (1978), 407–31.

14. See Envío 25, no. 162, Archivo del Instituto de Valencia de Don Juan, Madrid, November 1569. Supplies to build the *fragatas* were received in St. Augustine on December 2, 1571 (see AGI *CD* 548, no. 8, no. 5—*Data*).

15. The Pánuco contract was approved by Philip II at Madrid on February 23, 1573 (AGI *SD* 2528). Royal orders on the boundaries of the new grant were sent to Menéndez, the viceroy, and the *audiencias* of Mexico and Guadalajara on March 3, 1573 and August 20, 1574 (AGI *SD* 2528). Pedro Menéndez discussed the projected establishments on the road to New Spain in a letter to Francisco Borgia, from Madrid, January 18, 1568 (*Monumenta*, 228–34). Menéndez' power-of-attorney to Luis de Velasco is on record in the Archivo Histórico de Protocolos (Madrid), Protocolo no. 605 (*escribaniá* of Juan de Campillo, 1574, fol. 74).

16. A description of the clothing and household goods of Pedro Menéndez de Avilés, his family, and noble followers is in AGI *Ju* 817 (no. 5, piece 6). The tenure of Don Diego de Velasco as Florida lieutenant-governor was subjected to legal review by visitor Baltasar Castillo y Ahedo (see AGI *EC* 154-A, "Cargos," fol. 2vo–11 [1576–77]).

17. For the inheritance of Pedro Menéndez de Avilés, see Eugene Lyon, "The *Visita* of 1576 and the Change of Government in Spanish Florida," Congreso sobre el Impacto de España en la Florida, El Caribe y La Luisiana, 1500–1800, 1981 (in press). Menéndez' expansive claims were first outlined in AGI *EC* 1024-A, and later summarized by his heirs (in 1671) in AGI *SD* 231. Paul E. Hoffman calculated the crown's spending in Florida in "A Study of Florida Defense Costs," *Florida Historical Quarterly*, 51, 4 (April 1973), 401–22.

18. See Gonzalo Méndez Canzo, "Relación de la Tama y su Tierra . . . ," in Manuel Serrano y Sanz, ed., *Documentos históricos de la Florida y la Luisiana, siglos XVI al XVIII* (Madrid, 1912), 141–54, and Charles W. Arnade, *Florida on Trial* (Miami: University of Miami Press, 1959), 21–22.

19. "Discurso sobre el descubrimiento del Nuevo Méjico" (n.d., but ca. 1602), AGI *Pat* 22, ramo 2.

Chapter 10
"The Siege of Mobile, 1780" by William S. Coker and Hazel P. Coker

1. John Walton Caughey, *Bernardo de Gálvez in Louisiana, 1776–1783* (1934; rpt., Gretna: Pelican, 1972); J. Barton Starr, *Tories, Dons, and Rebels: The American Revolution in British West Florida* (Gainesville: University Presses of Florida, 1976). The formal presentation of the paper at The University of Alabama in 1981 included over 40 maps. However, space does not permit that many maps here; therefore only a few were selected to demonstrate the technique.

2. For all the maps, appendices, etc., see William S. Coker and Hazel P. Coker, *The Siege of Mobile, 1780, in Maps, with Data on Troop Strength, Military Units, Ships, Casualties and Prisoners of War, including a Brief History of Fort Charlotte (Condé)* (Pensacola: Perdido Bay Press, 1982).

3. Cecil Johnson, *British West Florida, 1763–1783* (1942; rpt., Hamden, Conn.: Archon, 1971), 1–7.

4. J. Barton Starr, "Campbell Town: French Huguenots in British West Florida," *Florida Historical Quarterly*, 54 (1976), 532–47.

5. Robin F. A. Fabel, "Anglo-Spanish Commerce in New Orleans during the American Revolution Era," in William S. Coker and Robert R. Rea, eds., *Anglo-Spanish Confrontation on the Gulf Coast during the American Revolution* (Pensacola: Gulf Coast History and Humanities Conference, 1982), 25–53.

6. James W. Covington, "The Cuban Fishing Ranchos: A Spanish Enclave within British Florida," in Coker and Rea, eds., *Anglo-Spanish Confrontation*, 17–24.

7. Johnson, *British West Florida*; Starr, *Tories*, 1–34.

8. Buchanan Parker Thomson, *Spain: Forgotten Ally of the American Revolution* (North Quincy, Mass.: Christopher, 1976).

9. John Preston Moore, *Revolt in Louisiana: The Spanish Occupation, 1766–1770* (Baton Rouge: Louisiana State University Press, 1976).

10. Fabel, "Anglo-Spanish Commerce in New Orleans," 31–38.

11. Caughey, *Gálvez*, 102–48; Starr, *Tories*, 78–121.

12. Caughey, *Gálvez*, 142–60.

13. Francisco de Borja Medina Rojas, *José de Ezpeleta: Gobernador de la Mobila, 1780–1781* (Seville: Escuela de Estudios Hispano-Americanos, 1980), 4.

14. Caughey, *Gálvez*, 145–47.

15. Borja, *Ezpeleta*, 4–5.

16. Caughey, *Gálvez*, 146.

17. Starr, *Tories*, 165–67.

18. Bernardo de Gálvez to José de Gálvez, Mobile, March 20, 1780, Archivo General de Simancas, Guerra Moderna, Legajo 6912; Borja, *Ezpeleta*, 5–6. The authors' decision to call it the *siege* of Mobile, instead of *battle*, followed the logic of Captain Durnford, who later wrote that "[Gálvez] was obliged, in consequence of the measures and precautions I used in the

defence of this paltry fort, to open trenches, and enter into all the formalities of a siege." See Mary Dunford, ed., *Family Recollections: Lieut. General Elias Durnford* (Montreal: John Lovell, 1863), 20.

19. Coker and Coker, *Siege of Mobile*, 5–97. There are 48 maps and illustrations and 8 appendices in the published volume.

20. Ibid., 14 and 28.

21. *Diario* of Don Bernardo de Gálvez, March 18, 1780 (Archivo General de Simancas; Guerra Moderna, legajo 6912), entry for January 10–11, 1780.

22. Coker and Coker, *Siege of Mobile*, 104–05.

23. Gálvez, *Diario*, January 20, 1780 (AGS GM 6912).

24. Details on Pickles' service with Gálvez during the Mobile campaign are lacking. The *West Florida*, however, *did* capture a small British sloop, which John Henderson, Pollock's clerk, sold as a prize at Mobile. Captain Joseph Calvert, an American privateersman, who visited Mobile during the siege (ca. February 21–26), later credited Pickles with having been "of greatest service" to Gálvez. (Pollock to Pickles, N.O., January 20, 1780; Pollock to the Commercial Committee, N.O., January 20, February 22, and July 19, 1780; John Henderson to Commercial Committee, Mobile Fort, April 17, 1780; Pollock to Calvert, N.O., March 3, 1780; Calvert to Robert Morris, Havana, April 24, 1780; Papers of the Continental Congress, microcopy 247, roll 64, pp. 123–28, 132–34, 347–48, 351, 357–62.) For the armament of the *West Florida* when Pickles captured it on Lake Ponchartrain, see Caughey, *Gálvez*, 159.

25. In 1784, acting under Gálvez' orders, José de Evia carefully surveyed the entrance to Mobile Bay. How unfortunate that Gálvez did not have that information in 1780! See Jack D. L. Holmes, "José de Evia and His Activities in Mobile, 1780–1784," *Alabama Historical Quarterly*, 34, no. 2 (Summer 1972), 110–11.

26. Gálvez, *Diario*, February 10–11, 1780 (AGS GM 6912); Caughey, *Gálvez*, 175–76.

27. Gálvez (*Diario*, February 25, 1780; AGS GM 6912) states that it was Juan Estuard (John Stuart), but he died on March 21, 1779; therefore it must have been Charles Stuart, John's cousin. See John Richard Alden, *John Stuart and the Southern Colonial Frontier* (1944; rpt., New York: Gordian Press, 1966), 171, 212n87.

28. Gálvez, *Diario*, February 23–25, 1780 (AGS GM 6912). Calvert blamed the report of 700 men lost on an Englishman, serving as a Spanish soldier, who had deserted immediately after being landed on Mobile Point. The deserter went to Pensacola, where he reported that "700 of Gen. Gálvez's Troops were lost with the Vessels." Calvert to Morris, Havana, April 24, 1780, Papers of the Continental Congress (microcopy 274, roll 64, p. 360).

29. Charles Stuart was appointed deputy Indian superintendent at Mobile in 1769. Before his capture, Stuart had ordered Indian agent Farquhar Bethune to secure a party of Choctaw to help defend Mobile. Bethune raised a force of 600 Choctaw, but they arrived too late to be of any assistance (see Starr, *Tories*, 177; Peter J. Hamilton, *Colonial Mobile, an Historical Study* [Boston: Houghton Mifflin, 1897], 183n4). Gilbert C. Din recently wrote that James Logan Colbert (a Scot trader), his sons, and a number of Chickasaws may have been at Mobile during the siege, and retired just before Durnford

surrendered. See "Loyalist Resistance after Pensacola: The Case of James Colbert," in Coker and Rea, eds., *Anglo-Spanish Confrontation*, 158.

30. Some 5,000 feet figured on a Spanish *vara* of roughly 33 inches.

31. Gálvez, *Diario*, March 2–3, 1780 (AGS GM 6912).

32. Ibid., March 9–10, 1780.

33. Ibid., March 15–17, 1780. The reports of the number of men captured vary: 16, 20, and 37. See Starr, *Tories*, 174n38; Caughey, *Gálvez*, p. 183.

34. Starr, *Tories*, 174.

35. Samuel Flagg Bemis, *Pinckney's Treaty: America's Advantage from Europe's Distress, 1783–1800* (New Haven: Yale University Press, 1960).

36. There is a difference of opinion whether Mobile was part of the Territory of Orleans between 1810 and 1812 or whether it was considered part of the Mississippi Territory as a result of the Mobile Act of 1803. Clarence Edwin Carter (ed., *The Territorial Papers of the United States: The Territory of Orleans, 1803–1812* [Washington, D.C.: G.P.O., 1940], 9:906n14) argued convincingly that Mobile was in the Territory of Orleans during those years. See Lucille Griffith, *Alabama: A Documentary History to 1900* (University: University of Alabama Press, 1972), 51–60. See also the Proclamation of 1810, in U.S. Congress, *American State Papers, Foreign Affairs* (Washington, D.C.: Gales and Seaton, 1832), 3:397–98; Isaac Joslin Cox, *The West Florida Controversy, 1798–1813: A Study in American Diplomacy* (1918; rpt., Gloucester: Peter Smith, 1967).

37. H. Wesley Odom, Jr., "Cayetano Pérez and the Fall of Mobile" (thesis, University of West Florida, 1977).

38. William S. Coker, "The Last Battle of the War of 1812: New Orleans, No, Fort Bowyer!" *Alabama Historical Quarterly*, 43, no. 1 (1981), 42–63.

39. Carter, *Territorial Papers*, 18, nos. 53–57, pp. 753–55.

Chapter 11
"Approaches to the Study of the Southeastern Borderlands" by Michael C. Scardaville

1. A prolific Southeastern Borderlands historian, Jack D. L. Holmes, has commented on the dearth of studies on Spanish Alabama. In 1970 he wrote that the "biggest lacuna in our knowledge of the Gulf Coast is Spanish Alabama from 1780 to 1813." (See Holmes, "Resources Outside the United States and Research Opportunities for Spanish Florida, 1781–1821," in *In Search of Gulf Coast History*, Ernest F. Dibble and Earle W. Newton, eds. [Pensacola: Historic Pensacola Preservation Board, State of Florida, 1970], 6.) He later noted that "this area has received the least emphasis of all Spanish Borderlands" and that "for young scholars, intent on making a name for themselves in a relatively virgin field, Spanish Alabama offers innumerable challenges" ("Research in the Spanish Borderlands: Alabama," *Latin American Research Review*, 7 [Summer 1972], 6–7).

2. Holmes, "Interpretations and Trends in the Study of the Spanish Borderlands: The Old Southwest," *Southwestern Historical Quarterly*, 74 (April 1971), 441–77; William S. Coker, Jack D. L. Holmes, Samuel Proctor, J. Leitch Wright, Jr., "Research in the Spanish Borderlands," *Latin American Research Review*, 7 (Summer 1972), 3–94. Also see John Francis Bannon, *The*

Spanish Borderlands Frontier, 1513–1821 (Albuquerque: University of New Mexico Press, 1974), 257–87, and Oakah L. Jones, "The Spanish Borderlands: A Selected Reading List," *Journal of the West*, 8 (January 1969), 137–42.

3. Herbert E. Bolton, *The Spanish Borderlands: A Chronicle of Old Florida and the Southwest*, vol. 23 of "The Chronicles of America" (New Haven: Yale University Press, 1921).

4. For a biography of Bolton by a former student, see John Francis Bannon, *Herbert Eugene Bolton: The Historian and the Man, 1870–1953* (Tucson: University of Arizona Press, 1978).

5. Bernard Moses, *The Establishment of Spanish Rule in America: An Introduction to the History and Politics of Spanish America* (New York: Cooper Square, 1898); William R. Shepherd, *Latin America* (New York: Holt, 1914). Also see Moses, "The Neglected Half of American History" (pp. 39–42), and Shepherd, "The Contribution of the Romance Nations to the History of the Americas" (pp. 66–67 in *Latin American History: Essays on Its Study and Teaching, 1898–1965*, ed. Howard F. Cline, vol. 1 [Austin: University of Texas Press, 1967]).

6. Bannon wrote that "Bolton broadened the concept of the West by adding another American frontier to the dimensions of [American history]." *Bolton and the Spanish Borderlands* (Norman: University of Oklahoma Press, 1964), 4.

7. Ibid., 25.

8. Ibid., 24–25.

9. Herbert E. Bolton and Thomas Maitland Marshall, *The Colonization of North America, 1492–1783* (New York: Macmillan, 1920).

10. Jack D. L. Holmes, "Research in the Spanish Borderlands: Louisiana," *Latin American Research Review*, 7 (Summer 1972), 35.

11. Herbert E. Bolton, "Defensive Spanish Expansion and the Significance of the Borderlands," in *Wider Horizons of American History* (Notre Dame: University of Notre Dame Press, 1939), 67–69.

12. Bannon, *The Spanish Borderlands Frontier, 1513–1821*, vii.

13. William Coker, "Research in the Spanish Borderlands: Introduction," *Latin American Research Review*, 7 (Summer 1972), 3–4.

14. Arthur P. Whitaker, *The Spanish-American Frontier, 1783–1795: The Westward Movement and the Spanish Retreat in the Mississippi Valley* (Boston: Houghton Mifflin, 1927) and *The Mississippi Question, 1795–1803: A Study in Trade, Politics, and Diplomacy* (New York: Appleton-Century, 1934); John Tate Lanning, *The Spanish Missions of Georgia* (Chapel Hill: University of North Carolina Press, 1935) and *The Diplomacy of Georgia* (Chapel Hill: University of North Carolina Press, 1934). Other Latin Americanists who started their careers in the Borderlands include Herbert I. Priestley (*Tristán de Luna: A Conquest of the Old South—A Study of Spanish Imperial Strategy* [Glendale: Arthur H. Clark, 1936]), Irving A. Leonard (*Spanish Approach to Pensacola, 1689–1693* [Los Angeles: Quivera Society, 1939]), and France V. Scholes (*Church and State in New Mexico, 1610–1650* [Albuquerque: University of New Mexico Press, 1937]).

15. See additional comments by John J. TePaske in "Spanish America: The Colonial Period," in *Latin American Scholarship since World War II: Trends in History, Political Science, Literature, Geography, and Economics*

(Roberto Esquenazi-Mayo and Michael C. Meyer, eds. [Lincoln: University of Nebraska Press, 1971], 8–9), and in John W. Caughey, "Herbert Eugene Bolton," in *Turner, Bolton, and Webb: Three Historians of the American Frontier* (Wilbur R. Jacobs, John W. Caughey, and Joe B. Frantz, eds. [Seattle: University of Washington Press, 1965], 66).

16. William Coker, "Research in the Spanish Borderlands: Mississippi, 1779–1798," *Latin American Research Review*, 7 (Summer 1972), 40.

17. Fanny and Adolph Bandelier, trans. and eds., *The Journey of Cabeza de Vaca from Florida to the Pacific, 1528–1536* (New York: A. S. Barnes, 1905); Edward G. Bourne, ed., *Narratives of the Career of Hernando de Soto in the Conquest of Florida*, 2 vols. (New York: A. S. Barnes, 1904); F. W. Hodge and T. H. Lewis, eds., *Spanish Explorers in the Southern United States, 1528–1543* (New York: Scribner, 1907); Woodbury Lowery, *The Spanish Settlements within the Present Limits of the United States, 1513–1574*, 2 vols. (New York: Russell and Russell, 1959); Jeanette Thurber Connor, trans. and ed., *The Colonial Records of Spanish Florida*, 2 vols. (De Land: Florida State Historical Society, 1925–30); Herbert Priestley, *The Luna Papers*, 2 vols. (De Land: Florida Historical Society, 1929), and *Tristán de Luna*. For more recent publications, see Eugene Lyon, *The Enterprise of Florida: Pedro Menéndez de Avilés and the Spanish Conquest of Florida of 1565–1568* (Gainesville: University Presses of Florida, 1976), and Robert S. Weddle, *Wilderness Manhunt: The Spanish Search for La Salle* (Austin: University of Texas Press, 1973).

18. Maynard Geiger, *The Franciscan Conquest of Florida, 1573–1618* (Washington, D.C.: Catholic University of America Press, 1937); Michael V. Gannon, *The Cross in the Sand: The Early Catholic Church in Florida, 1513–1870* (Gainesville: University of Florida Press, 1965).

19. Herbert E. Bolton and Mary Ross, *The Debatable Land: A Sketch of the Anglo-Spanish Contest for the Georgia Country* (rpt., New York: Russell and Russell, 1968), and Herbert E. Bolton, *Arredondo's Historical Proof of Spain's Title to Georgia* (Berkeley: University of California Press, 1925); John Tate Lanning, *The Diplomatic History of Georgia: A Study of the Epoch of Jenkins' Ear* (Chapel Hill: University of North Carolina Press, 1936); Charles W. Arnade, *The Siege of St. Augustine in 1702* (Gainesville: University of Florida Press, 1959); Jack D. L. Holmes, *Honor and Fidelity: The Louisiana Infantry Regiment and the Louisiana Militia Companies, 1766–1821* (Birmingham, 1965); Robert L. Gold, *Borderland Empires in Transition: The Triple Nation Transfer of Florida* (Carbondale: Southern Illinois University Press, 1969).

20. Jeanette Thurber Connor, trans. and ed., *Pedro Menéndez de Avilés, Adelantado, Governor and Captain-General of Florida* (De Land: Florida State Historical Society, 1923); Albert Manucy, *Florida's Menéndez: Captain-General of the Ocean Sea* (St. Augustine: St. Augustine Historical Society, 1965); Helen Hornbeck Tanner, *Zéspedes in East Florida, 1784–1790* (Coral Gables: University of Miami Press, 1963); Jack D. L. Holmes, *Gayoso: The Life of a Spanish Governor in the Mississippi Valley, 1789–1799* (Baton Rouge: Louisiana State University Press, 1965); John W. Caughey, *Bernardo de Gálvez in Louisiana, 1770–1783* (Berkeley, 1934).

21. For example, see Joyce Elizabeth Harman, *Trade and Privateering in Spanish*

Florida, 1732–1763 (St. Augustine: St. Augustine Historical Society, 1969);
Laura D. S. Harrell, "Preventive Medicine in the Mississippi Territory,
1799–1802," *Bulletin of the History of Medicine,* 40 (July–August 1966),
364–75; C. Richard Arena, "Land Settlement Policies and Practices in
Spanish Louisiana," in *The Spanish in the Mississippi Valley, 1762–1804,*
John Francis McDermott, ed. (Urbana: University of Illinois Press, 1974),
51–60; Jack D. L. Holmes, "Spanish Regulation of Taverns and the Liquor
Trade in the Mississippi Valley," in *The Spanish in the Mississippi Valley,
1789–1799,* 149–82; Theodore G. Corbett, "Migration to a Spanish Imperial
Frontier in the Seventeenth and Eighteenth Centuries: St. Augustine,"
Hispanic American Historical Review, 54 (August 1974), 414–30; Alicia V.
Tjarks, "Demographic, Ethnic and Occupational Structure of New Mexico,
1790," *The Americas,* 35 (July 1978), 45–88; Hans W. Baade, "Marriage
Contracts in French and Spanish Louisiana: A Study of 'Notarial' Jurispru-
dence," *Tulane Law Review,* 53 (December 1978), 1–92; Charles W. Arnade,
"Cattle Raising in Spanish Florida," *Agricultural History,* 35 (1961), 116–24;
John A. Ersterhold, "Lumber and Trade in the Lower Mississippi Valley and
New Orleans, 1800–1860," *Louisiana History,* 13 (1972), 71–91; Donald E.
Everett, "Emigres and Militiamen: Free Persons of Color in New Orleans,
1803–1815," *Journal of Negro History,* 38 (1953), 377–402; Jack D. L.
Holmes, "Some Economic Problems of Spanish Governors in Louisiana,"
Hispanic American Historical Review, 42 (1962), 521–43; Laura L. Porteus,
"Sanitary Conditions in New Orleans under the Spanish Regime, 1799–
1800," *Louisiana Historical Quarterly,* 15 (1932), 610–17.
22. Holmes, *Gayoso: The Life of a Spanish Governor in the Mississippi Valley,
1789–1799.*
23. John A. Garraty, *The American Nation: A History of the United States* (3d
ed.; New York, 1975), 9–11.
24. For sales of college history textbooks, see *Chronicle of Higher Education,*
November 17, 1980, 19–20.
25. John M. Blum et al., *The National Experience: A History of the United
States* (5th ed.; New York: Harcourt, Brace, Jovanovich, 1981), 4.
26. Henry Franklin Graff and John A. Krout, *The Adventure of the American
People* (New York: Rand McNally, 1973), 95–96.
27. Philip W. Powell, *Tree of Hate: Propaganda and Prejudices Affecting United
States Relations with the Hispanic World* (New York: Basic Books, 1971),
132.
28. Frances FitzGerald, *America Revised: History Schoolbooks in the Twentieth Century* (Boston: Little, Brown, 1979), 96.
29. Oakah L. Jones, "The Spanish Borderlands: Introduction," *Journal of the
West,* 8 (January 1969), 4.
30. See, for example, Stanley M. Hordes, "The Utilization of Local Eighteenth-
Century Records to Reconstruct Social and Economic History: The Case of
Louisiana" (paper presented at annual meeting of South Central Society for
Eighteenth-Century Studies, Albuquerque, 1980). Also see notes 1 and 2,
above.
31. John J. TePaske, *The Governorship of Spanish Florida, 1700–1763* (Durham:
Duke University Press, 1964).
32. Peter J. Hamilton, *Colonial Mobile: An Historical Study* (Boston: Houghton

Mifflin, 1897); Jack D. L. Holmes, "Livestock in Spanish Natchez," *Journal of Mississippi History*, 23 (1961), 15–37, and "Law and Order in Spanish Natchez, 1781–1798," *Journal of Mississippi History*, 25 (1963), 186–201. One exception is John G. Clark's *New Orleans, 1718–1812: An Economic History* (Baton Rouge: Louisiana State University Press, 1970).

33. See, for example, Eugene Lyon, *The Enterprise of Florida*; Charles W. Arnade, *The Seige of St. Augustine in 1702*; Robert L. Gold, *Borderland Empires in Transition.*

34. Research programs, sponsored by the Historic St. Augustine Preservation Board, the St. Augustine Restoration Foundation, Inc., and the Florida State University Field School, have begun in the last five years to examine urban development in Colonial St. Augustine.

35. Oakah L. Jones, *Los Paisanos: Spanish Settlers on the Northern Frontier of New Spain* (Norman: University of Oklahoma, 1979).

36. Bolton, "The Epic of Greater America," in *Wider Horizons of American History*, 51.

37. Lyon, *The Enterprise of Florida*; Paul E. Hoffman, *The Spanish Crown and the Defense of the Caribbean: Precedent, Patrimonialism, and Parsimony, 1535–1585* (Baton Rouge: Louisiana State University Press, 1980).

38. Pablo Tornero Tinajero, *Relaciones de dependencia entre Florida y Estados Unidos, 1783–1820* (Madrid: Ministerio de Asuntos Exteriores, Dirección General de Relaciones Culturales, 1979); Antonio Acosta Rodríguez, *La población de Luisiana española, 1763–1803* (Madrid: Ministerio de Asuntos Exteriores, Dirección General de Relaciones Culturales, 1979).

39. Michael V. Gannon, "Documents of the Spanish Borderlands: A Calendaring Project at the University of Florida," *William and Mary Quarterly*, 38 (October 1981), 718–22.

40. Hordes, "The Utilization of Local Eighteenth-Century Records."

41. Alistair Hennessy, *The Frontier in Latin American History* (London: Edward Arnold, 1978), 13.

42. Charles Fairbanks, "From Missionary to Mestizo: Changing Culture of Eighteenth-Century St. Augustine," in *Eighteenth Century Florida and the Caribbean*, Samuel Proctor, ed. (Gainesville: University Presses of Florida, 1976), 88–99; Kathleen Deagan, "*Mestizaje* in Colonial St. Augustine," *Ethnohistory*, 20 (1973), 53–64. For a comprehensive listing of site reports and material culture studies, see Thomas Ray Shurbutt and Janet Lois Gritzner, *Historical Archaeology of the Colonial Southeastern Atlantic Coast: A Bibliography* (Gainesville: University of Florida, Department of Anthropology, 1979).

43. In 1937, Bolton participated in the research on La Purísima Mission, one of the first major archaeological projects on a Spanish site in California. See Bannon, *Herbert Eugene Bolton: The Historian and the Man*, 207.

Bibliography

Articles, Monographs, Dissertations, and Theses

Antevs, Ernst. "Geologic-Climatic Dating in the West." *American Antiquity*, 20, no. 4 (1955), 317–35.

Arnade, Charles W. "Cattle Raising in Spanish Florida." *Agricultural History*, 35 (1961), 116–24.

———. *Florida on Trial, 1593–1602.* Hispanic American Studies, vol. 16. Miami: University of Miami Press, 1959.

The Siege of St. Augustine in 1702. University of Florida Monographs, Social Sciences No. 3. Gainesville: University of Florida Press, 1959.

Asch, David L., and Nancy B. Asch. "Chenopod as Cultigen: A Re-evaluation of Some Prehistoric Collections from Eastern North America." *Midcontinental Journal of Archaeology*, 2, no. 1 (1977), 3–45.

Baade, Hans W. "Marriage Contracts in French and Spanish Louisiana: A Study in 'Notarial' Jurisprudence." *Tulane Law Review*, 53, no. 1 (1978), 3–92.

Baker, Steven G. "Cofitachique: Fair Province of Carolina." Thesis, University of South Carolina, 1974.

Bender, Margaret M., David A. Baerreis, and Raymond L. Steventon. "Further Light on Carbon Isotopes and Hopewell Agriculture." *American Antiquity*, 46, no. 2 (1981), 346–53.

Brain, Jeffrey P., Alan Toth, and Antonio Rodriguez-Buckingham. "Ethnohistoric Archaeology and the De Soto Entrada into the Lower Mississippi Valley." In *Conference on Historic Site Archaeology Papers*, vol. 7. Ed. Stanley South. Columbia: Institute of Archeology and Anthropology, University of South Carolina, 1974, 232–89.

Brown, A. B. "Bone Strontium as a Dietary Indicator in Human Skeletal Populations." *Contributions to Geology*, 13 (1974), 47–48.

223

Brown, James A., ed. *Approaches to the Social Dimensions of Mortuary Practices.* Memoirs of Society of American Archaeology, vol. 25. Washington, D.C.: Society of American Archaeology, 1971.
Buikstra, Jane E. *Hopewell in the Lower Illinois Valley: A Regional Study of Human Biological Variability and Prehistoric Mortuary Behavior.* Northwestern Archaeological Program Scientific Papers, No. 2. Evanston: Northwestern University Press, 1976.
Bullen, Ripley P. "De Soto's Ucita and the Terra Ceia Site." *Florida Historical Quarterly,* 30, no. 4 (1952), 317–23.
_____. *The Terra Ceia Site, Manatee County, Florida.* Florida Anthropological Society Publications, No. 3. Gainesville: University of Florida, 1951.
Bushnell, Amy. " 'That Demonic Game': The Campaign to Stop Indian Pelota Playing in Spanish Florida, 1675–1684." *The Americas,* 35, no. 1 (1978), 1–19.
_____. "The Menéndez Marquez Cattle Barony at La Chua and the Determinants of Economic Expansion in Seventeenth-Century Florida." *Florida Historical Quarterly,* 56 (1978), 407–31.
Caldwell, Joseph R. *Trend and Tradition in the Prehistory of the Eastern United States.* American Anthropological Association Memoirs, 88. Menasha, Wis., 1958.
Carneiro, Robert. "A Theory of the Origin of the State." *Science,* 169, no. 3947 (1970), 733–38.
Chardon, Roland. "The Elusive Spanish League: A Problem of Measurement in Sixteenth Century New Spain." *Hispanic American Historial Review,* 60 (1980), 294–302.
Coker, William. "Research in the Spanish Borderlands: Introduction." *Latin American Research Review,* 7 (Summer 1972), 3–4.
_____. "Research in the Spanish Borderlands: Mississippi, 1779–1798." *Latin American Research Review,* 7 (Summer 1972), 40.
_____, Jack D. L. Holmes, Samuel Proctor, and J. Leitch Wright, Jr. "Research in the Spanish Borderlands," *Latin American Research Review,* 7 (Summer 1972), 3–94.
Corbett, Theodore, "Migration to a Spanish Imperial Frontier in the Seventeenth and Eighteenth Centuries: St. Augustine." *Hispanic American Historical Review,* 54 (August 1974), 414–30.
Cotter, John. "The Occurrence of Flints and Extinct Animals in Pluvial Deposits near Clovis, New Mexico." *Proceedings of the Academy of Natural Sciences of Philadelphia,* 89 (1937), 2–16.
Deagan, Kathleen. "The Material Assemblage of 16th Century Spanish Florida." *Historical Archaeology,* 12 (1978), 25–50.
_____. "*Mestizage* in Colonial St. Augustine." *Ethnohistory,* 20 (1973), 53–64.
Deevey, E., and Richard Flint. "Postglacial Hypsithemal Interval." *Science,* 125 (1957), 3240.
DeJarnette, David L., and Asael T. Hansen. *The Archeology of the Childersburg Site, Alabama.* Department of Anthropology, Florida State University, Notes in Anthropology, 6. Tallahassee: Florida State University Press, 1960.
_____, and Steven B. Wimberly. *The Bessemer Site: Excavation of Three Mounds and Surrounding Village Areas near Bessemer, Alabama.* Geological Survey of Alabama Museum Paper, 17, University of Alabama, 1941.

Delanglez, Jean, "El Rio del Espíritu Santo." *Mid-America*, 25, no. 4 (1943).

Deuel, Thorne. "Basic Cultures of the Mississippi Valley." *American Anthropologist*, 37 (1935), 429–45.

Drucker, Philip, Robert F. Heizer, and Robert J. Squier. *Excavations at La Venta, Tabasco*. Bureau of American Ethnology Bulletin, 170. Washington, D.C.: G.P.O., 1959.

Ersterhold, John A. "Lumber and Trade in the Lower Mississippi Valley and New Orleans, 1800–60." *Louisiana History*, 13 (1972), 71–91.

Everett, Donald E. "Emigres and Militiamen: Free Persons of Color in New Orleans, 1803–1815." *Journal of Negro History*, 38 (1953), 377–402.

Fairbanks, Charles H. "Early Spanish Colonial Beads." In *Conference on Historic Site Archaeology Papers*, 8th, vol. 2, pt. 1. Ed. Stanley South. Raleigh, N.C., 1968, 3–21.

Ford, James A. *Analysis of Indian Village Site Collections from Louisiana and Mississippi*. Department of Conservation, Louisiana Geological Survey, Anthropological Study 2. New Orleans: Department of Conservation, Louisiana Geological Survey, 1936.

———, and Gordon Willey. "An Interpretation of the Prehistory of the Eastern United States." *American Anthropologist*, 43, no. 3 (1941), 325–63.

Fowler, Melvin L. "Middle Mississippian Agricultural Fields." *American Antiquity*, 34, no. 4 (1969), 365–75.

Gannon, Michael V. "Documents of the Spanish Borderlands: A Calendaring Project at the University of Florida." *William and Mary Quarterly*, 38 (October 1981), 718–22.

Gasser, Robert E., and E. Charles Adams. "Aspects of Deterioration of Plant Remains in Archaeological Sites: The Walpi Archaeological Project." *Journal of Ethnobiology*, 1 (1981), 182–92.

Goldstein, Lynne G. *Mississippian Mortuary Practices: A Case Study of Two Cemeteries in the Lower Illinois Valley*. Northwestern University Archaeological Program Scientific Papers, 4. Evanston: Northwestern University Press, 1980.

Greenman, Emerson. "The Upper Paleolithic of the New World." *Current Anthropology*, 4, no. 1 (1963), 41–91.

Griffin, James B. "Eastern North American Archaeology: A Summary." *Science*, 156, no. 3772 (1967), 175–91.

———. "A Commentary on Some Archaeological Activities in the Mid-Continent, 1925–75." *Midcontinental Journal of Archaeology*, 1, no. 1 (1976), 5–38.

Hammond, Norman. "The Earliest Maya." *Scientific American*, 236 (1977), 116–23.

Harrell, Laura D. S. "Preventive Medicine in the Mississippi Territory, 1799–1802." *Bulletin of the History of Medicine*, 40 (July–August 1966), 364–75.

Haury, Emil W. "Artifacts with Mammoth Remains, Naco, Arizona." *American Antiquity*, 19, no. 1 (1953), 1–14.

———, E. B. Sayles, and William W. Wasley. "The Lehner Mammoth Site, Southeastern Arizona." *American Antiquity*, 25, no. 1 (1959), 2–30.

Hayashi, Kobayashi. "The Fukui Microblade Technology and Its Relationship in Northeast Asia and North America." *Arctic Anthropology*, 5, no. 1 (1968), 128–90.

Hill, Roscoe R. "The Office of Adelantado." *Political Science Quarterly,* 21, no. 4 (1913), 646–68.

Hoffman, Paul E. "A Study of Florida Defense Costs." *Florida Historical Quarterly,* 51, no. 4 (April 1973), 401–22.

Holmes, Jack D. L. "Interpretations and Trends in the Study of the Spanish Borderlands: The Old Southwest." *Southwestern Historical Quarterly,* 74 (April 1971), 441–47.

———. "Law and Order in Spanish Natchez." *Journal of Mississippi History,* 25 (1963), 186–201.

———. "Research in the Spanish Borderlands: Alabama." *Latin American Research Review,* 7 (Summer 1972), 6–7.

———. "Research in the Spanish Borderlands: Louisiana." *Latin American Research Review,* 7 (Summer 1972), 35.

———. "Some Economic Problems of Spanish Governors. In Louisiana." *Hispanic American Historical Review,* 42 (1962), 521–43.

———. "Livestock in Spanish Natchez." *Journal of Mississippi History,* 23 (1961), 15–37.

———. "José de Evia and His Activities in Mobile, 1780–84." *Alabama Historical Quarterly,* 34, no. 2 (Summer 1972), 105–12.

Holmes, William H. "Areas of American Culture Characterization Tentatively Outlined as an Aid in the Study of the Antiquities." *American Anthropologist,* 16, no. 3 (1914), 413–46.

———. "Aboriginal Pottery of the Eastern United States." In *Bureau of American Ethnology, 20th Annual Report, 1898–99.* Washington, D.C.: Bureau of American Ethnology, 1903.

———. "Ancient Pottery of the Mississippi Valley." In *Bureau of Ethnology, 4th Annual Report, 1882–83* (1886), 367–436.

———. "Law and Order in Spanish Natchez, 1781–1798." *Journal of Mississippi History,* 25 (1963), 186–201.

Jones, Oakah L. "The Spanish Borderlands: Introduction." *Journal of the West,* 8 (January 1969), 4.

———. "The Spanish Borderlands: A Selected Reading List." *Journal of the West,* 8 (January 1969), 137–42.

Kammen, Michael. "Clio and the Changing Fashions: Some Patterns in Current American Historiography." *American Scholar* (1975), 484–96.

Keeler, Robert Winston. "An Archaeological Survey of the Upper Catawba River Valley." Honors thesis, University of North Carolina, 1971.

Ketcham, Herbert E., trans. and ed. "Three Sixteenth Century Spanish Chronicles relating to Georgia." *Georgia Historical Quarterly,* 38 (1954), 81.

Klinger, Timothy. "Parkin Archeology: A Report on the 1966 Field School Test Excavations at the Parkin Site." *Arkansas Archeologist,* 16–18 (1975–77), 45–80.

Krieger, Alex D. *Culture Complexes and Chronology in Northern Texas with Extension of Puebloan Datings to the Mississippi Valley.* University of Texas Publication, 4640. Austin: University of Texas Press, 1946.

———. "The Eastward Extension of Puebloan Datings Toward Cultures of the Mississippi Valley." *American Antiquity,* 12, no. 3 (1947), 141–48.

Lafferty, Robert H., III. "An Analysis of Prehistoric Southeastern Fortifications." Thesis, Southern Illinois University, 1973.

Lankford, George E., III. "A New Look at de Soto's Route through Alabama." *Journal of Alabama Archaeology,* 23 no. 1 (1977), 10–36.

Larson, Lewis H., Jr. "Functional Considerations of Warfare in the Southeast during the Mississippian Period." *American Antiquity,* 37, no. 3 (1972), 383–92.

Lazarus, William C. "A Sixteenth Century Spanish Coin from a Fort Walton Burial." *Florida Anthropologist,* 17, no. 2 (1964), 134–37.

Lehmer, Donald J. *Introduction to Middle Missouri Archaeology.* National Park Service Anthropological Papers, 1. Washington, D.C.: G.P.O., 1971.

Lewis, Thomas M. N. *A Suggested Basis for Paleo-Indian Chronology in Tennessee and the Eastern United States.* Southern Indian Studies, 5. Chapel Hill: University of North Carolina Press, 1934.

Limp, W. Frederick, and Van A. Reidhead. "An Economic Evaluation of the Potential of Fish Utilization in Riverine Environments." *American Antiquity,* 44, no. 1 (1979), 70–78.

Lyon, Eugene. "Spain's Sixteenth-Century, North American Settlement Attempt: A Neglected Aspect." *Florida Historical Quarterly,* 59, no. 3 (January 1981), 275–92.

MacNeish, Richard S. "Early Man in the Andes." *Scientific American,* 224, no. 4 (1971), 36–46.

_____. "The Origins of New World Civilization." *Scientific American,* 211, no. 5 (1964), 29–37.

_____. "Ancient Mesoamerican Civilization." *Science,* 143 (1964), 531–37.

McKern, William C. "The Midwestern Taxonomic Method as an Aid to Archaeological Culture Study." *American Antiquity,* 4, no. 5 (1939), 301–13.

Martin, Paul S. "The Discovery of America." *Science,* 79 (1973), 969–74.

Martinez, Carlos A. "Culture Sequence on the Central Georgia Coast, 1000 B.C.–1650 A.D." Thesis, University of Florida, 1975.

Millon, Rene. "Teotihuacan: Completion of Map of Giant Ancient City in the Valley of Mexico." *Science,* 170 (1970), 1077–82.

Moore, Clarence B. "The Antiquities of the Ouachita Valley." *Journal of the Academy of Natural Sciences of Philadelphia,* 14, no. 1 (1909), 1–170.

_____. "Antiquities of the St. Francis, White and Black Rivers, Arkansas." *Journal of the Academy of Natural Sciences of Philadelphia,* 14, no. 2 (1910), 253–365.

_____. "Certain Aboriginal Remains of the Alabama River." *Journal of the Academy of Natural Sciences of Philadelphia,* 11 (1899), 320–28.

Nance, C. Roger. *The Archaeological Sequence at Durant Bend, Dallas County, Alabama.* Special Publication of Alabama Archaeological Society, 2. Orange Beach, Ala.: Alabama Archaeological Society, 1976.

Odom, H. Wesley, Jr. "Cayetano Pérez and the Fall of Mobile." Thesis, University of West Florida, 1977.

Pearce, James E. "The Significance of the East Texas Archaeological Field." In *Conference on Southern Prehistory.* Washington, D.C.: National Research Council, 1932.

Pearson, Charles. "Evidence of Early Spanish Contact on the Georgia Coast." *Historical Archaeology,* 11 (1977), 74–83.

Peebles, Christopher S. "Moundville: The Social Organization of a Prehistoric Community and Culture." Dissertation, University of California, 1974.

———— and Susan Kus. "Some Archaeological Correlates of Ranked Societies." *American Antiquity*, 42, no. 3 (1977), 421–48.

Phillips, Philip. "Introduction to the Archaeology of the Mississippi." Dissertation, Harvard University, 1939.

————, James A. Ford, and James B. Griffin. *Archaeological Survey in the Lower Mississippi Alluvial Valley, 1940–1947*. Papers of the Peabody Museum of American Archaeology and Ethnology, 25. Cambridge, Mass.: Peabody Museum, 1952.

Porteus, Laura L. "Sanitary Conditions in New Orleans under the Spanish Regime, 1799–1800." *Louisiana Historical Quarterly*, 15 (1932), 610–17.

Putnam, Frederick W. "Archaeological Explorations in Tennessee." *Eleventh Annual Report of the Peabody Museum*, 2, no. 2 (1878), 305–60.

Quimby, George I. "Cultural and Natural Areas before Kroeber." *American Antiquity*, 19, no. 4 (1954), 317–31.

Rathje, William L. "The Origin and Development of Lowland Classic Maya Civilization." *American Antiquity*, 36, no. 3 (1971), 275–85.

Reeves, Bryan O. K. "The Concept of an Altithermal Cultural Hiatus in Northern Plains Prehistory." *American Anthropologist*, 75, no. 5 (1973), 1221–53.

Reitz, Elizabeth J. "Spanish and British Subsistence at St. Augustine, Florida, and Frederica, Georgia, between 1565 and 1783." Dissertation, University of Florida, 1979.

Schoeninger, M. J. *Dietary Reconstruction at Chalcatzingo, a Formative Period Site in Morelos, Mexico*. Museum of Anthropology, University of Michigan, Technical Reports, 9, 1979.

Sears, William H. "The Study of Social and Religious Systems in North American Archaeology." *Current Anthropology*, 2, no. 3 (1961), 223–46.

Sheldon, Craig. "The Mississippian-Historic Transition in Central Alabama." Dissertation, University of Oregon, 1974.

Simpson, Anson. "Kingston (Illinois) Focus of the Mississippi Culture." *Papers in Anthropology, Transactions of the Illinois Academy of Science*, 27, no. 2 (1934), 25.

Skinner, Morris F., and O. C. Kaiser. "The Fossil Bison of Alaska and Preliminary Revision of the Genus." *Bulletin of the American Museum of Natural History*, 39. New York: American Museum of Natural History, 1947.

Smith, Bruce D. *Middle Mississippi Exploitation of Animal Populations*. University of Michigan, Museum of Anthropology, Anthropological Papers, 57. Ann Arbor: University of Michigan, 1975.

Smith, Marvin T. "The Route of de Soto through Tennessee, Georgia, and Alabama: The Evidence from Material Culture." *Early Georgia*, 4, no. 1–2 (1976), 27–48.

South, Stanley. *The Search for Santa Elena on Parris Island, South Carolina*. Research Manuscript Series, 150. Columbia: Institute of Archeology and Anthropology, University of South Carolina, 1979.

————. *The Discovery of Santa Elena*. Research Manuscript Series, 165. Columbia: Institute of Archeology and Anthropology, University of South Carolina, 1980.

Starr, J. Barton. "Campbell Town: French Huguenots in British West Florida." *Florida Historical Quarterly*, 54 (1976), 532–47.

228

Steponaitis, Vincas P. "Ceramics, Chronology, and Community Patterns at Moundville, a Late Prehistoric Site in Alabama." Dissertation, University of Michigan, 1980.

Steward, Julian B. *Basin-Plateau Aboriginal Socio-Political Groups*. Bureau of American Ethnology Bulletin, 120. Washington, D.C.: G.P.O., 1938.

Stirling, Matthew W. *An Initial Series from Tres Zapotes, Vera Cruz, Mexico*. National Geographic Society Contributed Technical Papers, 1. Washington, D.C., 1940.

Stuart, George E. "The Post-Archaic Occupation of Central South Carolina." Dissertation, University of North Carolina, 1975.

Swanton, John R. *Early History of the Creek Indians and Their Neighbors*. Bureau of American Ethnology Bulletin, 73. Washington, D.C.: G.P.O., 1922.

_____. *The Indians of the Southeastern United States*. Bureau of American Ethnology Bulletin, 137. Washington, D.C.: G.P.O., 1946.

Thomas, Cyrus, "Report on the Mound Explorations of the Bureau of American Ethnology, 1890–91." *Bureau of Ethnology, 12th Annual Report* (1894), 3–730.

Thomas, David H. "An Empirical Test for Steward's Model of Great Basin Settlement Patterns." *American Antiquity*, 38, no. 2 (1973), 155–76.

Tjarks, Alicia V. "Demographic, Ethnic and Occupational Structure of New Mexico, 1790." *The Americas*, 35 (July 1978), 45–88.

Vigneras, Louis-André. "A Spanish Discovery of North Carolina." *North Carolina Historical Review*, 46, no. 4 (October 1969), 398–414.

Vogel, J. C., and N. J. van der Merwe. "Isotopic Evidence for Early Maize Cultivation in New York State." *American Antiquity*, 42, no. 2 (1977), 238–42.

Woods, Patricia Dillon. *French-Indian Relations on the Southern Frontier, 1699–1762*. Studies in American History and Culture, 18. Ann Arbor: UMI Research Press, 1980.

Wycoff, Don G., and Timothy G. Baugh. "Early Historic Hasenai Elites: A Model for the Material Culture of Governing Elites." *Midcontinental Journal of Archaeology*, 5, no. 2 (1980), 225–88.

Yerkes, Richard. "The Potential of Fish Utilization in Riverine Environments." *Midcontinental Journal of Archaeology*, 6, no. 2 (1981), 207–17.

_____ and John R. Swanton. *The Indians of the Southeastern United States*. Bureau of American Ethnology Bulletin, 137. Washington, D.C.: G.P.O., 1946.

Zahler, James W., Jr. "A Morphological Analysis of a Protohistoric-Historic Skeletal Population from St. Simons Island, Georgia." Thesis, University of Florida, 1976.

Books and Chapters from Books

Acosta Rodríguez, Antonio. *La Población de Luisiana española, 1763–1803*. Madrid: Ministerio de Asuntos Exteriores, Dirección General de Relaciones Culturales, 1979.

Adair, James. *History of the American Indians* (1775). Reprint, New York: Johnson Reprints, 1968.

BIBLIOGRAPHY

Alden, John R. *John Stuart and the Southern Colonial Frontier: a Study of Indian Relations, War Trade and Land Problems in the Southern Wilderness, 1745–1775* (1944) Reprint, New York: Gordian Press, 1966.

———. *The South in the Revolution, 1763–1789.* Vol. 3 of *A History of the South.* Baton Rouge: Louisiana State University Press, 1957.

Bandelier, Fanny, and Adolph Bandelier, trans. and eds. *The Journey of Álvar Núñez Cabeza de Vaca and His Companions from Florida to the Pacific, 1528–1536.* New York: A. S. Barnes, 1905.

Bannon, John Francis. *The Spanish Borderlands Frontier, 1513–1821.* Albuquerque: University of New Mexico Press, 1974.

———. *Herbert Eugene Bolton: The Historian and the Man, 1870–1953.* Tucson: University of Arizona Press, 1978.

———, ed. *Bolton and the Spanish Borderlands.* Norman: University of Oklahoma Press, 1964.

Bemis, Samuel Flagg. *Pinckney's Treaty: America's Advantage from Europe's Distress, 1783–1800.* New Haven: Yale University Press, 1960.

Blum, John M., et al. *The National Experience: A History of the United States.* 5th ed. New York: Harcourt Brace Jovanovich, 1981.

Bolton, Herbert E. "Defensive Spanish Expansion and the Significance of the Borderlands." In *Wider Horizons of American History.* Notre Dame: University of Notre Dame Press, 1939, 67–69.

———. *The Spanish Borderlands: A Chronicle of Old Florida and the Southwest.* Vol. 23 of *The Chronicles of America.* New Haven: Yale University Press, 1921.

———, ed. *Arredondo's Historical Proof of Spain's Title to Georgia.* By Antonio de Arredondo. Berkeley: University of California Press, 1925.

——— and Mary Ross. *The Debatable Land: A Sketch of the Anglo-Spanish Contest for the Georgia Country.* Reprint, New York: Russell and Russell, 1968.

——— and Thomas Maitland Marshall. *The Colonization of North America, 1492–1783.* New York: Macmillan, 1920.

Borja Medina Rojas, Francisco de. *José de Ezpeleta: Gobernador de la Mobila, 1780–81.* Seville: Escuela de Estudios Hispanoamericanos de Sevilla, 1980.

Bourne, Edward G., ed. *Narratives of the Career of Hernando de Soto in the Conquest of Florida.* Trans. Buckingham Smith. 2 vols. New York: A. S. Barnes, 1904.

Brackenridge, Henry M. *Views of Louisiana Together with a Journal of a Voyage up the Missouri River in 1811* (1814). Reprint, Chicago: Quadrangle Books, 1962.

Brain, Jeffrey P. "Artifacts of the Adelantado." *Conference on Historic Site Archaeology Papers,* 8 (1975), 129–38.

———. *Tunica Treasure.* Cambridge, Mass.: Peabody Museum of Archaeology and Ethnology, Harvard University, 1979.

Brown, James A., ed. *Approaches to the Social Dimensions of Mortuary Practices.* Memoirs of the Society of American Archaeology, 25. Washington, D.C.: Society of American Archaeology, 1971.

Bryan, Alan L., ed. *Early Man in America from a Circum-Pacific Perspective.* Occasional Papers, I. Edmonton: University of Alberta Press, 1978.

Carter, Clarence Edwin, comp. and ed. *The Territorial Papers of the United States: The Territory of Orleans, 1803–1812.* Washington, D.C.: G.P.O., 1940.

Caughey, John W. "Herbert Eugene Bolton." In *Turner, Bolton, and Webb: Three Historians of the American Frontier.* Ed. Wilbur R. Jacobs, John W. Caughey, and Joe B. Frantz. Seattle: University of Washington Press, 1965.

_____. *McGillivray of the Creeks.* Norman: University of Oklahoma Press, 1938.

_____. *Bernardo de Gálvez in Louisiana, 1776–1783* (1934). Reprint, Gretna, Louisiana: Pelican, 1972.

Clark, John G. *New Orleans, 1718–1812: An Economic History.* Baton Rouge: Louisiana State University Press, 1970.

Cline, Howard F., comp. and ed. *Latin American History: Essays on Its Study and Teaching, 1898–1965.* Vol. 1. Austin: University of Texas Press, 1967.

Coe, Michael D. *Mexico.* New York: Praeger, 1962.

_____. *The Maya.* New York: Praeger, 1966.

Coker, William S. *The Last Battle of the War of 1812: New Orleans, No, Fort Bowyer!* Pensacola: Perdido Bay Press, 1981.

_____ and Hazel P. Coker. *The Siege of Pensacola, 1781, in Maps, with Data on Troop Strength, Military Units, Ships, Casualties and Related Statistics.* Pensacola: Perdido Bay Press, 1981.

_____. *The Siege of Mobile, 1780, in Maps, with Data on Troop Strength, Military Units, Ships, Casualties and Prisoners of War, including a Brief History of Fort Charlotte (Conde).* Pensacola: Perdido Bay Press, 1982.

Connor, Jeanette Thurber. *Pedro Menéndez de Avilés: Adelantado, Governor, and Captain-General of Florida.* De Land: Florida State Historical Society, 1923.

_____, trans. and ed. *The Colonial Records of Spanish Florida: Letters and Reports of Governors and Secular Persons.* 2 vols. De Land: Florida State Historical Society, 1925–30.

Corkran, David H. *The Creek Frontier, 1540–1783.* Norman: University of Oklahoma Press, 1967.

Cox, Isaac Joslin. *The West Florida Controversy, 1798–1813: A Study in American Diplomacy* (1918). Reprint, Gloucester, Mass.: Peter Smith, 1967.

Crane, Verner W. *The Southern Frontier, 1670–1732.* Durham: Duke University Press, 1928.

Craven, Wesley Frank. *The Southern Colonies in the Seventeenth Century, 1607–1689.* Vol. 1. Baton Rouge: Louisiana State Press, 1949.

Deetz, James J. F. *Invitation to Archaeology.* New York: Natural History Press, 1967.

Deuel, Thorne. "The Application of a Classificatory Method to Mississippi Valley Archaeology." In *Rediscovering Illinois,* by Fay-Cooper Cole and Thorne Deuel. Chicago: University of Chicago Press, 1937.

Dibble, Ernest F., and Earle W. Newton, eds. *In Search of Gulf Coast History.* Pensacola: Historic Pensacola Preservation Board, State of Florida, 1970.

Durnford, Mary, comp. and ed. *Family Recollections of Lieutenant General Elias Durnford.* Montreal: John Lovell, 1863.

Fagan, Brian M. *People of the Earth.* 3d ed. Boston: Little, Brown, 1980.

FitzGerald, Frances. *America Revised: History Schoolbooks in the Twentieth Century.* Boston: Little, Brown, 1979.

Flint, Richard F. *Glacial Geology and the Pleistocene Epoch.* New York: John Wiley, 1947.

Gannon, Michael V. *The Cross in the Sand: The Early Catholic Church in Florida, 1513–1870.* Gainesville: University of Florida Press, 1965.

Garcilaso de la Vega. *The Florida of the Inca.* Trans. and ed. John G. Varner and Jeannette J. Varner. Austin: University of Texas Press, 1962.

Garraty, John A. *The American Nation: A History of the United States.* 3d ed. New York: Harper & Row, 1975.

Geiger, Maynard J. *The Franciscan Conquest of Florida, 1573–1618.* Washington: Catholic University of America Press, 1937.

Gibbon, Guy. "A Model of Mississippian Development and Its Implications for the Red Wing Area." In *Aspects of Upper Great Lakes Anthropology,* ed. Elden Johnson. Duluth: Minnesota Historical Society, 1974.

Gibson, Arrell M. *The Chickasaws.* Norman: University of Oklahoma, 1971.

Gilbert, R. I. "Applications of Trace Element Research to Problems in Archaeology." In *Biocultural Adaptation in Prehistoric America,* ed. Robert L. Blakely. Athens: University of Georgia Press, 1977.

Giraud, Marcel. *Histoire de la Louisiane française.* Paris: Presses Universitaires de France, 1953–74.

Gold, Robert L. *Borderland Empires in Transition: The Triple Nation Transfer of Florida.* Carbondale: Southern Illinois University Press, 1969.

Graff, Henry Franklin, and John A. Krout. *The Adventure of the American People: A History of the United States.* New York: Rand McNally, 1973.

Griffin, James B. "Culture Change and Continuity in Eastern United States." In *Man in Northeastern North America.* Andover: Phillips Academy Foundation, 1946.

⸻, ed. *Archeology of Eastern United States.* Chicago: University of Chicago Press, 1952.

Griffith, Lucille. *Alabama: A Documentary History to 1900.* Revised and enlarged. University: University of Alabama Press, 1972.

Hally, David. *Archaeological Investigation of the Little Egypt Site (9Mu102), Murray County, Georgia, 1969 Season.* University of Georgia Laboratory of Archaeology Series, Report 18. Athens: University of Georgia Press, 1979.

Hamilton, Peter J. *Colonial Mobile, an Historical Study.* Boston: Houghton Mifflin, 1897.

Harman, Joyce Elizabeth. *Trade and Privateering in Spanish Florida, 1732–1763.* St. Augustine: St. Augustine Historical Society, 1969.

Heiss, Aloiss. *Descripción General de Las Monedas Hispano—Christianas desde la Invasión de los Arabes.* Madrid: R. N. Milagro, 1865.

Hennessy, Alistair. *The Frontier in Latin American History.* London: Edward Arnold, 1978.

Hester, James J., and James Grady. *Introduction to Archaeology.* 2nd ed. New York: Holt, Rinehart and Winston, 1982.

Hodge, Frederick W., and Theodore H. Lewis, eds. *Spanish Explorers in the Southern United States, 1528–1543.* New York: Scribner, 1907.

Hoffman, Paul E. *The Spanish Crown and the Defense of the Caribbean,*

1535–1585: Precedent, Patrimonialism, and Parsimony. Baton Rouge: Louisiana State University Press, 1980.

Holmes, Jack D. L. *Gayoso: The Life of a Spanish Governor in the Mississippi Valley, 1789–1799.* Baton Rouge: Louisiana State University Press, 1965.

––––––. *Honor and Fidelity: The Louisiana Infantry Regiment and the Louisiana Militia Companies, 1766–1821.* Birmingham, 1965.

Hopkins, David M., ed. *The Bering Land Bridge.* Stanford: Stanford University Press, 1967.

Hudson, Charles M. *The Southeastern Indians.* Knoxville: University of Tennessee Press, 1976.

Jennings, Jesse D. *Prehistory of North America.* New York: McGraw-Hill, 1968.

––––––and Edward Norbeck, eds. *Prehistoric Man in the New World.* Chicago: University of Chicago Press, 1964.

Jennings, Jesse D., ed. *Ancient Native Americans.* San Francisco: W. H. Freeman, 1978.

Johnson, Cecil. *British West Florida, 1763–1783* (1942). Reprint, Hamden, Conn.: Archon Books, 1971.

Jones, Oakah L. *Los Paisanos: Spanish Settlers on the Northern Frontier of New Spain.* Norman: University of Oklahoma Press, 1979.

Kidder, Alfred. *An Introduction to the Study of Southwestern Archaeology, with a Preliminary Account of the Excavation at Pecos.* New Haven: Yale University Press, 1968.

Lambert, Joseph C., trans. *The Reign of Louis XIV, 1698–1715.* Vol. 1 of *Histoire de la Louisiane française,* by Marcel Giraud. Baton Rouge: Louisiana State University Press, 1974.

Lanning, John Tate. *The Spanish Missions of Georgia.* Chapel Hill: University of North Carolina Press, 1935.

––––––. *The Diplomatic History of Georgia, A study of the Epoch of Jenkins' Ear.* Chapel Hill: University of North Carolina Press, 1936.

Leder, Lawrence H. *Historians of Nature and Man's Nature.* Vol. 3 of *The Colonial Legacy.* New York: Harper & Row, 1973.

Lehmer, Donald J. "Climate and Culture History in the Middle Missouri Valley." In *Pleistocene and Recent Environments of the Central Great Plains,* ed. Wakefield Dort, Jr. and J. Knox Jones. University of Kansas Special Publication 3, 1970.

Leonard, Irving A., ed. and trans. *Spanish Approach to Pensacola, 1689–1693.* Albuquerque: Quivera Society, 1939.

Lewis, Clifford M., and Albert J. Loomie. *The Spanish Jesuit Mission in Virginia.* Chapel Hill: University of North Carolina Press, 1953.

Linduska, Joseph. *Waterfowl Tomorrow.* U.S. Department of the Interior. Washington, D.C.: G.P.O., 1964.

Linne, Sigvald. *Archaeological Researches at Teotihuacan, Mexico.* Stockholm: Ethnographical Museum of Sweden, 1934.

Lowery, Woodbury. *The Spanish Settlements within the Present Limits of the United States, 1513–1574.* 2 vols. New York: Russell and Russell, 1959.

Lyon, Eugene. *The Enterprise of Florida: Pedro Menéndez de Avilés and the Spanish Conquest of 1565–1568.* Gainesville: University Presses of Florida, 1976.

233

MacNeish, Richard S. *The Nonceramic Artifacts.* Vol. 2 of *The Prehistory of the Tehuacan Valley.* Austin: University of Texas, 1967.

Manucy, Albert. *Florida's Menéndez: Captain General of the Ocean Sea.* St. Augustine: St. Augustine Historical Society, 1965.

McDermott, John Francis, ed. *The Spanish in the Mississippi Valley, 1762–1804.* Urbana: University of Illinois Press, 1974.

Meriwether, Robert L. *The Expansion of South Carolina, 1729–1765.* Kingsport, Tenn.: Southern, 1940.

Milanich, Jerald, and William C. Sturtevant, eds. *Francisco Pareja's 1613 Confesionario.* Trans. Emilio Moran. Tallahassee: Florida Division of Archives, History and Records Management, 1972.

———— and Samuel Proctor, eds. *Tacachale: Essays on the Indians of Florida and Southeastern Georgia during the Historic Period.* Gainesville: University Presses of Florida, 1978.

Moore, John Preston. *Revolt in Louisiana: The Spanish Occupation, 1766–1770.* Baton Rouge: Louisiana State University Press, 1976.

Moses, Bernard. *The Establishment of Spanish Rule in America: An Introduction to the History and Politics of Spanish America.* New York: Cooper Square, 1898.

Núñez Cabeza de Vaca, Álvar. *Narrative.* Trans. Fanny Bandelier. Barre: The Imprint Society, 1972.

O'Donnell, James H., III. *Southern Indians in the American Revolution.* Knoxville: University of Tennessee Press, 1973.

Peebles, Christopher S. *Excavations at Moundville, 1905–1951.* Ann Arbor: University Microfilms, 1979.

Peterson, Harold L. *Arms and Armor in Colonial America, 1526–1783.* Harrisburg: Stackpole Co., 1956.

Phillips, Philip. "Middle American Influences on the Southeastern United States." In *The Maya and Their Neighbors.* New York: D. Appleton, 1940.

Pickett, Albert T. *History of Alabama.* 2 vols. Charleston: Walker and James, 1851.

Pina Chan, Roman. *Tlatilco.* 2 vols. Mexico City: Instituto Nacional de Anthropologica e Historia, 1958.

Posner, Ernst. *American State Archives.* Chicago: University of Chicago Press, 1964.

Powell, Philip W. *Tree of Hate: Propaganda and Prejudices Affecting United States Relations with the Hispanic World.* New York: Basic Books, 1971.

Priestley, Herbert I. *Tristan de Luna: A Conquest of the Old South—A Study of Spanish Imperial Strategy.* Glendale: Arthur H. Clark, 1936.

————, ed. and trans. *The Luna Papers.* 2 vols. De Land: Florida State Historical Society, 1928.

Proctor, Samuel, ed. *Eighteenth-Century Florida and Its Borderlands.* Gainesville: University Presses of Florida, 1975.

Robinson, W. Stitt. *The Southern Colonial Frontier, 1607–1763.* Histories of the American Frontier Series. Albuquerque: University of New Mexico Press. 1979.

Rouse, Irving B. "The Inference of Migrations from Anthropological Evidence." In *Migrations in New World Culture History*, ed. Raymond H. Thompson. Tucson: University of Arizona Press, 1958.

Sanders, William T. "Hydraulic Agriculture, Economic Symbiosis, and the Evolution of States in Central Mexico." In *Anthropological Archeology in the Americas*, ed. Betty J. Meggers. Washington, D.C.: Anthropological Society of Washington, 1968.

_____ and Barbara J. Price. *Mesoamerica: The Evolution of a Civilization*. New York: Random House, 1968.

Schnell, Frank T., Vernon J. Knight, Jr., and Gail S. Schnell. *Cemochechobee: Archaeology of a Mississippian Ceremonial Center on the Chattahoochee River*. Gainesville: University Presses of Florida, 1981.

Scholes, France V. *Church and State in New Mexico, 1610–1650*. Albuquerque: University of New Mexico Press, 1937.

Sellards, Elias H. *Early Man in America*. Austin: University of Texas Press, 1952.

Serrano y Sanz, Manuel, ed. *Documentos históricos de la Florida y la Luisiana, Siglos XVI al XVIII*. Madrid: Suarez, 1912.

Service, Elman R. *The Origins of the State and Civilization: The Process of Cultural Evolution*. New York: W. W. Norton, 1975.

Shepherd, William R. *Latin America*. New York: Holt, 1914.

Shetrone, Henry C. *The Mound Builders*. New York: D. Appleton, 1931.

Shurbutt, Thomas Ray, and Janet Lois Gritzner. *Historical Archaeology of the Colonial Southeastern Atlantic Coast: A Bibliography*. Gainesville: University of Florida, 1979.

Sirmans, M. Eugene. *Colonial South Carolina: A Political History, 1663–1763*. Chapel Hill: University of North Carolina Press, 1966.

Smith, Bruce D., ed. *Mississippian Settlement Patterns*. New York: Academic Press, 1978.

Starr, J. Barton. *Tories and Rebels: The American Revolution in British West Florida*. Gainesville: University Presses of Florida, 1976.

Sturtevant, William C. "Black Drink and Other Caffeine-containing Beverages among Non-Indians." In *Black Drink, a Native American Tea*, ed. Charles M. Hudson. Athens: University of Georgia Press, 1979 (pp. 150–65).

Tanner, Helen Hornbeck. *Zéspedes in East Florida, 1784–1790*. Coral Gables: University of Miami Press, 1963.

Tate, Thad W., and David L. Ammerman, eds. *The Chesapeake in the Seventeenth Century: Essays on Anglo-American Society*. Chapel Hill: University of North Carolina, 1979.

TePaske, John J. *The Governorship of Spanish Florida, 1700–63*. Durham: Duke University Press, 1964.

_____. "Spanish America: The Colonial Period." In *Latin American Scholarship since World War II: Trends in History, Political Science, Literature, Geography, and Economics*, ed. Roberto Esquenazi-Mayo and Michael C. Meyer. Lincoln: University of Nebraska Press, 1971, 8–9.

Thomson, Buchanan Parker. *Spain: Forgotten Ally of the American Revolution*. North Quincy, Mass.: Christopher, 1976.

Thruston, Gates P. *The Antiquities of Tennessee and the Adjacent States and the State of Aboriginal Society in a Scale of Civilization Represented by Them*. Cincinnati: Robert Clark, 1890.

Tornero Tinajero, Pablo. *Relaciones de Dependencia entre Florida y Estados*

Unidos, 1783–1820. Madrid: Ministerio de Asuntos Exteriores, Dirección General de Relaciones Culturales, 1979.

Vaughan, Alden T., ed. *Early American Indian Documents.* Washington, D.C.: University Publications of America, 1979.

Wallace, David Duncan. *South Carolina: A Short History, 1520–1948.* Chapel Hill: University of North Carolina Press, 1951.

Wauchope, Robert. *Lost Tribes and Sunken Continents.* Chicago: University of Chicago Press, 1962.

Weddle, Robert S. *Wilderness Manhunt: The Spanish Search for La Salle.* Austin: University of Texas Press, 1973.

Wedel, Waldo R. *Prehistoric Man on the Great Plains.* Norman: University of Oklahoma Press, 1961.

Whitaker, Arthur P. *The Spanish-American Frontier, 1783–1795: The Westward Movement and the Spanish Retreat in the Mississippi Valley.* Boston: Houghton Mifflin, 1927.

———. *The Mississippi Question, 1795–1803: A Study in Trade, Politics, and Diplomacy.* New York: Appleton-Century, 1934.

Willey, Gordon R. *An Introduction to American Archeology.* 2 vols. Englewood Cliffs, N.J.: Prentice-Hall, 1966 and 1971.

——— and Philip Phillips. *Method and Theory in American Archaeology.* Chicago: University of Chicago Press, 1958.

Wing, Elizabeth S., and Antoinette B. Brown. *Paleonutrition: Method and Theory in Prehistoric Food Ways.* New York: Academic Press, 1979.

Wolf, Eric R. *Sons of the Shaking Earth.* Chicago: Phoenix Books, 1959.

Wood, W. Raymond, and R. Bruce McMillan, eds. *Prehistoric Man and His Environments: A Case Study in the Ozark Highland.* New York: Academic Press, 1976.

Wormington, Hannah M. *Ancient Man in North America.* 4th ed. Denver: Denver Museum of Natural History, 1957.

Wright, J. Leitch, Jr. *William Augustus Bowles, Director General of the Creek Nation.* Athens: University of Georgia Press, 1967.

———. *The Only Land They Knew: The Tragic Story of the American Indians of the Old South.* New York: The Free Press, 1981.

Zubillaga, Felix. *Monumenta Antiquae Floridae (1566–1572).* Rome: Monumenta Historica Societatis Iesu, 1956.

Documentary Collections

"Letter from the Secretary of War Relative to the Improvement of the Holston and Tennessee Rivers." 42d Cong., 2d sess., Exec. Doc. 167.

Archivo General de Indias: Secciones Contaduría, Secciones Justicia, Secciones Patronato, Secciones Escribanía de Camara, Secciones Contratación, Secciones Indiferente General, Secciones Santo Domingo.

Borja Medina Rojas, Francisco de. *José de Ezpeleta: Gobernador de la Mobila, 1780–81.* Archivo General de Simancas, Guerras Moderna, Legajos 6912. Sevilla: Escuela de Estudios Hispanoamericanos de Sevilla.

Coker, William S., and Robert R. Rea, eds. *Pensacola: The Gulf Coast History and Humanities Conference,* 1982.

Flannery, Kent V. "The Olmec and the Valley of Oaxaca." In *Dumbarton Oaks Conference on the Olmec*. Washington, D.C.: Dumbarton Oaks Research Library and Collection (Harvard University), 1968.

Gálvez, Bernardo de. Letter to José de Gálvez, Mobile, March 20, 1780. Archivo General de Simancas, Guerras Moderna, Legajos 6912.

_____. "Diario." Archivo General de Simancas: Guerras Moderna, Legajos 6912.

Guthe, Carl, ed. *Conference on Southern Prehistory*. National Research Council, Washington, D.C., 1932.

Martínez, Bartolomé. "Martirio de los padres y hermanos de la Compañia de Jesus." *Monumenta*. October 4, 1616, pp. 570–604.

Menéndez, Pedro. Letter to Francisco Borgia from Madrid. *Monumenta*. January 18, 1568, pp. 228–34.

Mooney, James. "Myths of the Cherokee." *Bureau of American Ethnology, 19th Annual Report*. Washington, D.C.: G.P.O., 1900.

South, Stanley. *The Conference on Historic Site Archaeology Papers*. Vol. 11. Columbia, S.C.: Institute of Archeology and Anthropology, University of South Carolina, 1977.

_____, ed. *The Conference on Historic Site Archaeology Papers*. Vol. 8. Columbia, S.C.: Institute of Archeology and Anthropology, University of South Carolina, 1975.

Swanton, John R. *Final Report of the United States De Soto Expedition Commission*. 76th Cong., 1st sess., Doc. 71. Washington, D.C.: G.P.O., 1939.

U.S. Congress. "Proclamation of 1810." In *American State Papers, Foreign Affairs*. Washington, D.C.: Gales and Seaton, 1832.

Willey, Gordon R. *Archeology of the Florida Gulf Coast*. Miscellaneous Collections, 113. Washington, D.C.: Smithsonian Institution, 1949.

Contributors

R. Reid Badger is Associate Professor of American Studies at The University of Alabama. A former Director of the University's Program in American Studies and Assistant Dean of the College of Arts and Sciences, he is the author of *The Great American Fair: The World's Columbian Exposition and American Culture.*

Jeffrey P. Brain is Curator of Southeastern Archaeology at The Peabody Museum, Harvard University. A recipient of the John M. Goggin Award for his work in the archaeology and history of the De Soto Expedition, Dr. Brain has also published numerous articles and monographs on Southeastern archaeology, including two major works on Mississippian Period sites.

Lawrence A. Clayton is Associate Professor of History and Director of the Latin American Studies Program at The University of Alabama. A specialist in the Andean region of South America and United States–Latin American relations, he has written two books and more than twenty articles and is currently writing a textbook on Latin American history.

Hazel P. Coker and William S. Coker are the founding editors of the Perdido Press of Pensacola, Florida, which specializes in publishing scholarly works on the Spanish Borderlands in the eighteenth century. The Cokers have collaborated on numerous works, including *The Siege of Pensacola (1781) in Maps, John Forbes' Description of the Spanish Floridas, 1804,* and *The Spanish Censuses of Pensacola, 1784–1820.*

Chester B. DePratter, who holds a doctoral degree from The University of Georgia, is an archaeologist whose primary research area is the paleogeography of the Georgia coastal region. His other interests include Southeastern United States ethnohistory and the exploration routes of Hernando de Soto and Juan Pardo. He is currently writing a book on the archaeology and ethnohistory of chiefdoms in the Southeast.

Charles H. Fairbanks, late Distinguished Service Professor of Anthropology at The University of Florida, was a major figure in the prehistoric and Colonial archaeology of the Southeastern United States. Through his studies of the Cherokee, Creek, and Seminole Indians, and in such works as *Florida Anthropology*, Dr. Fairbanks achieved an enviable reputation in ethnohistory and cultural anthropology as well. Dr. Fairbanks died July 17, 1984.

James B. Griffin is Professor Emeritus at The University of Michigan and one of the most influential American prehistorians of the twentieth century. A recipient of the Viking Fund Medal in Anthropology, Dr. Griffin is the author of more than one hundred articles and monographs. Two of his works, *The Prehistory of Eastern North America* and *The Fort Ancient Aspect*, are considered classics in American archaeology.

Charles M. Hudson is Professor of Anthropology at The University of Georgia and a leading scholar in Southeastern ethnohistory. A former Woodrow Wilson Scholar, Dr. Hudson is the author of numerous books and articles, including *The Catawba Nation* and, most recently, *Southeastern Indians.*

Richard A. Krause is Professor of Anthropology and former Chairman of the Department of Anthropology at The University of Alabama. Dr. Krause's scholarly interests include the archaeology and ethnology of the North American Great Plains, Sub-Saharan Africa, and Mesoamerica. He has published several works in archaeological theory and methodology.

Eugene Lyon is a widely recognized expert on the exploration and conquest of Florida in the sixteenth century. His *The Enterprise of Florida: Pedro Menéndez de Avilés and the Spanish Conquest of 1565–1568* is considered the definitive account of its subject, and his articles in *National Geographic* have brought the results of his research to a wide audience.

John H. Parry, late Gardiner Professor of Oceanic History and Affairs at Harvard University, was one of the world's outstanding authorities on the Age of Discovery and Exploration. The author of *The European Reconnaissance, The Establishment of the European Hegemony: 1415–1715*, and *The Spanish Seabourne Empire* (among others), Professor Parry distinguished himself by the breadth and scope of his examination of the expansion of Europe in the fifteenth and sixteenth centuries. He died August 25, 1982, at the age of 68.

Michael C. Scardaville is Associate Professor of History at the University of South Carolina. Dr. Scardaville has been instrumental in founding the Southeast Borderlands Association for scholars of all disciplines interested in advancing the knowledge of the Borderlands. Dr. Scardaville's works on demographic trends and society in St. Augustine are indicative of new techniques for studying the history of the region. He now directs the Public History Program at South Carolina.

Bruce D. Smith is Associate Curator of North American Archaeology at the Smithsonian Institution. He is a recognized authority on Mississippian Period subsistence and settlement practices, and has recently written a book on the prehistoric patterns of human behavior. Dr. Smith has a special interest in the human ecology of Eastern North America, and has published a number of articles on the human ecology of the late prehistoric period in the Southeastern United States.

Marvin T. Smith holds a doctoral degree in anthropology at The University of Florida, where he has concentrated on early Spanish exploration of the New World. He is the author of several articles, including "The Early Historic Period (1540–1670) on the Upper Coosa River Drainage of Alabama and Georgia," and has co-authored a book on the material remains of early Spanish-colonial trade.

Wilcomb E. Washburn is Director of the Office of American and Folklife Studies at the Smithsonian Institution and a past president of the American Studies Association. Dr. Washburn is the author of several distinguished works in colonial and nineteenth-century history, including, most recently, Red Man's Land, White Man's Law. His research interests include European expansion in the Age of Discovery, American colonial and political history, American Indian and white relations, and American museum history.

Index

Wallace, David Duncan: author, *South Carolina, A Short History, 1510–1948,* 150

War: conquest warfare, 24, 30; weapons, 93–94; of the Spanish Succession, 10; Queen Anne's, 10; of Jenkins' Ear, 11; of 1812, 12, 183; Yamassee, 150. *See also* Archery; Weapons

Warner, Jack: president, Gulf States Corporation, 153

Wateree River, 109, 126

Wauchope, Robert, 41

Weapons: Indian and Spanish, compared, 93–94. *See also* Archery; War

Webb, W. S.: archaeologist, 51

Weeden Island: pottery, 46; sand burial mounds, 131

Weekeewatchee Springs, 131, 132. *See also* Mounds; Sites, archaeological

Weogulfka Creek, 121

West Florida Royal Foresters: captured by Spanish, 180

Whitaker, Arthur P.: historian, 186

Wickliffe site, 50. *See also* Sites, archaeological

Willey, Gordon R., 54, 56, 128

Willing, Captain James, 164

Winyah Bay, 88

Withlacoochee River site, 131, 132. *See also* Mounds; Sites, archaeological

Wood, Peter, 145

Woodland period: characteristics of, 28, 60–61; transformation of, 28–30; priority over Mississippian, 43. *See also* Cultures, historical classification of

Woods, Patricia Dillion: author, *French-Indian Relations on the Southern Frontier, 1699–1762,* 149

Wright, J. Leitch, Jr.: historian, 149, 150

Wycoff, Don G., 57

Xuala: Soto expedition reaches, 108; location of, 109. *See* Soto expedition

Zéspedes, Manuel, 187

Zimmerman's Island: site of Chiaha, 109–11, 124. *See also* Sites, archaeological